THE FILMS OF GARY COOPER

THE FILMS

OF GARY COOPER

BY HOMER DICKENS

CITADEL PRESS   NEW YORK

ACKNOWLEDGEMENTS

Acknowledgement should be made of the services of various people who have contributed to one or another stage of work on this book, whether contributing pertinent information or photographs:

ALAN G. BARBOUR	BILL KENLY	G. SHANHINIAN
BOB BOARD	AL KILGORE	DICK SISSON
CARLOS CLARENS	ALBERT LORD	LEE SPARKS
JOHN COCCHI	NORMAN MILLER	ERIC SPILKER
JOHN DARTIGUE	PAUL NEMCEK	LOU VALENTINO
LESTER GLASSNER	GUNNARD NELSON	JERRY VERMILYE
PETER HANSON	JOE REGAN	JAMES WATTERS
RICHARD M. HUDSON	MARK RICCI	PEG WHEELER
NORMAN KAPHAN	GENE RINGGOLD	DOUGLAS WHITNEY
	MARY YUSHAK	

Also, the able staff of the New York Public Library's Theatre and Film Collection at Lincoln Center; the Museum of Modern Art/Film Stills Archive; the Memory Shop; United Press International (New York and Los Angeles); Metro-Goldwyn-Mayer, Inc.; and United Artists Corporation.

For extensive and invaluable research services, the author is most indebted to Dion McGregor, who has forgotten more about movies than anyone else knows, and Cliff McCarty, my West Coast liaison man.

Special thanks to Michael Sparks, editor and friend, for checking my tenses, repairing my split infinitives, and un-dangling those hateful participles.

Dedicated
with love and affection
to
H. J.
like Coop, always a gentleman

CONTENTS

Gary Cooper, the American Man   1
The Shorter Films of Gary Cooper   23

Filmography
 1 The Winning of Barbara Worth   29
 2 It   31
 3 Children of Divorce   33
 4 Arizona Bound   35
 5 Wings   37
 6 Nevada   39
 7 The Last Outlaw   42
 8 Beau Sabreur   44
 9 The Legion of the Condemned   47
10 Doomsday   50
11 Half a Bride   52
12 Lilac Time   54
13 The First Kiss   57
14 The Shopworn Angel   59
15 Wolf Song   62
16 Betrayal   65

17 The Virginian   68
18 Only the Brave   71
19 Paramount on Parade   73
20 The Texan   75
21 Seven Days Leave   78
22 A Man From Wyoming   80
23 The Spoilers   83
24 Morocco   85
25 Fighting Caravans   87
26 City Streets   92
27 I Take This Woman   95
28 His Woman   97
29 Make Me a Star   99
30 Devil and the Deep   101
31 If I Had a Million   104
32 A Farewell to Arms   106
33 Today We Live   109
34 One Sunday Afternoon   113
35 Design for Living   115
36 Alice in Wonderland   117

37	Operator 13	*119*
38	Now and Forever	*123*
39	The Wedding Night	*126*
40	The Lives of a Bengal Lancer	*129*
41	Peter Ibbetson	*132*
42	Desire	*136*
43	Mr. Deeds Goes to Town	*139*
44	Hollywood Boulevard	*142*
45	The General Died at Dawn	*144*
46	The Plainsman	*147*
47	Souls at Sea	*150*
48	The Adventures of Marco Polo	*153*
49	Bluebeard's Eighth Wife	*156*
50	The Cowboy and the Lady	*159*
51	Beau Geste	*162*
52	The Real Glory	*166*
53	The Westerner	*169*
54	North West Mounted Police	*174*
55	Meet John Doe	*178*
56	Sergeant York	*181*
57	Ball of Fire	*184*
58	The Pride of the Yankees	*187*
59	For Whom the Bell Tolls	*190*
60	The Story of Dr. Wassell	*194*
61	Casanova Brown	*197*
62	Along Came Jones	*199*
63	Saratoga Trunk	*201*
64	Cloak and Dagger	*204*
65	Unconquered	*206*
66	Variety Girl	*209*
67	Good Sam	*211*
68	The Fountainhead	*214*
69	It's a Great Feeling	*218*
70	Task Force	*220*
71	Bright Leaf	*223*
72	Dallas	*225*
73	You're in the Navy Now	*227*
74	Starlift	*229*
75	It's a Big Country	*231*
76	Distant Drums	*233*
77	High Noon	*235*
78	Springfield Rifle	*238*
79	Return to Paradise	*241*
80	Blowing Wild	*243*
81	Garden of Evil	*245*
82	Vera Cruz	*248*
83	The Court-Martial of Billy Mitchell	*252*
84	Friendly Persuasion	*255*
85	Love in the Afternoon	*259*
86	Ten North Frederick	*262*
87	Man of the West	*265*
88	The Hanging Tree	*267*
89	Alias Jesse James	*269*
90	They Came to Cordura	*271*
91	The Wreck of the Mary Deare	*274*
92	The Naked Edge	*276*

Two Tributes *280*

Cooper in the 1940s

GARY COOPER, THE AMERICAN MAN

Of all the men who have acted in motion pictures, none has come as close to portraying the embodiment of the American man as Gary Cooper. The image he projected from the screen was the personification of the ideal American, i.e., the tall, handsome, soft-spoken gentleman with unswerving integrity and sincerity, overcoming adversity regardless of the odds—or the situation. He was popular with men and women alike, and was the hero of children.

Cooper had a way of injecting his own likeable self into whatever he did or with whomever he played. For the most part, it seemed to work. Some consider him the greatest of *natural* screen actors; others, however, think of him only as a "personality star." During his peak period, 1935-1945, he proved, even to his detractors, that he was an *actor* of subtlety and depth.

While he was never known for his loquacity, neither was "yup" and "nope" his total vocabulary, although no one enjoyed kidding about this more than he did. This "man of few words" myth came about through his natural shyness with strangers, but close friends like Ernest Hemingway, the Duke and Duchess of Windsor, Jack Benny, Jock Whitney, and James Stewart knew better.

Cooper possessed a keen business mind and an uncanny intuitive sense about what was theatrically right. He seemed to know when and where to make the right move, much to the consternation of those around him. A simple man at heart, he was as much at home sitting on the hard ground by a campfire as he was on a plush sofa in an elegant drawing room.

Hollywood, sometimes a cruel master, didn't seem to affect Cooper. He was always the same person. His friend Richard Arlen once said, "Some people are just nice guys, and nothing—not even Hollywood—can change it. . . . Coop just likes people; it's as simple as that."

1

At age two

ity poll, conducted by *Variety,* still included Cooper and Clark Gable, whose movies continue to be a source of pleasure to millions, despite the fact that both men have long since passed from the scene.

Frank James Cooper was born on May 7, 1901, in Helena, Montana. His father, Charles Henry Cooper, who emigrated at nineteen from England, in 1885, later became a Montana State Supreme Court Justice. His mother, the former Alice Brazier, left her native Gillingham, Kent, to visit a brother in America and stayed to marry Charles.

In 1906, Charles Cooper bought the Seven-Bar-Nine, a 600-acre railroad-landgrant ranch just forty miles from Helena, in the bend of the Missouri River near the Big Belt Mountains, but he didn't do too well with ranching. His town house, in Helena, was a large, two-story brick structure on Eleventh Avenue, which backed on the original Last Chance Gulch.

In 1910, Mrs. Cooper, convalescing from a serious illness, was advised to take a sea voyage by her doctor. Her husband decided they should return to England, where Frank and his older brother, Arthur (born in 1895), were schooled until the outbreak of the World War. Young Frank was then a pupil in the Dunstable School, Mr. Cooper's alma mater.

The Coopers returned home when the United States entered World War I. Arthur, twenty-two, enlisted shortly thereafter. However, young Frank, who had just turned sixteen, stayed on his father's ranch. Help was hard to get on the ranch, since all of the available manpower had left the Montana plains to fight, and soon he became a regular ranch hand. Speaking of his life of the Seven-Bar-Nine, Cooper later recalled, "Getting up at five o'clock in the morning in the dead of Winter to feed 450 head of cattle and shoveling manure at forty below ain't romantic." "But," he added, "Dad was a true Westerner. And I take after him."

Before attending Wesleyan, College, an agricultural school at Bozeman, Montana, Frank took some art courses and developed a certain flair for cartoons and caricatures. While at Wesleyan, he was involved in a serious automobile accident with a fellow student, which fractured Cooper's hip. He convalesced at his father's ranch, during which time he perfected his horsemanship.

At Iowa's Grinnell College, in 1921, Frank began to perfect his artistic ability by filling the school paper with political caricatures. He was

Once the six-foot-two-and-three-quarters actor, with brown hair and blue eyes, got a foothold in Hollywood, his rise was swift. Audiences liked him from the start and, over the years, would go to see him in any role. His first substantial part came in 1926, he was a star by 1928, and was making $6,000 a week by 1933. Said Cooper modestly: "I guess I just picked up things here and there from the directors and actors I worked with."

His career as an actor spanned thirty-six years—one of the longest in motion picture history. He was one of the top ten money-makers for sixteen of those years and at the time of his death it was estimated that his films had grossed well over $200 million. In 1968, a nation-wide television popular-

2

vastly impressed by the work of Western artist Charles M. Russell whose paintings, Cooper found out, were worth more than a herd of beef. Leaving Grinnell, in 1923, Cooper submitted many delightful cartoons and caricatures to the Helena *Independent*. During the summers he worked as a guide in Yellowstone National Park.

His father, after serving just one year as a State Supreme Court Judge, resigned from the bench to administer the estates of two cousins in San Diego, California. On Thanksgiving Day, 1924, Frank joined his parents in Los Angeles, hoping to interest local newspaper editors in his artistic talents. His efforts proved fruitless, so he then sought any work he could get. "I was down to the essential starting point for all actors," he recalled, "I was broke."

He worked for a few weeks as a canvassing salesman for a local photographer, then sold advertising space for theatrical curtains. Then, during the 1924 Christmas season, Cooper ran into two boyhood friends from Montana while strolling along busy Hollywood Boulevard. Jimmy Galeen and Jimmy Calloway, lawyer's sons like Cooper, were working for the movie studios as cowboy extras. Cooper listened with interest as the boys gave him the rundown on what they did (riding and stunt work)

for ten dollars a day. Yet another of his Montana friends, Jay "Slim" Talbot, was also doing quite well. Said Cooper: "When he was eighteen, Slim was one of the best riders, ropers and bulldoggers in the West." Talbot explained to Coop that "in rodeo, you're paid to stay on the horse; in films, to fall off."

Once these fellows had introduced Coop to the various casting directors, he never lacked for work as a cowboy extra during 1925 and the first half of 1926. Much of the time he didn't know what film he was working on—poverty row directors did crowd scenes themselves—for the bigger productions and directors had second unit directors to handle action sequences. Often, the action footage was cut and re-cut to service several films in production at the same time. Cooper may have been in as many as fifty films before his break came in *The Winning of Barbara Worth*.

Cooper, who remembered holding the hind hoof of a horse in an early Western while it was being shod by Dustin Farnum, once told a reporter that "some days I was a cowboy before lunch and an Injun in the afternoon." He also recalled that he had been in a campfire sequence of a Rin Tin Tin picture, but the dog, alas, was the great star's "stand-in."

During
his college
days

With his father, Judge Charles H. Cooper, in 1929

With his mother
and brother Arthur
in 1932

Exercising at home

With Lupe Velez
and Frank Yaconelli

5

"On my third picture, a Tom Mix Western (*The Lucky Horseshoe*), I saw Mix act and was told that he got $17,500 a week. I figured I could do that kind of acting, too."

As near as can be figured, Cooper's first released film was *The Thundering Herd* (March 1, 1925). Then came *Wild Horse Mesa; The Lucky Horseshoe;* Richard Dix's *The Vanishing American,* in which he was a cowboy (and possibly an "Injun"); the part of a masked Cossack in Valentino's *The Eagle;* another cowboy, in *The Enchanted Hill* with Florence Vidor; and a patron in the night club sequence of Universal's *Watch Your Wife* and also in the outdoor café scene, in which star Virginia Valli appeared. Walter Brennan was also in the former. Meanwhile, Cooper's father was settling some business for a client whose daughter was actress-producer Marilyn Mills, a former stand-in for Mary Pickford and Norma Talmadge, among others. Her specialty was churning out two- to five-reel Westerns, starring herself and J. Frank Glendon. They just happened to need a heavy at that time, and Cooper filled the bill.

The first of these featurettes, directed by Bruce Mitchell, was called *Tricks* and released just after *Wild Horse Mesa.* The next one, *Three Pals,* came out in November of 1925. Cooper also appeared in a two-reeler called *Lightnin' Wins* for producer Hans Tiesler's Independent Pictures Corporation. The stars were Lightnin', The Super Dog and Eileen Sedgwick. Although Cooper was not billed in the credits, his name appeared on the title card that introduced his character to the audience.

Cooper soon had a series of photographs of himself taken, in the style of Valentino, Ramon Novarro, Wallace Reid, Tom Mix, et al., and flooded studio casting offices with them, but to no avail. It seems the studios were looking for someone new and different. It was at this time that he made contact with Nan Collins, a studio casting director and, later, an actor's agent. She immediately took an interest in Frank, albeit a motherly one, and her suggestions and guidance at this early, uncertain period were responsible for his later successes.

"Nan came from Gary, Indiana, and suggested I adopt that name. She felt it was more exciting than Frank. I figured I'd give it a try. Good thing she didn't come from Poughkeepsie." There were already two Frank Coopers in films at that time, so, *Gary* Cooper it became and Gary Cooper it remained.

Cooper's new agent also thought it advisable that he make a quickie filmstrip, demonstrating his

riding skill, so casting people could see what he looked like on film. This film test, which cost him approximately $75.00, showed him riding toward the camera on a horse, galloping at a fast speed, reining to a sudden stop for a closeup, then falling from his horse in a cloud of dust.

Miss Collins sent the test to John Waters, the director of the popular Zane Grey Westerns at Paramount, who made a note for future reference. She also had new pictures of Cooper taken—natural ones, not of the Valentino genre—which were sent to studio casting directors.

About the time Cooper's test was returned by John Waters, Miss Collins learned that Bob McIntyre, Samuel Goldwyn's casting director, was interviewing riders for Henry King's film version of Harold Bell Wright's *The Winning of Barbara Worth,* so she sent Gary over with the can of film under his arm. When director King saw the test, he hired Cooper at fifty dollars a week for a small part. Many key scenes with stars Vilma Banky and Ronald Colman had already been shot, and King was awaiting the services of Herold Goodwin, whom he had hired for the pivotal role of Abe Lee, the man whose love for Vilma is never fulfilled. Since Goodwin was tied up at Warner Bros. filming *The Honeymoon Express,* King decided to give the role of Abe Lee to Cooper. His salary rose to $65.00 a week.

Gary Cooper's personality and naturalness were very apparent and, once the film was released, he established an immediate rapport with audiences. Everyone found this charming young man far more "winning" than *Barbara Worth.* Nan refused Samuel Goldwyn's contract offer of $65.00 a week and hustled Cooper back to John Waters, who had already heard about his Abe Lee performance. Paramount Pictures came up with a contract for $150.00 a week, which was acceptable to both agent and client.

While Waters was preparing a Western called *Arizona Bound,* Paramount gave Cooper a two-scene bit as a reporter in Elinor Glyn's *It*—starring the "It" girl herself, Clara Bow. Bow asked that Cooper be in her next picture, *Children of Divorce,* and Paramount executives were only too happy to comply, since the couple was already being seen around the film capital. The publicity hounds sang out, "The 'It' Girl Finds Her 'It' Boy."

Gary's rushes were dreadful and proved he wasn't the lover-boy type (although he looked it), and B. P. Schulberg fired him. However, director Frank Lloyd wanted to keep him, so he re-cut his scenes, making them "passable." Cooper was re-hired and completed his part. The film itself also went through some "re-cutting," by an assistant director on the lot named Josef von Sternberg. He worked the leading actors, at night, applying great pressure, and gave this sagging film some life. Although he made no friends among these actors, the finished *Children of Divorce* fared much better due to his fantastic drive.

John Waters filmed *Arizona Bound* in two weeks' time. The location work was shot at Bryce Canyon, Utah, and Cooper did his own stunt work. This was his first starring role.

Paramount's publicity campaign for Gary was now in full swing and he was immediately shipped off to Kelly Field, near San Antonio, Texas, for a brief, but key role in William A. Wellman's *Wings*. He had one scene and spoke one line, but, just as in *The Winning of Barbara Worth,* he died. Audiences remembered him, however, and the fan mail poured in.

Back in Hollywood, Cooper then starred in two more Westerns. *Nevada,* from Zane Grey's novel, had Thelma Todd as the heroine and William Powell as the villain. *The Last Outlaw,* another Western by the author of *Arizona Bound,* was a well-mounted quickie directed by Arthur Rosson and featuring Cooper opposite Betty Jewel and Jack Luden. He rode Flash, the Wonder Horse.

Paramount had overshot on the Ronald Colman-Neil Hamilton *Beau Geste* and decided to create *Beau Sabreur,* to satisfy the demand for a sequel film from exhibitors. Despite the ideal combination of Cooper and Evelyn Brent, the sequel was not particularly good.

Instead of trying to find a suitable vehicle for Cooper and Miss Brent, Paramount then worked overtime on a campaign expounding Fay Wray and Gary Cooper as "Paramount's Glorious Young Lovers." The film was *The Legion of the Condemned* and its creators were William A. Wellman and John Monk Saunders, Miss Wray's husband, the pair who had *Wings* to their credit. They did not equal their previous success, despite stunning aerial scenes and an exciting climax in which Gary rescues Fay from a German firing squad. The Wray-Cooper duo was "blah."

In less than two years, Cooper went from cowboy extra in Florence Vidor's *The Enchanted Hill* to her co-star in Warwick Deeping's soap opera *Doomsday.* Cooper was winning a large following with female movie-goers and, more important, he was learning to handle himself well in love scenes.

He swiftly went into *Half a Bride,* a cute little comedy with Esther Ralston, directed by Gregory La Cava. This gave him a chance at comedy and he learned a great deal from one of the best of comic directors.

Colleen Moore, then making her pictures at First National, thought Cooper would be ideal as her leading man in *Lilac Time* and had him borrowed. Once again, he was in a flyer's uniform and his scenes with Miss Moore were warm and tender. Alvin Knechtel's aerial photography was especially noteworthy, but it was generally felt that director George Fitzmaurice put too much emphasis on the sentimental scenes, a facet which was further accented by the Nathaniel Shilkret-L. Wolfe Gilbert song, "Jeannine, I Dream of Lilac Time," which was played in conjunction with the film showings around the country. *Lilac Time* boasted "Photophone Sound Effects."

Paramount—and Fay Wray—were awaiting Gary's return for the filmization of Tristram Tupper's *Four Brothers,* which they had the nerve to call *The First Kiss.* It received a mild reception.

Sound was already very much on the movie scene by mid-1928 and Paramount eased two of its biggest stars, Nancy Carroll and Cooper, before the microphone in the final scenes of *The Shopworn Angel.* Cooper's voice recorded well and Nancy Carroll not only spoke, but sang the tearful ballad, "A Precious Little Thing Called Love." Both players had no worries about the talkies.

The studio hoped to re-team Cooper and Carroll in *Half Sinner,* but, instead, put him in *Wolf Song,* which also became a part-talkie when they injected a bit of dialogue for Cooper and co-star Lupe Velez before the "Mexican Spitfire" sang two songs: "Mi Amado" and "Yo Te Amo Means I Love You." This saga of the Southwest boasted beautiful photography and vigorous direction by Victor Fleming and his assistant, Henry Hathaway, who was later to direct many of Cooper's best performances. Cooper's off-screen romance with Lupe caused a sensation in the press, especially when it became known they shared a Laurel Canyon hideaway.

Mrs. Cooper, who was now living in Los Angeles with her husband, soon stepped into the picture. Gary, respecting his mother's opinion, never saw Lupe again. Later, Mrs. Cooper had this to say about his close friendship with Evelyn Brent: "Evelyn Brent has been good to Gary; she has given him poise, she has taught him to think; her influence has been excellent, and I will always regard her with affection and gratitude."

Lupe was furious, telling the press "I'm not good enough for him, I know that. But I tried to make him happy. I *did* make him happy. I would have done anything in the world for him. His mother!—I hope she never cries the tears that I have cried. I hope she never knows the suffering I have known. I don't hate her—that much. She said I wasn't good enough for Gary. She told him that when I was in New York, I was seeing other men. She told him that I wasn't faithful to him. He believed what she told him."

Betrayal was Cooper's last silent film. It was hoped that it could also become a "part-talkie," but, in testing star Emil Jannings, they found his heavy German accent a liability and Esther Ralston's voice registered too thin to record well. For whatever reason, it did poorly at the box office.

Paramount then announced plans to produce Joseph Conrad's *Victory*, with Cooper, Jean Arthur, Baclanova and ZaSu Pitts. At the same time, however, someone came up with the idea of re-making Owen Wister's *The Virginian*, which executives felt was better suited to introduce Cooper to the talkies. The story was a winner, which had been proven twice before. Victor Fleming and Henry Hathaway again directed with verve. Cooper gave self-assurance to the title role, while Walter Huston menaced all as the evil Trampas. The best technical talents were assembled for this auspicious event. Although *The Virginian* seems a bit primitive and static by today's standards, its use of sound was most commendable.

Cooper's second sound·film was *Seven Days Leave,* based on James M. Barrie's "The Old Lady Shows Her Medals," which was directed by Richard Wallace and assisted by stage director John Cromwell. Paramount was afraid of this "little gem" and held up its release for more than a year. However, it contains one of Cooper's finest portrayals.

He then stepped into a mire called *Only the Brave,* a tepid romance-actioner set in the Civil War. After escaping this drivel, he was assigned to Paramount's all-star musical extravaganza *Paramount on Parade*. With this production, Paramount joined the other major film studios in showcasing its big-name talent in various sketches and musical numbers to help usher in the sound era. Its predecessors included *The Show of Shows* (Warners); *The Hollywood Revue of 1929* (Metro-Goldwyn-Mayer); *The Fox Movietone Follies* (Fox); and *King of Jazz* (Universal).

Cooper appeared in the "Let Us Drink to the

Celebrating the flow of legal beer in 1933, with Mae West

Girl of My Dreams" segment, which consisted of two scenes, a modern-day black-and-white sequence which faded into a period piece shot in the new two-color Technicolor process.

John Cromwell then directed Cooper and Fay Wray in *The Texan,* based on O. Henry's short story "A Double-Dyed Deceiver." The photography by Victor Milner was especially beautiful.

In May of 1930, plans were being formulated to star Cooper in a talkie re-make of DeMille's *Rose of The Rancho* (and the studio even took out big ads in the trade magazines) with Rosita Moreno, Lillian Roth and Nino Martini. However, Cooper was used to replace George Bancroft in Rex Beach's *The Spoilers* instead. This Alaskan saga proved to be a popular success. Kay Johnson and Betty Compson co-starred, but this story is always best remembered for the fierce knock-down, drag-out fight between the two principal men, Cooper and William "Stage" Boyd.

Cooper then reported to work on *Morocco* for director Josef von Sternberg, who used this film to introduce Marlene Dietrich to the American public. Cooper, remembering his past experiences with the German director, was most uncomfortable. To add insult to injury, von Sternberg spent most of his time and energies working with, on, and for Dietrich. To top it off, then the initial advertisements for *Morocco* billed Marlene Dietrich first, "with Gary Cooper and Adolphe Menjou." Cooper complained to the top brass and, since he was their biggest money-making male star, executives listened. The ads were changed.

Perhaps it was through his discomfort that Cooper gave one of his finest performances as the moody, sullen Legionnaire Tom Brown. His anger and annoyance was put to good use, creating a vivid anti-hero, and he received fine reviews. The studio wanted to follow up *Morocco* with Cooper and Dietrich in *Dishonored,* but Cooper refused.

Zane Grey's 1929 novel *Fighting Caravans* provided him with a wonderful Western adventure comedy-drama. His youthful glee and comic ability were a good match for his spirited co-star Lily Damita, and Ernest Torrence and Tully Marshall supplied some humorous interludes. The full-scale production was heightened by the gorgeous photography of Lee Garmes, who had photographed *Morocco,* and Henry Gerrard. The William Shea editing was also most effective.

In 1931, Paramount was considering filming Charles Dickens' classic *A Tale of Two Cities.* Gary wanted the part of Sydney Carton so much that he actually made up as the character and had photographs taken to show to studio brass. What they thought of his eagerness is not known, since they abandoned the project soon afterward.

Cooper then began a salary battle that was to last for several years. As punishment, he was put in *City Streets* in *support* of Clara Bow. This proved a lucky break for him, since Bow was soon involved in a legal hassle with her secretary Daisy DeVoe and was unable, alas, to make the film.

New York director Rouben Mamoulian, who had brilliantly directed Helen Morgan in *Applause* at Paramount's Astoria Studios in 1929, came West for his first Hollywood picture. Sylvia Sidney, better known for her stage work than her two previous film appearances, made her star debut in *City Streets,* replacing Clara Bow. Mamoulian, photog-

rapher Lee Garmes and the cast, which included Paul Lukas, Wynne Gibson and William "Stage" Boyd, made an otherwise ordinary gangster yarn sizzle with excitement.

Hoping to create a new screen team, Paramount put Cooper and Sidney into the remake of the old Lon Chaney silent *The Miracle Man,* but Cooper was soon replaced by Fredric March who was replaced by Chester Morris. Cooper went into a trifle called *I Take This Woman.* His health was not good during its filming. He lost ten pounds and was in a weakened condition; his doctor told him he had anemia and jaundice.

For a complete rest cure, Cooper left for Europe, staying first in Paris and then journeying to Italy, where he became the hit of the International set through his romance with Countess Dorothy di Frasso, the American-born daughter of multi-millionaire Bertrand L. Taylor. When he became bored with society, Cooper took off for Africa to hunt, and the Countess followed with a fully-equipped safari. Later, news reached him in Tanganyika that Paramount had found its new "Gary Cooper" and had merely switched Cooper's initials around in doing so. He was told that the young man's name, which had been Archibald Leach, was now *Cary Grant.*

Although Cooper had returned to New York briefly, months earlier, to make *Sal of Singapore* with Claudette Colbert at Paramount's Astoria Studios (released as *His Woman*), he took his time returning to Hollywood. By the time he arrived, with Countess Dorothy right behind him, Cary Grant had already been given assignments in three pictures that had been slated for Cooper: *Hot Saturday* with Nancy Carroll, *Madame Butterfly* with Sylvia Sidney, and *The Eagle and the Hawk* with Fredric March and Carole Lombard.

Back in Hollywood, Cooper began working with Tallulah Bankhead and Charles Laughton in a sour script entitled *Devil and the Deep.* The only one with a substantial part with which to work was Laughton, and he was marvelous. Bankhead and Cooper were given routine leading roles, as was Cary Grant, who appeared in the earlier scenes as a love-smitten lieutenant mad for Tallulah.

During the filming, Cooper and Bankhead did "box office duty" by making a guest appearance in the Stuart Erwin-Joan Blondell film *Make Me a Star,* a talkie re-make of Harry Leon Wilson's *Merton of the Movies.* This was followed by a brief segment in the eight-episode *If I Had a Million.*

The overall idea was good, but not all of the pieces of the puzzle fit together. Norman McLeod directed Gary's scenes.

Paramount had originally purchased Ernest Hemingway's *A Farewell to Arms* with Fredric March and Claudette Colbert in mind, but then assigned Nancy Carroll to appear with Cooper. Carroll, unfortunately, was tied up with another film and was soon replaced by Eleanor Boardman. Soon it was announced that Paramount had borrowed Helen Hayes from MGM. As Lt. Fredric Henry, Cooper gave a grand account of himself, which he attributed to the knowing direction of Frank Borzage. Helen Hayes gave one of her better performances as Catherine Barkley and Adolphe Menjou was a near-perfect Major Rinaldi. The production was technically superb and a hit with critics and public alike, despite its "happy ending."

After he refused to co-star with Sylvia Sidney in *Pick-Up* (George Raft replaced him), Paramount loaned Cooper to Metro-Goldwyn-Mayer to appear opposite Joan Crawford in *Today We Live,* based on William Faulkner's "Turnabout." Howard Hawks directed and Cedric Gibbons was the picture's art director. Like Hemingway's *A Farewell to Arms,* this was the first Faulkner work to be filmed.

Cooper was then invited to a party given by Cedric Gibbons and his wife, Dolores Del Rio, where he was introduced to the host's niece, socialite Veronica Balfe, known to her friends as "Rocky." Miss Balfe attended the Todhunter School in New York City and the Bennett School in Millbrook, New York, and had been introduced to society in 1931. She had also had a fling in movies, under the name of Sandra Shaw. Her only two appearances were in *King Kong* (she was thrown to her death from a high building when Kong realized that she wasn't Fay Wray, a bit that was cut after the first showings) and Fox's *Blood Money,* with George Bancroft, a delicious Frances Dee and a sensational Judith Anderson.

They quickly became friends and, soon, Miss Balfe's mother and stepfather (Mr. and Mrs. Paul Shields) announced the engagement at their Park Avenue home. They were married on December 15, 1933, in New York City. He was thirty-two, and she twenty. After their wedding, they left for Phoenix, Arizona, and soon moved into a house in Van Nuys. They then rented a house in Brentwood, because his schedule was so full—giving up a plan to get a farm somewhere. Their only daughter, Maria Veronica Balfe Cooper, was born on September 15,

1937. Her godparents were Dolores Del Rio and Cedric Gibbons.

Cooper did fairly well in the role of Biff Grimes in the screen adaptation of James Hagan's Broadway hit *One Sunday Afternoon.* His co-stars were: Fay Wray, in their fifth and final film together; Neil Hamilton; and Frances Fuller, repeating her original stage role as the girl who wins Cooper away from Fay, and later wins his love, too.

Paramount then co-starred him with Fredric March and Miriam Hopkins in Noël Coward's *Design for Living.* The role of George Curtis was originally felt best suited for Robert Montgomery or Douglas Fairbanks, Jr. (and one of them should have done it), but Cooper was the final choice. It wasn't his cup of tea, although he tried to make it work. Ernst Lubitsch directed with a firm hand, but all of the lightness of Coward's original was gone.

In December 1933, he made his stage debut, with Sari Maritza and Raquel Torres, at New York's Paramount Theatre, in a skit directed by Lubitsch. The theatre was jammed and the skit was awful.

Next, Cooper appeared in the multi-star *Alice in Wonderland.* As the White Knight, he wore a suit of armor, donned a bald pate, a Cyrano de Bergerac nose, a gigantic mustache and sideburns. The

10

With the elite of Hollywood: Leslie Howard,
Douglas Fairbanks, Norma Shearer, and Fredric March

critics didn't think he was particularly effective, nor did the public.

Marion Davies then borrowed Cooper for her Cosmopolitan Production of *Operator 13* at MGM. Cooper was required to do little except look handsome in this sumptuously-mounted Civil War spy story, but Miss Davies was especially good in the title role. Scenes and music from this production were later broadcast nationally over the Columbia Broadcasting System, so that people could get a sampling of what the picture contained.

Paramount announced, in June of 1933, that Gary Cooper, now under a *new* contract ($6,000.00 weekly), was to appear next with Claudette Colbert in *Honor Bright*. By the time filming began, his leading lady was Carole Lombard and the title had been changed to *Now and Forever*. Henry Hathaway, who had assisted directors on three earlier Cooper films, directed the star for the first time. They got along well and, although it isn't one of his best films, Cooper was most effective as a cynical ne'er-do-well who tries to sell his little girl (Shirley Temple) to relatives, but is eventually won over by the child's charm.

In 1934, Cooper was mentioned for several film ventures that never came about. Paramount kept trying to re-team him with Claudette Colbert and it announced, first, that they would appear in something called *52 Weeks for Fleurette* and, second, Ernst Lubitsch's *Carmen*. Cooper and Miriam Hopkins were mentioned for the remake of the Adolphe Menjou-Florence Vidor silent *The Grandduchess and the Waiter* and he was also to appear with Gertrude Michael and Claude Rains in the adventure yarn *The Last Outpost*, a role that later went to Cary Grant.

While Paramount was searching madly for a suitable script, independent producer Samuel Goldwyn found one and borrowed back the young man, who might have been a Goldwyn star, to appear with a lady Goldwyn wished very much to make a star, Anna Sten, in *The Wedding Night*. Cooper was never better, under the keen direction of King Vidor, in his portrayal of novelist Tony Barrett, who becomes involved with a Polish peasant girl while staying at his Connecticut farm. Sten also did superb work, but was the victim of an over-blown publicity campaign she failed to live up to. The surprise, however, was the magnetic performance of Helen Vinson, as Cooper's possessive wife Dora.

Goldwyn was so excited by Cooper's portrayal that he offered him the lead opposite Edward G. Robinson and Miriam Hopkins in *Barbary Coast*. However, Paramount had purchased W. R. Burnett's *Dr. Socrates* for Cooper, but when he didn't feel he was right for it, the property was sold to Warners, who made it with Paul Muni and Ann Dvorak.

Paramount then needed a vehicle for Cooper and took a second look at Major Francis Yeats-Brown's novel *The Lives of a Bengal Lancer*, which had just been cast with Clive Brook, Cary Grant and Phillips Holmes. A complete reversal was quickly executed and *The Lives of a Bengal Lancer* then starred Gary Cooper, Franchot Tone and Richard Cromwell, supported most ably by C. Aubrey Smith, Sir Guy Standing, Douglass Dumbrille and Kathleen Burke, who replaced Katherine DeMille after shooting began. Henry Hathaway directed with non-flagging action and Ellsworth Hoagland edited the film brilliantly. This remains one of the greatest adventure films ever made, a joy to see time and time again.

Hathaway was next assigned to direct an adaptation of George du Maurier's somber fantasy *Peter Ibbetson* with Robert Donat and Irene Dunne, but the pair was soon replaced by Brian Aherne and Ann Harding, who had just made an impression in RKO-Radio's *The Fountain*. Soon, however, Aherne was replaced by Cooper, who was then preparing to start shooting the murder-mystery *The Glass Key*.

Cooper's Peter Ibbetson was a remarkably shaded portrayal of a man caught in a dream world created by the woman he loved. It was an unusual change of pace for him and, while it didn't fare well in the United States, it was a tremendous hit throughout Europe. In 1935, Cooper was the most popular star in France, closely followed by Clark Gable.

Desire re-united him with Marlene Dietrich, but this time the production was supervised by Ernst Lubitsch and directed by Frank Borzage. It was a fun-fest from start to finish, with La Dietrich as an international jewel thief ensnaring a vacationing auto engineer from Detroit into her plot to sneak a pearl necklace across the Spanish border. The Cooper-Dietrich duo put an otherwise routine script into high gear.

Cooper and Carole Lombard then turned down *The Case Against Mrs. Ames*, which was handed to George Brent and Madeleine Carroll. Lombard was shipped off to Universal and made history in *My Man Godfrey*, while Cooper went to Columbia for *Mr. Deeds Goes to Town*, a film that was to do for him what *It Happened One Night* had done for Clark Gable.

Longfellow Deeds, a bashful millionaire in a disillusioned world, suited Cooper like a glove and his work, under Frank Capra's witty direction of Robert Riskin's agile script, proved even to his detractors that he was an actor of quality and depth, not just a "movie star." Jean Arthur and an excellent supporting cast helped make this one of the happiest films of all time. For his performance, Cooper received his first Academy Award nomination.

He then won the leading role in King Vidor's large-scale Western *The Texas Rangers* and on May 2, 1936, he and Jack Oakie left Hollywood for New Mexico to shoot the location scenes for the picture. Cooper never did this assignment, for he was replaced by Fred MacMurray.

Goldwyn then made another bid for Cooper's services, for his proposed filming of *Maximilian of Mexico*, which was to co-star Merle Oberon, Joel McCrea and Miriam Hopkins, but Paramount had hired Broadway's *enfant terrible,* Clifford Odets, to write a scenario for Cooper, tentatively entitled *Chinese Gold.* Before he appeared in this production, however, Cooper did an unbilled guest bit in Robert Florey's *Hollywood Boulevard,* which starred his good friend John Halliday. *Chinese Gold* became the beautifully-mounted production *The General Died at Dawn.* Odets provided Cooper with the life-size part of an American soldier of fortune who risks life and death to come to the aid of poor Chinese peasants.

This was followed by a deliciously grandiose Western melodrama called *The Plainsman,* which Cecil B. DeMille produced and directed. Cooper was Wild Bill Hickok, Jean Arthur was Calamity Jane, and James Ellison was Buffalo Bill Cody. *Souls at Sea,* which followed, was a robust sea saga in which Cooper's pal George Raft goes down to the sea in a ship carrying his dead ladylove as Cooper escapes to safety with Frances Dee.

Cooper and Irene Dunne were slated for *Swing High, Swing Low,* but were replaced by Fred MacMurray and Carole Lombard as Cooper went back to Goldwyn for *The Adventures of Marco Polo,* a tongue-in-cheek mish-mash by Robert E. Sherwood.

Comedies were again on his agenda, and Cooper first appeared in *Bluebeard's Eighth Wife.* Finally cast again with Claudette Colbert, he seemed uncomfortable as a sophisticate under the direction of Ernst Lubitsch. Next was *The Cowboy and the Lady* for Goldwyn, which was less sophisticated, but much more fun, and let him utilize all of his natural qualities representative of the "simple man." He was most appealing as the cowboy. The lady was Merle Oberon.

Director William A. Wellman then resurrected P. C. Wren's *Beau Geste* and gave it a superb production. The photography, art direction and second unit work were all first-rate. The fine cast included Ray Milland, Robert Preston and Brian Donlevy, who was outstanding as Sergeant Markoff. The small role of Isobel was originally assigned to Patricia Morison, but she was replaced by a young lady well on her way at Paramount, Susan Hayward.

While Cooper returned to the Goldwyn Studio once again, Paramount filmed *The Light That Failed* with Ronald Colman in a part that was originally offered to Cooper in 1935. Henry Hathaway directed *The Real Glory,* which depicted the 1900 Moro uprisings of the Philippine Islands, and Cooper was excellent as a doctor fighting great odds in a disease-ridden village.

The U.S. Treasury Department reported in 1939 that Gary Cooper was the nation's top wage earner, at $482,819.

He stayed on to work under William Wyler, whom Goldwyn had set to direct *The Westerner* after his great production of *Wuthering Heights.* Even though his friend Walter Brennan had the showier role of Judge Roy Bean, Cooper was wise enough to stand his ground. His delineation of Cole Hardin, often overlooked, is a sound example of his skill at finding the common denominator of a character and knowing how to proceed from there. This "psychological" Western seemed to do more thinking and talking than getting itself involved with physical action, but Wyler handled the situation with keen foresight. Gregg Toland's masterful use of the camera made each frame seem like a celluloid poem.

North West Mounted Police was Cecil B. DeMille's first Technicolor film and Cooper's first feature-length venture into the new three-color process. The vast locales enhanced a vigorous tale, full of Mounties, Texas Rangers, Indians and romance.

Frank Capra's 1941 *Meet John Doe* was definitely a *protest,* long before that idiom became commonplace in the 1960's. Robert Riskin's script, which began on a humorous note and became more serious as it unfolded, was really warning America to be on its guard against fascism. The production and the acting were of a high caliber and director Capra never let his action lag or waver for a minute. Cooper's John Doe remains one of his finest characterizations, full of subtle nuances few thought him capable of conveying. Barbara Stanwyck, as the girl who "created" John Doe and later saved him from self-destruction, was splendid.

Warner Bros. then offered him another role which gave him a fine opportunity to create a solid piece of acting, that of Alvin C. York, America's most decorated hero of the first World War. His transition from rowdy hillbilly to a man who "gets religion" to conscientious objector to fine soldier to humble war hero was skillfully executed. *Sergeant York,* directed by Howard Hawks was one of the best film biographies to come out of Hollywood—but, that it did come out of Hollywood resulted in the film's only noticeable defect, the tacky, unnecessary, "glossy" ending.

This film brought Cooper his due when he was voted the Best Actor of the Year by the New York Film Critics, and, in February 1942, at the Hollywood Biltmore Hotel, James Stewart presented Cooper with the Oscar of the Academy of Motion Picture Arts and Sciences. The Best Actress Award went to Joan Fontaine for *Suspicion.*

Cooper then made two more excellent pictures for Samuel Goldwyn. *Ball of Fire* was a sprightly comedy, in which he portrayed a young, scholarly, but somewhat dull, professor who is taught some wonderful slang by burlesque queen Barbara Stanwyck. The scenario by Charles Brackett and Billy Wilder was glib and full of fun under Howard Hawks' direction.

Sam Wood's production *The Pride of the Yankees,* which followed, provided Cooper with what many consider his greatest screen portrayal. As Lou Gehrig, the New York Yankee baseball star whose life was cut short by a rare paralysis, Cooper was warm, real and sincere in his depiction of Gehrig the man. The fact that Cooper knew little of baseball was of minor importance, for he worked for weeks with various coaches to affect the proper demeanor. For this role, he received his third Academy Award nomination.

Barred from military service during World War II, because of his age (forty-one) and ailments, Cooper made a 23,000 mile tour of the Southwest Pacific. His recitation of Gehrig's farewell speech in Yankee Stadium left few with dry eyes, and was extremely popular with the GIs.

Cooper and director Sam Wood then made Ernest

Hemingway's *For Whom the Bell Tolls* at Paramount, with Ingrid Bergman, in short-clipped hair, as his co-star. The production was lush, the romance vivid, the politics muddled, the color photography breathtaking, the length *long.* Cooper, Hemingway's own personal choice for the role of Robert Jordan, was rewarded with his fourth Academy Award nomination. In subsequent showings abroad, and in the late 1950's in the States, *For Whom the Bell Tolls* was drastically cut, but, miraculously Cooper and Bergman escaped the scissors.

Wood, Cooper and Bergman then packed their bags and moved to Warner Bros. to film Edna Ferber's *Saratoga Trunk.* Cooper was just perfect in the kind of adventurous role to which he added so much. Bergman playing in a dark wig, proved that comedy was a game she could easily play. Filming was completed by June, 1943, the picture edited, scored and ready for release by the end of the year, but Warners held up general release until the War was over. The general public first saw this gem in November, 1945.

Cecil B. DeMille and Cooper were together again in *The Story of Dr. Wassell* at Paramount. It was a Technicolored saga of a U.S. naval doctor who saved the lives of some marines and sailors in Java during the early years of the war in the Pacific. This single, courageous act was destined to become a DeMille epic of heroism and was considerably overblown.

The early 1940's were Gary Cooper's prime years, with one hit after another and performances which delighted audiences and pleased critics and top quality productions. His growth as an actor rivaled his importance as a "star." The only trouble lay in the fact that such a trend does not continue forever. Everyone expected a blockbuster. However, the picture that followed, *Casanova Brown,* his fourth film directed by Sam Wood, was a delightful comedy in a light vein, not a blockbuster.

It was produced and written by Nunnally Johnson for the newly-formed International Pictures, Inc. Cooper was charming in the title role and was backed up by young pros like Teresa Wright and old pros like Frank Morgan. Again, his simple-man characterization contained some of his best work.

Said Sam Wood: "You're positive he's going to ruin your picture. I froze in my tracks the first time I directed him. I thought something was wrong with him, and I saw a million-dollar production go glimmering. I was amazed at the results on the screen. What I thought was underplaying turned out to be just the right approach. On the screen he's perfect, yet on the set you'd swear it's the worst job of acting in the history of motion pictures."

Cooper became a producer in 1945 with *Along Came Jones,* also starring as the shy cowboy who is mistaken for a notorious outlaw. Loretta Young was his beautiful leading lady. Next, intrigue and danger were his in *Cloak and Dagger,* which introduced Continental actress Lilli Palmer to U.S. audiences, a better-than-average spy yarn directed by Fritz Lang.

Unconquered re-united Cooper with Paulette Goddard and was his fourth and final picture for Cecil B. DeMille, although the three of them appeared in the all-star *Variety Girl,* filmed at the same time, which was released just after *Unconquered.*

Cooper then testified before the 1947 House Committee on Un-American Activities. He had noticed certain Communist elements at Hollywood gatherings and once turned down a script because "its leading character was a man whose ambition was to organize an army in the United States that wouldn't fight to defend the country."

Along with Ann Sheridan, Cooper then appeared in a film for Producer-Director Leo McCarey (Rainbow Productions) called *Good Sam.* McCarey's original conception was Cooper's screen image personified, but his idea got lost somewhere during the filming. However, *Good Sam* is still a joy to watch, if only for all of the laugh-packed bits McCarey injected into it. Cooper and Sheridan were a delight.

Cooper next ventured into Ayn Rand's *The Fountainhead* as the idealistic architect Howard Roark and gave a most interesting interpretation of a difficult role. His co-star was Patricia Neal, who was quite effective, and King Vidor directed.

Before going into the extremely good naval actioner *Task Force,* Cooper did box-office duty for Warners by appearing as himself on the Warner lot, in David Butler's *It's a Great Feeling. Task Force* is the kind of actioner that is always a pleasure to sit through. It had much to offer: action, romance, comedy, drama and Technicolor newsreel footage of World War II edited in, which gave credibility to the action which preceded it. Jane Wyatt, as his wife, gave a warm and moving performance.

Patricia Neal was again cast with Cooper in a routine melodrama set in the South—along with Lauren Bacall and Jack Carson—called *Bright Leaf* and what the script lacked was more than made up

for in its handsome mounting. Gary played his role almost effortlessly, but he was still effective, as was Jack Carson. The women, however, were not as lucky.

In 1950, it was rumored that Cooper would make his "legitimate" stage debut in Horton Foote's *The Chase,* but it was never more than a rumor.

Bright Leaf was followed-up by a clanker called *Dallas,* a Technicolor western romp with Ruth Roman. He then went to 20th Century-Fox for Henry Hathaway's delightful comedy *U.S.S. Teakettle.* As a Naval Reserve Officer who takes command of a ship during World War II only to find all but one of his crew are "90-day wonders," like himself, he gave a humorous characterization. Cooper actually made a rare personal appearance when *U.S.S. Teakettle* opened at the Roxy in New York City and he clowned with the Ritz Brothers. In an interview, he said, "Only reason I made the appearance was because I like the picture very much and I wanted to help it along." Despite fine reviews when the film opened, there was little deposited in the box office till, so Fox withdrew it and quickly re-titled it *You're in the Navy Now,* which it has remained ever since.

In 1951, he separated from "Rocky" for a period and dated such women as Patricia Neal and Kay Topping (later Mrs. Clark Gable.) The gossip columnists were delighted to have some "dirt" with which to fill their reader's hearts, but Cooper disappointed them a short time later when he told reporters, "It's true we've had a little difficulty, but it's not serious."

Cooper then appeared as himself—again—in Warner's *Starlift,* satirizing his own image as a Western hero in a sketch with Frank Lovejoy, Phil Harris and Virginia Gibson. This foursome sang "Look Out, Stranger, I'm a Texas Ranger." Next, he went to MGM for an engaging bit in their eight-episode view of America entitled *It's a Big Country.* Cooper's section, called "Texas," was written by Dorothy Kingsley and directed by Clarence Brown. The episode that critics always singled out for comment, it was clever and humorous.

Back at Warner Bros., Cooper got trapped in a low-adventure creation called *Distant Drums,* and, from the look of things, they weren't distant enough. Everything relied on Cooper's name, but while his name was big at the box office, it wasn't big enough to overcome a rotten story and sluggish direction.

He next made a perfect move; he agreed to take a cut in salary for a percentage of the profits, which

With lifelong friend,
and his stand-in
for many years,
Jay "Slim" Talbot

With his wife "Rocky,"
Dolores Del Rio, and Cedric Gibbons

Cooper in the 1920s

With Joan Fontaine at
Academy Award ceremonies,
February 1942

At San Simeon with Hostess-with-the-Mostess
Marion Davies (right) and guest Mary Pickford

Eating with the troops
in the South Pacific, 1943

The Ernest Hemingways flanking
the Gary Coopers at the Stork Club

17

enabled producer Stanley Kramer to bring in a Western picture for $750,000. That was the beginning of big star participation in the business side of movie-making. Later, Cooper would continue to get "a piece of the action," without having to take a cut in regular salary. Such was his power at the box office.

Kramer's picture was *High Noon*. Cooper came back into the foreground with his superlative performance of Marshal Will Kane, who is forced to face four killers as the corrupt townspeople turn away from him. Fred Zinnemann's direction, Dimitri Tiomkin's musical score and Elmo William's editing proved that even a conventional Western's framework could achieve variations on the age-old theme and fully demonstrated that the motion picture is indeed the twentieth century's most dynamic art form. His sixth Academy Award nomination won him his second Oscar.

The next few years produced no films in the caliber of *High Noon*, but Cooper's salary—and percentage—grew and grew. While not artsy-craftsy, the following films *were* enjoyable, for one reason or another: *Springfield Rifle, Return to Paradise, Blowing Wild, Garden of Evil* (his first film in CinemaScope), *Vera Cruz* and *The Court-Martial of Billy Mitchell.*

Cooper, himself, purchased two properties during the 1950's which he hoped to produce and star in, but, in both cases, nothing came about. He purchased Alfred Hayes' book *The Girl on the Via Flaminia* with the intention of co-starring Ingrid Bergman or Valli, but he eventually sold the rights to Anatole Litvak and Leland Hayward for $50,000. He also bought the film rights to A. B. Guthrie, Jr.'s *The Way West* for $65,000, with similar plans.

In 1956, Cooper "told" his memoirs to *Saturday Evening Post* writer George Scullin and they appeared in eight installments, entitled "Well, It Was This Way."

Director William Wyler then got Cooper's services for the role of Jess Birdwell in his production of Jessamyn West's *Friendly Persuasion.* This totally beautiful picture was, with little doubt, Cooper's finest film since *High Noon.* In it, he gave a charming, sincere and wholesome portrayal of a Quaker husband and father in Indiana at the time of the Civil War. Wyler, who had directed him in *The Westerner,* sixteen years earlier, gave this production such a human touch, that it appealed to just about every type of audience. Wyler later

Cooper in the 1930s

said of Cooper "He's a superb actor, a master of movie acting."

He invaded the recording industry in August of 1956, when he cut a disc of Dimitri Tiomkin's "Marry Me, Marry Me" from *Friendly Persuasion.* Said he: "I hope all of this won't ruin my career."

Billy Wilder's *Love in the Afternoon* followed and, although his co-star Audrey Hepburn gave a radiant performance, many felt that Cooper was too old to appear opposite so young an actress. The basic faults were probably miscasting him again as a sophisticate and the fact that he appeared extremely tired.

He then assumed the role of Joe Chapin, which Spencer Tracy had turned down, in the filmization of John O'Hara's *Ten North Frederick* and gave a good performance, despite a hackneyed script and uninspired direction. Acting honors fell to ex-model Suzy Parker, whose delineation of Kate Drummond, who had an affair with the older politician, went deeper than what the scenarist provided.

He was treated for a stomach ulcer and had minor facial surgery in 1958, thus creating the rumors that Cooper had had his face "lifted." The following year he converted to Catholicism, the faith of his wife and daughter.

After the second-rate *Man of the West,* Cooper appeared in Delmer Daves' *The Hanging Tree,* which was based on the excellent novelette by Dorothy M. Johnson, one of the best Western writers. Most everyone expected another routine picture, but they were treated to an intelligent drama, ably handled by a first-rate cast.

He was then picked off by gun-totin' Bob Hope in an unbilled guest bit at the climax of *Alias Jesse James.*

Cooper made a few appearances on television, which were both good and bad. He was good when he appeared with Dick Powell on "The Steve Allen Show," but he was bad on "The Ed Sullivan Show," for which he re-created a scene from *The Court-Martial of Billy Mitchell.*

Because of his illnesses, doctors advised against his making the long journey to Australia to appear opposite Deborah Kerr in Fred Zinnemann's *The Sundowners* and the role went to Robert Mitchum (and became one of his best). However, Cooper did make Robert Rossen's strange all-star opus *They Came to Cordura,* which was followed by MGM's *The Wreck of the Mary Deare* co-starring Charlton Heston. The latter was a fine sea suspense story, but Cooper again appeared tired and

Cooper in the 1950s

19

spent. No one knew, or realized, just how ill he was, not even himself.

In 1960, his doctors discovered that he was suffering from cancer, but didn't tell him. Two major abdominal operations were performed and, after his convalescence, he went to England to make *The Naked Edge* for director Michael Anderson, who had directed him in *Mary Deare*. Deborah Kerr, back from Australia, was his leading lady. Filming was done at the Elstree Studios, plus several location scenes in and around London.

After Cooper's return to the United States, in December, 1960, he spent a few weeks at Sun Valley, Idaho, and then narrated and appeared in the excellent television documentary *The Real West*, produced on NBC-TV's "Project 20" series. In it, the West was shown as it was before it was glamorized by dime novels, Hollywood epics, and weekly television sagas. Cooper's handling of the narrative was a perfect piece of casting. He appeared against the background of a ghost town. When viewed on March 29, 1961, *Time* magazine remarked "Aided by Gary Cooper's relaxed narration of a fine script, the program looked deep into the eyes of settlers, cowboys, Indians, Westerners of all conditions." Jack Gould in *The New York Times* noted "Gary Cooper, in one of his infrequent appearances on the home screen, acted as narrator of the hour and showed to fine advantage in the drawl for which he is famed."

In January of 1961, a testimonial dinner was given for him by the Friars, during which poet Carl Sandburg called him "one of the most beloved illiterates this country has ever known." Cooper, embarrassed by the various remarks, said, "The only achievement I am really proud of is the friends I have made in this community."

The next month, he learned from his doctors the truth about his cancer, and they began treating him with radioactive cobalt, which was a well-kept secret until the Academy Award presentations several weeks later, when his close friend James Stewart accepted an honorary Oscar on his behalf. The citation read as follows: "Gary Cooper for his many memorable screen performances and the international recognition he, as an individual, has gained for the motion picture industry." Stewart, in his almost tearful tribute, said, "We're all very proud of you, Coop. All of us are tremendously proud."

Two days later, his agent released to the press the news of Gary Cooper's mortal illness. The public responded with thousands of letters sent to his lavish, one-story home (on three hillside acres in the plush Holmby Hills area of West Los Angeles). Among them were messages from President John F. Kennedy and Queen Elizabeth II of Great Britain, an honor accorded few film personalities.

As the end drew near, Cooper was confined to his bed and kept under heavy sedation. His friend of many years, Ernest Hemingway, then bedridden in a hospital, phoned Cooper during those last few days. He was told by Coop, "I'll bet I make it to the barn before you do."

On May 13, 1961, just six days after his sixtieth birthday, Cooper was gone. His death left a void no other actor can ever fill.

Services were held at the Church of the Good Shepherd in Beverly Hills, and only his family and

close friends went to Holy Cross Cemetery where he was buried. His eighty-six-year-old mother was there, with Cooper's sixty-five-year-old brother Arthur. Cooper's father had passed away in 1946.

His pallbearers included James Stewart, William Goetz, Jack Benny and Samuel Goldwyn.

The press of the world eulogized him:

Perhaps with him there is ended a certain America . . . that of the frontier and of innocence which had or was believed to have an exact sense of the dividing line between good and evil.
— *Corriere Della Sera* (ROME)

He had the soul of a boy, a pure, simple, nice, warm boy's soul . . . he was the incarnation of the honorable American.
— *Svenska Dagbladet* (STOCKHOLM)

He was the symbol of trust, confidence and protection . . . He is dead now. What a miracle that he existed.
— *Die Welt* (HAMBURG)

But the peoples of the world carry another impression of Gary Cooper, for he left them a legacy of the kind of person he stood for during his thirty-six-year span as a public figure, which is perhaps best described in Cooper's own words: "I looked at it this way. To get folks to like you—as a screen player, I mean—I figured you had to sort of be their ideal. I don't mean a handsome knight riding a white horse, but a fella who answered the description of a right guy."

At home
with his daughter
Maria and wife "Rocky"

With Marilyn Mills in *Three Pals*

THE SHORTER FILMS OF GARY COOPER

THE EXTRA FILMS:

The task of reconstructing Gary Cooper's career as an extra is not an easy one, since the prime necessity for searching out these bit performances is being able to see all, or nearly all, of the films released during 1925 and 1926. Most of these films, however, with the exception of noted classics, are unavailable for study purposes, even to bona fide film societies. The following list represents probably about one-eighth of these extra appearances and has been substantiated through Mr. Cooper's own recollections, actual screenings of the films, or through still photographs. They are in order of *release* date:

1) THE THUNDERING HERD (Paramount), 1925. Director: William K. Howard. From the novel by Zane Grey. Cast: Noah Beery, Raymond Hatton, Lois Wilson, Jack Holt.

2) WILD HORSE MESA (Paramount), 1925. Director: George B. Seitz. From the novel by Zane Grey. Cast: Jack Holt and Billie Dove.

3) THE LUCKY HORSESHOE (Fox), 1925. Director: John G. Blystone. Scenarist: John Stone. Cast: Tom Mix, Billie Dove and Ann Pennington.

4) THE VANISHING AMERICAN (Paramount), 1925. Director: George B. Seitz. From the novel by Zane Grey. Scenarist: Lucien Hubbard and Ethel Doherty. Photographer: Bert Glennon. Cast: Richard Dix, Lois Wilson, Noah Beery.

5) THE EAGLE (United Artists), 1925. Director: Clarence Brown. Scenarist: Hans Kraly. Photographer: George Barnes. Cast: Rudolph Valentino, Vilma Banky and Louise Dresser.

6) THE ENCHANTED HILL (Paramount), 1926. Director: Irwin Willat. Scenarists: James Shelley Hamilton and Victor Irwin. Cast: Florence Vidor, Jack Holt and Noah Beery.

7) WATCH YOUR WIFE (Universal), 1926.

22

Director: Sven Gade. Scenarists: Charles E.
Whittaker and Sven Gade. Cast: Virginia Valli,
Pat O'Malley and Nat Carr.

THE SHORT SUBJECTS:

The films included in this section are not of
feature length, although the first two were five-
reelers (featurettes).

1) TRICKS (Davis Distributing Company), 1925.
Director: Bruce Mitchell. Scenarist: Mary C.
Bruning. Cast: Marilyn Mills and J. Frank
Glendon.

2) THREE PALS (Davis Distributing Company),
1925. Director: Bruce Mitchell. Scenarist:
Mary C. Bruning. Cast: Marilyn Mills and J.
Frank Glendon.

3) LIGHTNIN' WINS (Independent Pictures
Corporation), 1926. Director: Hans Tiesler.
Cast: Lightnin', The Super Dog and Eileen
Sedgwick.

4) THE SLIPPERY PEARLS (1932). Little is
known about this two-reel short except that
it was one of the famous, but almost forgotten, shorts made by the Masquers Club. Stars
from all the studios made appearances in them
and salaries were donated to worthy Hollywood charities. This particular film concerned the theft of pearls belonging to Norma
Shearer. Others in the big-name cast included
Edward G. Robinson, Irene Dunne, Buster
Keaton, Barbara Stanwyck, Joan Crawford,
Gary Cooper, Laurel & Hardy, Loretta Young,
Wynne Gibson, Fay Wray, and Wallace Beery,
among many others.

5) VOICE OF HOLLYWOOD (Tiffany), 1932.
Twelve-minute short featuring Farina as the
studio M.C., John Wayne as the announcer
and Thelma Todd as "Miss Information."
The guests included George Bancroft, El
Brendel, Jackie Cooper, Lupe Velez, and Gary
Cooper.

6) STAR NIGHT AT THE COCONUT
GROVE, 1935. A candid glimpse of Hollywood notables arriving at the famous night
spot (in gorgeous Colourtone, according to the
ads) with such stars as Mary Pickford, Bing
Crosby, Gary Cooper, Jack Oakie, John Mack
Brown and Leo Carrillo. This item was a part
of the bill that accompanied *Naughty Marietta*
at the Empire Theatre in New York, in 1935,
when short subjects were popular.

As an extra in *The Thundering Herd* (1925)

23

Cooper (left) with Vilma Banky
and Rudolph Valentino in *The Eagle* (1925)

7) LA FIESTA DE SANTA BARBARA (Metro-Goldwyn-Mayer), 1936. Shot in Technicolor, this 19-minute M-G-M short subject used the Santa Barbara Mission, during fiesta days, as its background. There was loads of singing, dancing and humor supplied by stars like Cooper, Buster Keaton, Ida Lupino, Binnie Barnes, Robert Taylor, Toby Wing, Edmund Lowe, Warner Baxter, and Harpo Marx, among others. Steffi Duna and Maria Gambarelli did dance numbers and Joe Morrison sang "The Last Round-Up."

8) LEST WE FORGET (Metro-Goldwyn-Mayer), 1937. Director and Scenarist: Frank Whitbeck. Musical Score: David Snell. This one-reel short subject was a pictorial message in behalf of the Will Rogers Memorial Hospital at Saranac Lake, New York. Gary Cooper and Harry Carey spoke informally about Will Rogers, Allan Jones sang "a song of the hills," and Robert Taylor made the direct plea to the audience for funds.

9) MEMO FOR JOE (Produced by RKO Pathé for the National War Fund), 1944. Director: Richard O. Fleischer. Producer: Frederick Ullman, Jr. Scenarist: Ardis Smith. Narrator: Quentin Reynolds. Eight minutes. Released: August 10, 1944. Cooper was seen briefly entertaining troops in the Pacific on his USO tour. Other clips included such stars as Bob Hope, Frances Langford, Joe E. Brown, Ray Bolger and John Wayne.

With Marilyn Mills,
J. Frank Glendon
and Wesley Barry in *Tricks*

24

10) SNOW CARNIVAL (Warner Bros.), 1949. Cooper narrated, produced and performed in this Technicolor sports short.

11) HOLLYWOOD MOTHERS (Columbia), 1955. Director: Ralph Staub. Editor: Edwin Bryant. Musical Conductor: Mischa Bakaleinikoff. One of the popular Columbia "Screen Snapshots," this one featured clips of famous movie personalities with their mothers. Gary Cooper and his mother were joined by Joan Crawford, Jane Powell and Cesar Romero and their mothers.

COMPILATION FILM:

LAND OF LIBERTY (Metro-Goldwyn-Mayer), 1939-1941. Editor: Cecil B. DeMille. Assistants: Herbert L. Moulton, Francis Stuart Harmon, Arthur H. DeBra and William H. Pine. Narrative by Jeanie MacPherson and Jesse Lasky, Jr. Historical Consultant and Commentary by James T. Shotwell. Presented by the Motion Picture Industry of the U.S.

This impressive compilation film featured ap-

Cooper, extreme left, as an extra with Virginia Valli and Pat O'Malley (center table) in Universal's *Watch Your Wife*

proximately 140 stars in clips from 112 feature pictures and short subjects over a period of twenty-five years. Cuttings from newsreels and stock footage material were also used. Included were scenes from *OPERATOR 13, THE PLAINSMAN,* and *THE ADVENTURES OF MARCO POLO.*

The central theme, although slight deviations occurred, was to show great moments in American history.

His television debut (1955)
with Steve Allen
and Dick Powell on "The Steve Allen Show"

With J. Frank Glendon
and Marilyn Mills in *Tricks*

FILMOGRAPHY

THE WINNING OF BARBARA WORTH

A Samuel Goldwyn Production
Released Thru United Artists   1926

CAST:

RONALD COLMAN *(Willard Holmes)*; VILMA BANKY *(Barbara Worth)*; CHARLES LANE *(Jefferson Worth)*; PAUL MC ALLISTER *(The Seer)*; E. J. RATCLIFFE *(James Greenfield)*; GARY COOPER *(Abe Lee)*; CLYDE COOKE *(Tex)*; ERWIN CONNELLY *(Pat)*; SAM BLUM *(Blanton)*; EDWIN BRADY.

CREDITS:

HENRY KING *(Director)*; SAMUEL GOLDWYN *(Producer)*; FRANCES MARION *(Scenarist)*; GEORGE BARNES *(Photographer)*; VIOLA LAWRENCE *(Editor)*; CARL OSCAR BORG *(Art Director)*; GREGG TOLAND *(Associate Photographer)*; RUPERT HUGHES *(Titler)*; TED HENKEL *(Musical Score)*. *Based on the novel by* HAROLD BELL WRIGHT.

SYNOPSIS:

Jefferson Worth, who owns a valuable stretch of land in the Colorado River country, together with a group of New York financiers, undertakes an enormous irrigation plan to turn arid land into fertile soil. Willard Holmes, an engineer from the East, is put in charge of the project. During a routine inspection of the dam, another young engineer, Abe Lee, discovers that it is faulty. He therefore warns the men, but no one believes his report.

Financier James Greenfield, who plans to double-cross his partners, tries to break up a romance between Holmes and Barbara Worth, Jefferson's adopted daughter. Meanwhile, the dam is about to burst and, after an exhausting race, Lee is able to alert Holmes just in time to avoid a catastrophe. Holmes saves the day, thus winning the beautiful Barbara, as Lee, her other suitor, dies—a victim of his own courage.

NOTES:

Harold Bell Wright's 1911 novel *The Winning of Barbara Worth* has little to do with its title, for the

With Ronald Colman

With Vilma Banky and Ronald Colman

main concentration is on Jefferson Worth, whose men find a little desert waif, whom he adopts and brings up as his own daughter. Barbara appears only in the last fifty or so pages of the novel.

Henry King's filmization is noteworthy for three reasons: its superb photography, by George Barnes and Gregg Toland; the fantastic flood scene, which highlights the film's climax; and the film debut of a young Montana cowboy named Gary Cooper. Cooper had only a few scenes in this epic story of the Southwest, but he established an immediate rapport with audiences.

Although this film was one of the biggest box-office hits of 1926, it is of relatively minor importance today. Not only did the public like Cooper, but the critics did too. Said *Variety Weekly:* "An outstanding performance was given by Gary Cooper as Abe Lee, played in a most sympathetic manner, who came near taking the stuff away from Colman. Cooper is a youth who will be heard of on the screen and possibly blossom out as an 'ace' lead, of which there seems to be a scarcity on the coast right now."

The *New York Herald Tribune* found the film ". . . at times annoying, but at other times it has moments of real beauty. . . . The flood rivals the Red Sea overflow in *The Ten Commandments.*" *Motion Picture* thought "Gary Cooper played the most consistent and convincing characterization of the picture as Abe Lee." *Picture Play* wrote, "Barbara Worth set a high price on her fair hand, but if she had valued herself lightly there would have been nothing for Harold Bell Wright to call *The Winning of Barbara Worth,* and less for Samuel Goldwyn to film. There is too little as it is to have enlisted the fine skill of Henry King and the talents of Vilma Banky and Ronald Colman. They are all out of their element."

30

With Vilma Banky

With William Austin

IT

A Paramount Picture   1927

CAST:

CLARA BOW *(Betty Lou)*; ANTONIO MORENO *(Cyrus Waltham)*; WILLIAM AUSTIN *(Monty)*; JACQUELINE GADSDON *(Adela Van Norman)*; JULIA SWAYNE GORDON *(Mrs. Van Norman)*; PRISCILLA BONNER *(Molly)*; ELEANOR LAWSON *(First Welfare Worker)*; ROSE TAPLEY *(Second Welfare Worker)*; GARY COOPER *(Reporter)*; ELINOR GLYN *(Herself)*; LLOYD CORRIGAN *(Cabin Boy on Yacht)*.

CREDITS:

CLARENCE BADGER *(Director)*; CLARENCE BADGER, ELINOR GLYN *(Producers)*; B. P. SCHULBERG *(Associate Producer)*; HOPE LORING, LOUIS D. LIGHTON *(Scenarists)*; ELINOR GLYN *(Adaptation)*; H. KINLEY MARTIN *(Photographer)*; E. LLOYD SHELDON *(Editor)*;

GEORGE MARION, JR. *(Titler)*. *Based on the novel by* ELINOR GLYN.

SYNOPSIS:

Young Cyrus Waltham has just had a department store business turned over to him by his father. Waltham's old pal, Monty, comes in to congratulate him and the two decide to make a tour of inspection. The two young men, who have just read Elinor Glyn's story of "It" in a magazine, decide to look for "it" among the shop girls. Waltham catches the eye of sassy Betty Lou, who made sure he would, and they later date.

After a night at the Ritz with her boss, Betty Lou makes a bet with her girl friend Molly that the next time he sees her he won't know her. She

31

wins her bet. Complications set in, but, in the end, she hooks him after a thrilling struggle in the water, which is her way of easing herself into a yachting party given by Waltham.

NOTES:

Once Cooper had completed his role in Goldwyn's *The Winning of Barbara Worth,* he was snapped up by Paramount. While they were checking through scripts in which to use Cooper, word was already spreading about his performance in Henry King's new picture. One who heard this news was Clara Bow, then the darling money-maker of Paramount. She insisted that Cooper be given a part—any part—in her new film, *It.*

Thus, Cooper played a reporter in a tenement scene. His two shots had him first on the street in front of the apartment building and then on the landing outside the apartment. Clara Bow was inside that apartment, but Cooper never got past the doorway. Clara Bow did a beautiful job as the Jazz-age baby who had "it" and her co-star, Antonio Moreno, fresh from co-starring with Garbo in MGM's *Torrent,* was excellent as Waltham.

Said *Variety:* "Best picture that the big, new Broadway house [New York's Paramount Theatre] has had to date. Clara Bow really does it all, and how!" *Motion Picture,* however, felt "The picture is streaky—sometimes dreadfully dull, but just as often fresh and amusing, and worth a trial."

With Esther Ralston

CHILDREN OF DIVORCE

A Paramount Picture   1927

CAST:

CLARA BOW *(Kitty Flanders);* ESTHER RALSTON *(Jean Waddington);* GARY COOPER *(Ted Larrabee);* EINAR HANSON *(Prince Ludovico de Sfax);* NORMAN TREVOR *(Duke de Gondreville);* HEDDA HOPPER *(Katherine Flanders);* EDWARD MARTINDEL *(Tom Larrabee);* JULIA SWAYNE GORDON *(Princess de Sfax);* TOM RICKETTS *(The Secretary);* ALBERT GRAN *(Mr. Seymour);* IRIS STUART *(Mousie);* MARGARET CAMPBELL *(Mother Superior);* PERCY WILLIAMS *(Manning);* JOYCE MARIE COAD *(Little Kitty);* YVONNE PELLETIER *(Little Jean);* DON MARION *(Little Ted).*

CREDITS:

FRANK LLOYD *(Director);* E. LLOYD SHELDON *(Producer);* HOPE LORING, LOUIS D. LIGHTON *(Scenarists);* VICTOR MILNER *(Photographer);* E. LLOYD SHELDON *(Editor);* B. P. SCHULBERG *(Associate Producer). Based on the novel by* OWEN MCMAHON JOHNSON.

SYNOPSIS:

Jean Waddington, Ted Larrabee and Kitty Flanders have grown up together in a rich, spoiled society. Jean and Ted, like many of their friends, are children of divorce and are, thus, hesitant about getting married, though they love one another deeply. Although most of the young people in their crowd are flippant and have a cynical attitude toward love, like Kitty Flanders, Jean and Ted are much too serious.

After a night of wild partying, Kitty tricks Ted into marriage and, on the morning after, he receives a note from the girl he really loves, Jean. She, too, marries a man she doesn't love and soon learns that he is unfaithful. Shortly thereafter, Kitty dies tragically and Jean divorces her husband. Now the two can marry.

NOTES:

Clara Bow, by this time, liked Gary Cooper and,

while Paramount was preparing the western, *Arizona Bound* for him, asked that he be given the romantic lead in this drama. The hero, Ted Larrabee, was a weakling and Cooper wasn't good in this role. He was actually replaced once, because his love-scenes were "awful." However, it turned out that his replacement was just as bad, so he was asked to finish the picture.

Children of Divorce also wasn't the kind of film-fare that director Frank Lloyd did well and the end result wasn't to be believed. In a desperate move, Paramount called in Josef von Sternberg to give the film some "spunk," which he certainly did. The rough edges were ironed out and many scenes were re-shot at night (the stars were already on other assignments), until the desired effect was achieved. Paramount was impressed with this stream-lining job by von Sternberg and quickly assigned him a melodramatic script which, in his hands, began a trend of gangster films. The movie was *Underworld*.

Said *Photoplay:* "This starts out to be a preach-ment against divorce and ends in convincing audiences that circumstances alter cases and divorce isn't such a terrible thing after all." *Variety* felt "Miss Ralston rings true on her 'class' impersona-tion and there is little doubt that both starred girls take the picture away from the men. Gary Cooper will likely find himself more at home in Westerns." *Film Daily* lauded that "Clara Bow in her every gesture stamps herself a great actress. Esther Ralston's regal and blonde beauty shows up well next to Miss Bow's flapperish charms, and she renders a thoroughly sympathetic performance. The choice of the featured male was not so happy. Einar Hansen is very unimpressive, nor does Gary Cooper do anything to distinguish himself."

With Clara Bow

With Albert Gran

With Hedda Hopper, Esther Ralston, Clara Bow, Einar Hanson, and Julia Swayne Gordon

34

ARIZONA BOUND

A Paramount Picture   1927

CAST:

GARY COOPER *(The Cowboy);* BETTY JEWEL *(The Girl);* JACK DOUGHERTY *(Buck O'Hara);* CHRISTIAN J. FRANK *(The Stranger); and* EL BRENDEL, CHARLES CROCKETT, JOE BUTTERWORTH, GUY OLIVER, GUINN "BIG BOY" WILLIAMS.

CREDITS:

JOHN WATERS *(Director);* JOHN STONE, PAUL GANGELON *(Scenarists);* MARION JACKSON *(Adaptation);* C. EDGAR SCHOENBAUM *(Photographer);* ALFRED HUSTWICK *(Titler). Based on a story by* RICHARD ALLEN GATES.

SYNOPSIS:

A rambling young cowboy happens into a small Western town the day a big gold shipment is leaving by stagecoach. As it happens, two different parties plan to rob the stage. Buck O'Hara, the driver, who has public confidence, is one, and a stranger also plans to hi-jack the shipment for himself.

The young cowboy is embroiled in the following action and, accused of being one of the bandits, he narrowly escapes lynching. In the end, he retrieves the gold, establishes his innocence and wins the girl.

NOTES:

This was Gary Cooper's first starring film and, despite the fact that it was a routine western programmer, it helped establish him with movie-going audiences. Paramount's ad campaign's proclaimed, "You're headed in the right direction for thrills if you're 'Arizona Bound.'" *Variety* remarked, "Cooper is a tall youth, with a boyish smile and enough swagger to give him character. *Arizona Bound* will give him a respectable introduction to his future public."

The *Exhibitors Daily Review* commented, "Gary Cooper has the physique, the ability to ride, as well as histrionic ability, for a Western hero and Paramount has done well to assign such parts to him. He is equally effective in the action business and he and Betty Jewel, who is charmingly vivacious as the heroine, make an appealing pair."

Cooper did most of his own stunt tricks in *Arizona Bound,* which included jumping from a horse onto a swiftly-moving stagecoach. His future in Westerns was assured.

With Betty Jewel

With Richard Arlen

WINGS

A Paramount Picture   1927

CAST:

CLARA BOW *(Mary Preston);* CHARLES "BUDDY" ROGERS *(Jack Powell);* RICHARD ARLEN *(David Armstrong);* JOBYNA RALSTON *(Sylvia Lewis);* GARY COOPER *(Cadet White);* ARLETTE MARCHAL *(Celeste);* EL BRENDEL *(Herman Schwimpf);* "GUNBOAT" SMITH *(the Sergeant);* RICHARD TUCKER *(Air Commander);* JULIA SWAYNE GORDON *(Mrs. Armstrong);* HENRY B. WALTHALL *(Mr. Armstrong);* GEORGE IRVING *(Mr. Powell);* HEDDA HOPPER *(Mrs. Powell);* NIGEL DE BRULIER *(Peasant);* ROSCOE KARNS *(Lt. Cameron);* JAMES PIERCE *(MP);* CARL VON HAARTMAN *(German Officer).*

CREDITS:

WILLIAM A. WELLMAN *(Director);* LUCIEN HUBBARD *(Producer);* HOPE LORING, LOUIS D. LIGHTON *(Scenarists);* HARRY PERRY *(Photographer);* LUCIEN HUBBARD *(Editor);* ROY POMEROY *(Engineering Effects);* B. P. SCHULBERG *(Associate Producer);* JULIAN JOHNSON *(Titler);* E. LLOYD SHELDON *(Editor-In-Chief);* JOHN S. ZAMECNIK *(Musical Score);* RICHARD JOHNSTON *(Assistant Director);* E. BURTON STEENE, AL WILLIAMS, SERGEANT WARD *(Aerial Cinematographers);* HERMAN SCHOOP, GENE O'DONNELL, FAXON M. DEAN, RUSSELL HARLAN, PAUL PERRY, ART LANE, CLIFF BLACKSTONE, HARRY MASON, RAY OLSEN, BERT BALDRIDGE, AL MEYERS, WILLIAM CLOTHIER, GUY BENNETT, L. GUY WILKY, FRANK COTNER, ERNEST LAZELL (LASZLO) *(Aerial Cameramen). Based on an original story by* JOHN MONK SAUNDERS.

SYNOPSIS:

When the United States enters the World War, Jack Powell and David Armstrong join the Air Service. Jack is loved by Mary, but carries a locket from Sylvia, who sent it to David, whom she loves. Rivalry between the boys arouses a deep enmity, but events at training camp produce a strong

37

The men of *Wings*: Richard Arlen,
Charles "Buddy" Rogers and Gary Cooper

friendship. Mary, meanwhile, joins a truck outfit and is sent to France. Soon the boys are decorated for bravery, although Jack is threatened with a court martial until Mary sacrifices her reputation to save him and is sent home.

At camp, Jack and David, arguing over Sylvia, are interrupted by orders to attack two observation balloons. During this engagement, David is shot down, but escapes alive. The next day, he steals a German plane from a nearby base and crosses into his own lines. Meanwhile, a German aviator brings word to the American camp that David is dead. Filled with regret, Jack takes off and terrorizes German forces all day. Returning home, he spots a German plane and, unaware that David is piloting it, shoots it down.

David, dying, is taken into a small French farmhouse. Jack lands, in hopes of cutting the insignia from the plane, and discovers he has shot down David, who dies in his arms. Going through his buddy's belongings, Jack learns of Sylvia's love for David and is brokenhearted. Back home, later, after the war, Jack discovers his love for Mary.

NOTES:

Paramount, realizing the potential star-power of Gary Cooper, put him into a small, but distinguished, role in one of their biggest pictures as part of his build-up. Both director William A.

38

Wellman and John Monk Saunders, who wrote the original story, were ace pilots during the "great war" and paid close attention to every detail concerning air combat and the flyers themselves. The result was one of the finest flying pictures ever made —for few since have equalled its authenticity and exciting air sequences.

Cooper's one scene emphasized the empathy which he could draw from audiences, for the studio was flooded with letters asking the name of the pilot who ate the chocolate bar and then went to his death. That was his only scene, shot in a tent in the training camp sequence, with eager recruits Arlen and Rogers. As the hard-bitten, experienced pilot who offers advice to the boys, he accepts a candy bar from Arlen, takes a bite and says "When your time comes, you're going to get it." With that, he sets the candy bar down and leaves. Moments later, as the audience learns that his plane has crashed, the camera pans to the half-eaten chocolate bar in the tent.

Wellman photographed all location shots in San Antonio, Texas, and, while Cooper was there, hoped to use him in another scene which never materialized. *Wings* was one year in production and cost an estimated $2,000,000 before its release August 21, 1927. There was no studio process photography—everything was shot in the sky. Dick Grace, Hollywood's best stunt pilot, did two fantastic crashes in this film, one for Buddy Rogers and another for Richard Arlen.

Wings won the first Academy Award for "Best Picture of the Year" for the 1927-28 film season. It also won Roy Pomeroy an Academy Award for Best Engineering Effects, a category that was discontinued after the first presentations were made.

The *Literary Digest* said, "*Wings* is a fine picture, largely by virtue of its success in reproducing scenes of actual combat in airplanes." The *Christian Science Monitor* critic noted that it was a "... thrilling picture ... Mr. Wellman has employed his splendid ensemble of fighting men with veracity and dramatic effect."

With Charles "Buddy" Rogers

With Thelma Todd

NEVADA

A Paramount Picture   1927

CAST:

GARY COOPER *(Nevada)*; THELMA TODD *(Hettie Ide)*; WILLIAM POWELL *(Clan Dillion)*; PHILIP STRANGE *(Ben Ide)*; ERNIE S. ADAMS *(Cash Burridge)*; CHRISTIAN J. FRANK *(Sheriff of Winthrop)*; IVAN CHRISTY *(Cawthorne)*; GUY OLIVER *(Sheriff of Lineville)*.

CREDITS:

JOHN WATERS *(Director)*; JOHN STONE, L. G. RIGBY *(Scenarists)*; C. EDGAR SCHOENBAUM *(Photographer)*; JACK CONWAY *(Titler)*. *Based on the novel by* ZANE GREY.

SYNOPSIS:

Nevada, a young "bad boy" of the plains who is trying to reform, protects Hettie Ide and her brother Ben from cattle rustlers and, in doing so, unmasks the leader of the gang, who is trusted ranchman Clan Dillion.

NOTES:

While *Nevada* was hardly one of Paramount's better silent Zane Grey Westerns, it did contain some rousing action and good performances from its principals.

Photoplay remarked that the film "Thrills with suspense, dazzles with fine performances, glamorous outdoor photography and a hero with a sense of humor, Gary Cooper." *Variety Weekly* noted, "Paramount has Gary Cooper now riding the plains, tall, two-fisted, gun toting and lightning fast on the draw, who has done his darndest to step into the shoes of Jack Holt. Cooper does well but the stories seem to be getting thinner. . . . Cooper is improving in his work and serving his masters well in everything but his love making. There comparisons creep in and, as a consequence, Cooper suffers thereby."

With Thelma Todd

With Ernie S. Adams

40

THE LAST OUTLAW

A Paramount Picture   1927

CAST:

GARY COOPER *(Sheriff Buddy Hale)*; BETTY JEWEL *(Janet Lane)*; JACK LUDEN *(Ward Lane)*; HERBERT PRIOR *(Bert Wagner)*; JIM COREY *(Butch)*; BILLY BUTTS *(Chick); and* FLASH, *the Wonder Horse.*

CREDITS:

ARTHUR ROSSON *(Director)*; JOHN STONE, J. WALTER RUBEN *(Scenarists)*; J. WALTER RUBEN *(Adaptation)*; JAMES MURRAY *(Photographer)*; GEORGE CROOK *(Assistant Director). Based on a story by* RICHARD ALLEN GATES.

SYNOPSIS:

Buddy Hale meets Janet Lane, whose brother Ward is suspected of murdering the local sheriff. Buddy becomes the new sheriff, but loses Janet's admiration when it evolves that he must arrest her brother, who actually did kill the sheriff, because he suspected him of being the head of a rustler gang. There follows a series of exciting chases, fights and blood-and-thunder gunplay which last until the murderer himself is killed and Buddy and Janet are reunited.

NOTES:

In yet another program western utilizing his resources to fullest advantage, Cooper had many fine scenes riding the beautiful Flash, the Wonder Horse, and pulled off some terrific stunts.

Said *Variety Weekly:* "Gary Cooper is Paramount's new western star whom they are trying to put over. Cooper first came to attention in *The Winning of Barbara Worth* and was finally starred in *Arizona Bound.* Paramount can stand a western star and has a personality bet in Cooper, but they're not doing right by him if *The Last Outlaw* is a sample of the best story material they can offer. The blood-and-thunder title is very Biograph-y in its import and the plot is just as Broncho Billy with its cattle rustling, double-dealing sheriffs and other central ingredients.

"Cooper does some good work, rides fast and flashy on his horse, 'Flash,' and impresses with his gun totin' generally. Screen mechanics are against him. He labors against story shortcomings and creaking directorial machinations."

With Betty Jewel

With Betty Jewel

With Betty Jewel and Jack Luden

43

BEAU SABREUR

A Paramount Picture   1928

CAST:

GARY COOPER *(Major Henri de Beaujolais)*; EVELYN BRENT *(Mary Vanbrugh)*; NOAH BEERY *(Sheikh El Hamel)*; WILLIAM POWELL *(Becque)*; ROSCOE KARNS *(Buddy)*; MITCHELL LEWIS *(Suleiman the Strong)*; ARNOLD KENT *(Raoul de Redon)*; RAOUL PAOLI *(Dufour)*; JOAN STANDING *(Maudie)*; FRANK REICHER *(General de Beaujolais)*; OSCAR SMITH *(Djikki)*; and ALBERTO MORIN.

CREDITS:

JOHN WATERS *(Director)*; TOM J. GERAGHTY *(Scenarist)*; C. EDGAR SCHOENBAUM *(Photographer)*; MILTON E. HOFFMAN *(Production Supervisor)*; RICHARD JOHNSTON *(Assistant Director)*; E. LLOYD SHELDON *(Editor-in-Chief)*; ROSE LOWENGER *(Film Editor)*; JULIAN JOHNSON *(Titler)*. *Based on the novel "Beau Geste" by* PERCIVAL CHRISTOPHER WREN.

SYNOPSIS:

Major Henri de Beaujolais, a handsome French officer sworn to live and die for France and never look at a woman, is sent to a French garrison in the Sahara. He is soon assigned the task of negotiating a treaty with Sheikh El Hamel, to stand off the Touareg uprising and save the territory for France.

Young Beaujolais' troubles are complicated by Mary Vanbrugh, an American authoress in the area to soak up atmosphere, with whom he quickly falls in love, and Becque, an insurgent Foreign Legion member who leaves the service to steam up the disciples of Allah. As it turns out Sheikh El Hamel, wants the American authoress for himself and, for a time, he holds up the treaty in hopes of getting her. Beaujolais battles all for the hand of this fascinating woman.

44

With Evelyn Brent

With Evelyn Brent

NOTES:

Paramount, which had a great deal of desert footage left from its brilliant 1926 production of *Beau Geste,* needed a suitable vehicle for Evelyn Brent (a success in von Sternberg's *Underworld*) and, further, wanted to try Gary Cooper out in a romantic part, so *Beau Sabreur* was whipped up. The end result was totally unsatisfactory, despite the facts that Cooper and Brent were a good team and the production was given good mounting. As a "studio sequel" to a literary classic, the film disappointed the public and critics alike.

Motion Picture News knocked, "*Beau Sabreur* merely goes over familiar ground. It is well-enough staged, and is competently acted by Noah Beery. Gary Cooper is too grim as the hero, but Evelyn Brent reveals acting ability which shows that her talent flashed in *Underworld* is genuine." *Film Daily* disagreed, saying "Gary Cooper carries the hero part well. Evelyn Brent makes silly love interest worthwhile. William Powell a great heavy, as usual."

Variety declared, "Cooper makes a passable hero, Miss Brent leaves the imprint of having been miscast, and Beery is under heavy wraps, histrionically and physically, so that he doesn't help much on performance. This tale is far under the horsepower of which "Geste" could boast, and all in all is amongst the weakest features that Paramount has shown lately. It's hardly likely to receive favorable word-of-mouth exploitation."

With Evelyn Brent

With Arnold Kent and Raoul Paoli

46

THE LEGION OF THE CONDEMNED

A Paramount Picture   1928

CAST:

FAY WRAY *(Christine Charteris)*; GARY COOPER *(Gale Price)*; BARRY NORTON *(Byron Dashwood)*; LANE CHANDLER *(Charles Holabird)*; FRANCIS MC-DONALD *(Gouzalo Vasques)*; ALBERT CONTI *(Von Hohendorff)*; CHARLOTTE BIRD *(Tart in Cafe)*; VOYA GEORGE *(A Gambler)*; FREEMAN WOOD *(A Bored Man)*; E. H. CALVERT *(The Commandant)*; TOTO GUETTE *(A Mechanic)*.

CREDITS:

WILLIAM A. WELLMAN *(Director and Producer)*; E. LLOYD SHELDON *(Associate Producer)*; JOHN MONK SAUNDERS, JEAN DE LIMUR *(Scenarists)*; HENRY GERRARD *(Photographer)*; ALYSON SHAFFER *(Editor)*; GEORGE MARION, JR. *(Titler)*; RICHARD JOHNSTON *(Assistant Director)*; E. LLOYD SHELDON *(Editor-in-Chief)*. *Based on an original story by* JOHN MONK SAUNDERS.

SYNOPSIS:

Four young men join "The Legion of the Condemned," a French flying escadrille during World War I, which is very much like the famed Foreign Legion. Their reasons for doing so vary (murder—gambling—automobile accident which resulted in death of girl—boredom), but they all draw high cards for sure-death assignments. At the first drawing, Gale Price loses to Byron Dashwood, who flies off to drop a spy behind the lines. Caught with his passenger, he is shot.

The next man to draw an assignment is Gale. While he awaits the arrival of his spy-passenger, his thoughts travel back to the days when he was a reporter assigned to cover an Embassy ball. He takes young Christine Charteris, not knowing that she's a French secret service agent, and is crushed when he later finds her drunk and on the knees of a German baron. This, we find out, is the reason why he joined the "Legion of the Condemned."

When his spy-passenger arrives, Gale discovers it's

With Charlotte Bird

Christine. Quick explanations are exchanged before they're off and he drops her in enemy territory. However, she is caught and put before a firing squad. A bombing postpones the execution and Christine is rescued by Gale.

NOTES:

Director Wellman and his friend John Monk Saunders, who wrote the original story (which was later novelized by Eustace H. Ball) had not yet finished re-hashing the World War's gallant air service but, unfortunately, the result was a second-rate re-telling of *Wings*, plot changes not withstanding.

One critic noted that "Gary Cooper typifies strength and courage in his portrayal of Gale," while *Variety* said, "Fay Wray looks good, but Cooper is up against a pretty fair assortment of trouping from the male contingent." *Motion Picture News* felt, "This new opus can be safely compared to *Wings* in its collection of thrills." The *New York Herald Tribune* found that the film "moves rapidly," while the *New York Post* announced that the film ". . . has its tense moments, with a far-fetched and romantic plot."

Paramount took out tremendous ads everywhere hailing its new screen team, Fay Wray and Gary Cooper, which caused *Photoplay* to comment, "It is their bow as a co-starring team, and they are sure to register in a big way with the motion picture public." They didn't.

With Fay Wray

48

With Fay Wray

With Florence Vidor

DOOMSDAY

A Paramount Picture   1928

CAST:

FLORENCE VIDOR *(Mary Viner)*; GARY COOPER *(Arnold Furze)*; LAWRENCE GRANT *(Percival Fream)*; CHARLES A. STEVENSON *(Captain Hesketh Viner)*.

CREDITS:

ROWLAND V. LEE *(Director and Producer)*; DONALD W. LEE *(Scenarist)*; DORIS ANDERSON *(Adaptation)*; HENRY GERRARD *(Photographer)*; ROBERT BASSLER *(Editor)*; JULIAN JOHNSON *(Titler)*. *Based on the novel by* WARWICK DEEPING.

SYNOPSIS:

Mary Viner lives with her father, a retired English captain in poor health, in a cottage owned by Percival Fream. Down the road lives Arnold Furze, a good-looking young farmer who considers it a privilege to work hard at Doomsday, a property that has built up since the war. Fream wants to marry Mary and make her a symbol of his wealth, and so proposes to her. A few days later, Mary and Arnold meet by accident near his farm, and a mutual attraction soon develops into love. She promises to marry him, until she sees his house and is disillusioned. On the way home, she meets Fream in his chauffeur-driven limousine and, dazzled by all that money can buy, she foolishly marries Fream, instead of the man she truly loves.

Captain Viner is left in a nurse's care while the Freams travel abroad for a year. After her return, Mary realizes that money cannot buy happiness. At her first reception she learns, from Arnold, that her father is ill. He dies soon afterward. After the funeral, Mary returns to the old cottage and applies for an annulment. She then goes to Arnold's farm and offers to be his housekeeper for six months to prove she'll work hard for her man. He accepts.

NOTES:

Gary Cooper gave a good account of himself in this Florence Vidor vehicle, which was based on the novel by Warwick Deeping, the author of *Sorrell and Son*. Definitely of the soap opera genre, *Doomsday* did much to further impress Cooper's image on the female members of the movie-going public. However, critics were divided as to his effectiveness in the role of Arnold Furze. The *New York Sun* said, in part, ". . . Gary Cooper [had] nothing much to do but look bucolic as a young English farmer unwilling to take back the girl who once had fooled him until convinced that drudgery was really what she felt to be her career." In contrast, the critic of the *New York World* thought, "Acting honors must be given to Gary Cooper, admirably cast as Arnold, the young officer who is so bitterly disappointed in the girl he loves. Cooper gives the role a sympathetic understanding that makes you realize that there is a screen star in the making."

With Florence Vidor

With Florence Vidor

With Florence Vidor

With Esther Ralston

HALF A BRIDE

A Paramount Picture   1928

CAST:

ESTHER RALSTON (*Patience Winslow*); GARY COOPER (*Captain Edmunds*); WILLIAM J. WORTHINGTON (*Mr. Winslow*); FREEMAN WOOD (*Jed Session*); MARY DORAN (*Betty Brewster*); GUY OLIVER (*Chief Engineer*); RAY GALLAGHER (*Second Engineer*).

CREDITS:

GREGORY LA CAVA (*Director*); DORIS ANDERSON, PERCY HEATH (*Scenarists*); VICTOR MILNER (*Photographer*); VERNA WILLIS (*Editor*); JULIAN JOHNSON (*Titler*); RUSSELL MATHEWS (*Assistant Director*); B. P. FINEMAN (*Production Supervisor*). *Based on the story "White Hands" by* ARTHUR STRINGER.

SYNOPSIS:

Patience Winslow, a spoiled darling of the rich, is marooned on a desert island in the Pacific with the handsome skipper of her yacht, Captain Edmunds.

Patience, it seems, was enjoying a honeymoon cruise with her much-older husband when the mishap occurred.

Since they are the only inhabitants of the island, they enter into a trial marriage (in name only) for three months, soon concluding that any man would fall in love with any girl if they were alone on an island together. Eventually, however, they are rescued and returned to the mainland, only to find they cannot live without each other.

NOTES:

Despite the thinness of the plot, director Gregory LaCava injected many wonderfully comic touches, for which he was later to become so famous in films like *My Man Godfrey* and *Stage Door*. This was Cooper's second film with lovely Esther Ralston, with whom he had appeared in *Children of Divorce*. They made a delightful comic duo.

With Esther Ralston

Said *Photoplay:* "This is advertised as a 'compassionate marriage' but don't be misled, it's nothing of the sort. The heroine marries one man and spends her honeymoon with another, but not 'with malice aforethought.' Esther Ralston and Gary Cooper, in their respective roles, handle this delicate situation with commendable restraint. Good entertainment." *Motion Picture* felt, "Gary Cooper is at his best and Esther Ralston is particularly winning."

With Esther Ralston

With Esther Ralston

With Colleen Moore

LILAC TIME

*A First National Picture
with* Photophone Sound Effects   *1928*

CAST:

COLLEEN MOORE *(Jeannine);* GARY COOPER *(Captain Philip Blythe);* EUGENIE BESSERER *(Widow Berthelot);* BURR MC INTOSH *(General Blythe);* KATHRYN MC GUIRE *(Lady Iris);* CLEVE MOORE *(Flight Commander);* ARTHUR LAKE *(The Unlucky One);* JACK STONE *(The Kid);* DAN DOWLING, STUART KNOX, JACK PONDER, HARLAN HILTON *(Aviators);* GEORGE COOPER *(Sergeant Hawkins);* EDWARD DILLON *(Corporal "Smitty");* EMILE CHAUTARD *(The Mayor);* EDWARD CLAYTON *(The Enemy Ace);* PAUL HURST *(Hospital Orderly);* PHILO MC CULLOUGH *(German Officer);* NELSON MC DOWELL *(A French Drummer);* and RICHARD JARVIS.

CREDITS:

GEORGE FITZMAURICE *(Director and Producer);* CAREY WILSON *(Scenarist);* WILLIS GOLDBECK *(Adaptation);* GEORGE MARION, JR. *(Titler);* NATHANIEL SHILKRET *(Musical Score);* AL HALL *(Editor);* ALVIN KNECHTEL *(Aerial Photographer);* SID HICKOX *(Photographer).* SONG: *"Jeannine, I Dream of Lilac Time" by* NATHANIEL SHILKRET *(Music) and* L. WOLFE GILBERT *(Lyrics). Based on the play by* JANE COWL *and* JANE MURFIN *and the book by* GUY FOWLER. *"Presented by John McCormick."*

SYNOPSIS:

A group of Royal Air Corps flyers are being billeted near their air field in France at the widow Berthelot's farmhouse. Her daughter, Jeannine, has become their mascot. When one of them is killed, Captain Philip Blythe is sent as a replacement. However, while landing his plane, he crashes rather than run down young Jeannine, who just happens to be in his way.

A series of humorous misunderstandings develop between the young pair but, eventually, they find themselves in love. Soon the flyers depart on a mission and, one by one, they are shot down in action. Jeannine promises she will wait for Blythe and she does so, even through a bombardment. His plane crashes near the farmhouse and he is rushed to the local hospital. She tries to visit him, but is told by his stern father that his son is dead. Jeannine, heartbroken, sends lilacs—their favorite flower—to his room and starts back home as Blythe, having noticed the lilacs, sees her from his window and calls her back.

NOTES:

Lilac Time was re-vamped from an old Jane Cowl stage play to suit Miss Moore's particular talents. Besides handling her dramatic chores well, she again demonstrated with flair what a deft comedienne she was, especially in scenes like the one in which she accidently started the aircraft across the field. In the panic that followed she turned the wrong switch and began firing the machine gun, sending all who are trying to help her scrambling to safety.

The film's chief asset, however, was superb aerial photography, ranking it alongside *Wings* and, later, *Hell's Angels* and *The Dawn Patrol*. George Fitzmaurice directed with a knowing hand, although there was a heavy accent on sentiment. This was Cooper's first loan-out film, about which Marquis Busby, in the *Los Angeles Times,* noted, "Gary Cooper, as Blythe, gives a fine performance. He is a sincere and manly lover. I have never seen him to better advantage."

Motion Picture Classic, on the other hand, felt, "Gary Cooper, had he been less restrained and colored his role more, would have added considerable to the film's appeal. But he is too restrained—and the best part of the sentiment misses some necessary heartbeats."

With Colleen Moore

With Colleen Moore

With Colleen Moore

56

THE FIRST KISS

A Paramount Picture   1928

CAST:

FAY WRAY *(Anna Lee)*; GARY COOPER *(Mulligan Talbot)*; LANE CHANDLER *(William Talbot)*; LESLIE FENTON *(Carol Talbot)*; PAUL FIX *(Ezra Talbot)*; MALCOLM WILLIAMS *("Pap")*; MONROE OWSLEY *(Other Suitor); and* GEORGE NASH.

CREDITS:

ROWLAND V. LEE *(Director and Producer)*; JOHN FARROW *(Scenarist)*; ALFRED GILKS *(Photographer)*; LEE HELEN *(Editor)*; TOM REED *(Titler). Based on the story "Four Brothers" by* TRISTRAM TUPPER.

SYNOPSIS:

Handsome young Chesapeake Bay fisherman Mulligan Talbot, proud son of a once-respected old Maryland family, does everything from oyster fishing to cooking for his three shiftless brothers. Anna Lee, the town's richest girl, sees Mulligan openly, despite protests from her father. One day when Mulligan kisses her she flares up, even though she loves him, calling him "White Trash!" Though she apologizes, Mulligan is now painfully aware of their social differences.

To boost his family socially, he thrashes his brothers and forces each to learn a profession, financing them through pirating activities under the guise of a rich relative. Six years later each brother is successful, but Mulligan is still an oysterman—to the disappointment of Anna. He begins paying back all the money he stole but, in so doing, is detected and ultimately arrested.

Anna causes a sensation at his trial by testifying in his behalf. She also informs his brothers that it was Mulligan who paid for their education, and they come to his aid. His lawyer brother defends him and he is paroled in Anna's custody and, together, on a schooner he built for her, they set sail.

57

With Leslie Fenton,
Monroe Owsley and Fay Wray

This was the second time Paramount teamed Cooper and Fay Wray and, again, the publicity hounds at the studio blew hard on their horns. Perhaps Paramount was hoping for a screen team to match Fox's Janet Gaynor-Charles Farrell combo. What they should have concentrated on was a good script. As one critic put it, "As it is told on the screen, this narrative is rather dull and unbelievable. Gary Cooper, however, gives a sterling account of himself as Mulligan, and Miss Wray is fair as the haughty girl who subsequently falls in love with Mulligan."

Motion Picture News added, "The Paramount team of Gary Cooper and Fay Wray haven't the strongest dish in the world here, but they, with some assistance from a few others in the cast, make it more than tolerable. The stars do well by their roles, though Cooper might have injected more fire into his performance." *Photoplay* was moved to write, "The work of the principals is pleasant enough and the backgrounds are charmingly photographed." The location work was filmed at St. Michaels, Maryland.

With Fay Wray

With Malcolm Williams
and Fay Wray

With Nancy Carroll

THE SHOPWORN ANGEL

A Paramount Picture   1928

CAST:

NANCY CARROLL *(Daisy Heath);* GARY COOPER *(William Tyler);* PAUL LUKAS *(Bailey);* EMMETT KING *(The Chaplain);* MILDRED WASHINGTON *(Daisy's Maid); and,* ROSCOE KARNS, BERT WOODRUFF.

CREDITS:

RICHARD WALLACE *(Director);* LOUIS D. LIGHTON *(Producer);* HOWARD ESTABROOK, ALBERT SHELBY LE VINO *(Scenarists);* CHARLES LANG *(Photographer);* ROBERT BASSLER *(Editor);* TOM MIRANDA *(Titler);* SONG: *"A Precious Little Thing Called Love"* by LEW DAVIS *and* J. FRED COOTS. *Based on the story by* DANA BURNET.

SYNOPSIS:

Wise show girl Daisy Heath becomes aware of America's part in the World War when she witnesses a parade of soldiers. That evening, she becomes humorously involved in an auto accident with Pvt. William Tyler, a tall Texas doughboy. They become friends and, soon, the idealistic Tyler finds himself hopelessly in love. The sophisticated Daisy, amused by her soldier, plays it for laughs, all the while maintaining a liaison with suave man-about-town Bailey. Bailey senses a threat in young Tyler and persuades Daisy not to see him again. Believing him, she stops seeing Tyler.

Tyler is ordered to embark for France, but, because of his love for Daisy and his growing fear of war, he panics and goes A.W.O.L. He spends the day with Daisy and tells her of his love. For the first time, Daisy finally experiences love and promises to marry him. At the wedding ceremony, Daisy, overcome with emotion, faints and Tyler is torn away from the uncompleted ceremony to sail with his regiment. However, before going, he tells her that now he can face anything. Daisy's life has been changed drastically by her relationship with

With Nancy Carroll

With Nancy Carroll

With Mildred Washington

Tyler and she avoids all her old contacts. While preparing for a new chorus job, she thinks of Tyler in France and—with a new spirit within her, begins to rehearse.

NOTES:

This bittersweet romance, originally called *The Hard Boiled Angel,* gave audiences a preview of the voices of Nancy Carroll and Gary Cooper in the closing scenes. Thus, it is officially a part-talkie. Both stars proved to have pleasing tones and their continuation in films, with the advent of the talkies, was well assured.

Nancy Carroll's Daisy was sheer bliss and, as a team, she and Cooper complimented one another admirably. One of the film's most touching moments is in the closing scene, when Nancy sings "A Precious Little Thing Called Love" while recalling good times with Cooper and visualizing him overseas.

Not only did the public make this a box-office hit, but the critics cheered too. Said *Picture Play:* "Acted with rare feeling, delicacy and intelligence by Gary Cooper, Nancy Carroll, and Paul Lukas, with complete absence of the maudlin. Mr. Cooper heard for the first time in talking sequence. He's there!" Mordaunt Hall in *The New York Times* found that "Gary Cooper gives a wonderfully sensitive performance as the love-smitten doughboy. Nancy Carroll's acting shows a nice appreciation for Daisy's mood. Several minor roles are nicely played by men not mentioned on the program."

Photoplay commented that "Gary Cooper's charming boyishness is an effective foil for the scintillating Nancy. An unexpected and artistic ending saves this from the tawdriness of the usual city-girl country-boy picture." The *New York Herald Tribune* remarked that "Nancy Carroll has never been as good as she is in the role of the chorus girl. Gary Cooper is engaging, ingenuous." The *New York Daily Mirror* thought, "Nancy Carroll plays her role magnificently. Gary Cooper amazes fans. He gives a great performance." The *New York Sun* wrote, "Nancy Carroll and Gary Cooper give expert and charming performances. Richard Wallace has turned out a thoroughly fresh and fascinating film."

With Nancy Carroll and Emmett King (center)

WOLF SONG

A Paramount Picture   1929

CAST:

GARY COOPER *(Sam Lash)*; LUPE VELEZ *(Lola Salazar)*; LOUIS WOLHEIM *(Gullion)*; CONSTANTINE ROMANOFF *(Rube Thatcher)*; MICHAEL VAVITCH *(Don Solomon Salazar)*; ANN BRODY *(Duenna)*; RUSSELL (RUSS) COLUMBO *(Ambrosia Guiterrez)*; AUGUSTINA LOPEZ *(Louisa)*; GEORGE RIGAS *(Black Wolf)*; LEONE LANE *(Dance Hall Girl)*.

CREDITS:

VICTOR FLEMING *(Director and Producer)*; JOHN FARROW, KEENE THOMPSON *(Scenarists)*; ALLEN SIEGLER *(Photographer)*; EDA WARREN *(Editor)*; IRVIN TALBOT *(Musical Synchronization)*; MAX TERR *(Recording Supervisor)*; B. P. FINEMAN *(Associate Producer)*; HENRY HATHAWAY *(Assistant Director)*. SONGS: *"Mi Amado"* and *"Yo Te Amo Means I Love You"* by RICHARD WHITING *(Music)* and ALFRED BRYAN *(Lyrics)*; JULIAN JOHNSON *(Titler)*. *Based on the novel by* HARVEY FERGUSSON.

62

SYNOPSIS:

Sam Lash and his two partners, Gullion and Rube Thatcher, are hardy fur trappers and incipient wanderers who usually unwind at the Taos Cantina. Young Sam is the sort of roving swain who always loves 'em and leaves 'em, until he meets a beautiful well-bred, yet fiery, Mexican girl named Lola Salazar. Romance engulfs them, but Lola's strong-willed father, Don Solomon Salazar, stands in the way of their happiness.

So Sam kidnaps Lola and carries her off to his beloved mountains and, later, marries her. However, after a brief period of domesticity, Sam finds he misses his comrades and the rousing times they had together. He truly hears the "wolf song," the pagan call of the wanderlust, deserts his bride, leaving her broken hearted at Bent's fork. On the way back to his chums, he has second thoughts and reverses his trek for a return home. He is ambushed by Black Wolf and some of his braves, but finally gets into the eager arms of Lola.

With Lupe Velez

With Lupe Velez

NOTES:

This torrid romance of the great outdoors was advertized as a "Part-Talkie" because of the addition of two songs for Lupe Velez and the lead-in dialogue preceding them between Cooper and Lupe. When originally completed, this "silent" was 6,070 feet; as a Part-Talkie, it became 7,021 feet.

Motion Picture News reported "Lupe Velez indulges in a flock of respiratory acrobatics whenever she has a love scene with Gary. Lupe's voice is pleasing enough but she is difficult to understand. Gary is far from being a lady killer in his make-up in this offering and it is difficult to visualize this picture adding to his lists of conquests among the fair fans. Louis Wolheim gives the best performance of the entire cast."

The off-screen Cooper-Velez romance, through the benefit of a full-scale publicity campaign, together with a cross-country public appearance tour by the stars in conjunction with the opening of *Wolf Song* in dozens of cities, helped make this picture the commercial success it was. The nude swimming scene with the two stars ended up being miles away from the camera in the released prints.

With Constantine Romanoff
and Louis Wolheim

With Michael Vavitch and Lupe Velez

With Esther Ralston

BETRAYAL

A Paramount Picture   1929

CAST:

EMIL JANNINGS *(Poldi Moser);* ESTHER RALSTON *(Vroni);* GARY COOPER *(André Frey);* JADA WELLES *(Hans);* DOUGLAS HAIG *(Peter);* BODIL ROSING *(Andre's mother); and* ANN BRODY, PAUL GUERTMANN, LEONE LANE.

CREDITS:

LEWIS MILESTONE *(Director);* HANS KRALY, LEO BIRINSKY *(Scenarists);* HENRY GERRARD *(Photographer);* J. S. ZAMECNIK *(Musical Score);* DEL ANDREWS *(Editor);* NATHAN WATT *(Assistant Director);* DAVID O. SELZNICK *(Associate Producer);* JULIAN JOHNSON *(Titler). Based on a story by* VICTOR SCHERTZINGER *and* NICHOLAS SOUSSANIN.

SYNOPSIS:

A handsome young Viennese artist, André Frey, vacations in a little Alpine village, where he meets Vroni, a beautiful Swiss peasant girl, and has a summer-long affair with her. When he is forced to return to Vienna, they vow to keep their love secret and he promises to come back as soon as he can. Upon his return some time later, André finds Vroni married to Poldi Maser, the village burgomaster, a well-to-do middle-aged man, whom her father forced her to marry. She introduces André to Poldi as an old friend who has just lost his sweetheart. Poldi is sympathetic and welcomes the young man to his home.

Seven years later, Poldi again invites André to his home, as a surprise birthday present for Vroni. Before long, André sends Vroni a note begging her to leave with him, threatening suicide if she doesn't. She refuses, thus sacrificing love for honor. That evening, the pair join a throng on a toboggan slide and, in a tremendous crash, Vroni is killed and André badly injured. Vroni's body is brought home to Poldi and the note falls from her pocket. After

65

With Emil Jannings

With Emil Jannings
and Esther Ralston

the funeral he reads it and is enraged, until he learns that André, too, has just died. Fortunately, he is left with happy memories of Vroni and the two sons she has given him.

NOTES:

Betrayal was Gary Cooper's last silent film and also ended the silent film career of Emil Jannings in Hollywood. This old-hat melodrama was not particularly well received by the critics or the public. The reviewer in *Picture Play* said "Gloomy, somber, and slow, *Betrayal* nevertheless offers Emil Jannings at his best—if any star can be said nowadays to be at his best in a totally silent picture. Furthermore, he finds able support in the popular Gary Cooper and Esther Ralston. . . . Mr. Cooper, in a role devoid of sympathy, plays with that repressed eloquence which is so wholly his own." *Motion Picture* warned, "Be sure to arrive on time, for the film's most charming moments are the opening love scenes between Esther and Gary Cooper."

Still another critic pointed out that "Mr. Jannings' performance would have been helped by more natural scenery. The sight of a village here looks woefully cramped. Miss Ralston gives an intelligent interpretation of her part. Mr Cooper, looking very tall, is sincere as the artist." Location shots were filmed at Lake Tahoe, but the village itself was a studio set.

David O. Selznick, later one of Hollywood's greatest producers, worked on *Betrayal* as Associate Producer.

With Esther Ralston

With Esther Ralston

With Mary Brian

THE VIRGINIAN

A Paramount Picture   1929

CAST:

GARY COOPER (*The Virginian*); WALTER HUSTON (*Trampas*); RICHARD ARLEN (*Steve*); MARY BRIAN (*Molly Wood*); CHESTER CONKLIN (*Uncle Hughey*); EUGENE PALLETTE (*Honey Wiggin*); E. H. CALVERT (*Judge Henry*); HELEN WARE ("*Ma*" *Taylor*); VICTOR POTEL (*Nebraskey*); TEX YOUNG (*Shorty*); CHARLES STEVENS (*Pedro*); JACK PENNICK (*Slim*); GEORGE CHANDLER (*Ranch Hand*); WILLIE FUNG (*Hong, the cook*); GEORGE MORRELL (*Reverend Dr. McBride*); ERNIE S. ADAMS (*Saloon singer*); ETHAN LAIDLAW (*Posseman*); ED BRADY (*Greasy*); BOB KORTMAN (*Henchman*); JAMES MASON (*Jim*); FRED BURNS (*Ranch Hand*); NENA QUARTERO (*Girl in Bar*).

CREDITS:

VICTOR FLEMING (*Director*); LOUIS D. LIGHTON (*Producer*); HOWARD ESTABROOK (*Scenarist*); J. ROY HUNT, EDWARD CRONJAGER (*Photographers*); WILLIAM SHEA (*Editor*); M. M. PAGGIE (*Sound Recorder*); HENRY HATHAWAY (*Assistant Director*); JOSEPH L. MANKIEWICZ (*Titler*). *Based on the novel by* OWEN WISTER *and play by* KIRK LA SHELLE.

SYNOPSIS:

The Virginian, foreman of the Box H ranch, near Medicine Bow, Wyoming, gives his old buddy Steve a job. Soon after, they meet Molly Wood, the new schoolteacher from Vermont. In the local saloon, the Virginian meets Trampas and they quarrel over a dancing girl. Meanwhile, Steve and the Virginian attend a christening and both dance with Molly. Both fun-loving boys play practical jokes on each other, but Molly finds Steve out and lets the Virginian take her home.

Just after he tells Molly of his love, the Virginian catches Steve putting Trampas' brand on Box H stock. He warns him, believing his friend has gone straight, until a posse of ranchers seizes Steve and two other rustlers. The Virginian is forced to superintend the hanging of the three men but knows Trampas, who escaped, is to blame, and swears to get him.

When Molly learns that the Virginian participated in the hanging of Steve, she spurns him. However, later, when he is wounded by Trampas, she nurses him back to health. On their wedding day, Trampas comes into town and orders the Virginian out by sundown. He shoots it out with Trampas and kills him. Molly rushes into his arms.

NOTES:

The Virginian was Cooper's first all-talking picture and the third film version of the Owen Wister classic. Dustin Farnum was the first Virginian in 1921, followed shortly by Kenneth Harlan, in 1923. It was subsequently filmed in 1946, with Joel McCrea, and in 1962 it was adapted to television as a 90-minute weekly series with James Drury in the title role.

Victor Fleming directed the 1929 version with a certain gusto and made good use of sound. The photography, on location near Sonora in the High Sierras, was a great asset, while the Howard Estabrook script contained such great dialogue as Coo-

per's retort to the menacing Walter Huston in the saloon, "When you call me that, smile!" This tagline, which was to become famous in filmic dialogue, was even printed on the publicity stills. It is one of the most misquoted lines in movie history. What Cooper actually said to Huston was, *"If you want to call me that, smile!"*

Randolph Scott, a native of Virginia, worked with Gary as a coach for the proper accent required of a Virginian. It is interesting to note that two of the foremost directors of films had assignments on *The Virginia.* Henry Hathaway, who was later to direct Cooper in many films, worked as an assistant to Victor Fleming. Joseph L. Mankiewicz wrote all of the transition titles, which were still employed although sound had firmly arrived.

One reviewer for a New Jersey paper thought, "Gaunt-faced Gary is difficult to accept as the drawling, sunny hero of the author's conception, and Arlen is hardly the type for the lazy weakling, Steve." The London *Times* critic didn't agree, saying "Mr. Gary Cooper is everything he should be as the Virginian, strong, attractive and serious, without being over-solemn." The film was a popular success and Cooper's reign in the talkies was fully assured. Paramount re-issued *The Virginian* nationally in 1935, by popular demand.

With Mary Brian and Richard Arlen

With Fred Burns (extreme left),
Tex Young, Victor Potel,
Eugene Pallette,
James Mason, Richard Arlen
and Charles Stevens

ALL
TALKING
ACTION
SPECIAL

Gary Cooper, new male idol of American fans. Walter Huston, stage star. Richard Arlen, Mary Brian and a big cast. In a swift-moving love-drama from Owen Wister's well known novel. With all the far-flung panorama of the gorgeous West as a background. Directed by Victor Fleming, who made "Abie's Irish Rose."

THE "VIRGINIAN"

**GARY COOPER, WALTER HUSTON,
RICHARD ARLEN and MARY BRIAN**

With Walter Huston

With Mary Brian

ONLY THE BRAVE

A Paramount Picture   1930

CAST:

GARY COOPER (*Captain James Braydon*); MARY BRIAN (*Barbara Calhoun*); PHILLIPS HOLMES (*Captain Robert Darrington*); JAMES NEILL (*Vance Calhoun*); MORGAN FARLEY (*Tom Wendell*); GUY OLIVER (*General U. S. Grant*); JOHN H. ELLIOT (*General Robert E. Lee*); E. H. CALVERT (*The Colonel*); VIRGINIA BRUCE (*Elizabeth*); ELDA VOELKEL (*Lucy Cameron*); WILLIAM LE MAIRE (*The Sentry*); FREEMAN S. WOOD (*Elizabeth's Lover*); LALO ENCINAS (*General Grant's secretary*); CLINTON ROSEMOND (*Butler*); WILLIAM BAKEWELL (*Young Lieutenant*).

CREDITS:

FRANK TUTTLE (*Director*); EDWARD E. PARAMORE, JR. (*Scenarist*); AGNES BRAND LEAHY (*Adaptation*); HARRY FISCHBECK (*Photographer*); DORIS DROUGHT (*Editor*); RICHARD DIGGES, JR. (*Titler*); J. A. GOODRICH (*Sound Recorder*). *Based on a story by* KEENE THOMPSON.

SYNOPSIS:

Cavalry captain James Braydon leaves Union headquarters to visit his sweetheart Elizabeth, but finds her in the arms of a civilian. Back at HQ, full of bitterness, he volunteers for spy duty. Carrying false papers and planning to get himself captured, Braydon arrives at the home of Barbara Calhoun, a Virginia belle, during a ball for Southern officers. Barbara is captivated by the tall and handsome "Confederate" stranger, much to the chagrin of Captain Robert Darrington, the hot-headed Southerner who loves her.

Braydon tries to pique Darrington's jealousy in order to come into ill-favor and subsequent arrest, but Barbara defends his every action. He later goes to her room loaded with military maps, thus convincing her that he is a spy, but she refuses to reveal him. Finally, Braydon has to leap from a window to get captured.

The Confederates, acting on false dispatches, leave the plantation while Braydon is left under guard. Soon, however, the retreating Confederates return. Enraged at Braydon's trickery, they stand him before a firing squad, but, at that moment, a Union detachment arrives and, although he is not executed, he is wounded in the battle. After peace is made at Appomatox, Darrington is best man at Braydon's marriage to Barbara.

NOTES:

This was one of the low points in Gary Cooper's film career. The romantic melodrama just plodded along and critics and public alike stayed away. Said the *New York Times:* "Gary Cooper's performance as the spy is not up to his usual standards while the *New York World* noted that "Once in hostile territory Mr. Cooper rode gallantly to his task until overtaken by soldiers with drawls."

Motion Picture News felt that "Gary Cooper fits well as the Northern hero. Phillips Holmes comes pretty near taking all the thunder away from Cooper for an outstanding performance. Mary Brian is blah and meaningless."

With Mary Brian

With Mary Brian and Phillips Holmes

With William Bakewell

72

With Jack Oakie and Mary Brian

PARAMOUNT ON PARADE

A Paramount Picture   1930

CAST:

(in alphabetical order) RICHARD ARLEN, JEAN ARTHUR, WILLIAM AUSTIN, GEORGE BANCROFT, CLARA BOW, EVELYN BRENT, MARY BRIAN, CLIVE BROOK, VIRGINIA BRUCE, NANCY CARROLL, RUTH CHATTERTON, MAURICE CHEVALIER, GARY COOPER, LEON ERROL, STUART ERWIN, KAY FRANCIS, SKEETS GALLAGHER, HARRY GREEN, MITZI GREEN, JAMES HALL, PHILLIPS HOLMES, HELEN KANE, DENNIS KING, ABE LYMAN AND HIS BAND, FREDRIC MARCH, NINO MARTINI, DAVID NEWELL, JACK OAKIE, WARNER OLAND, ZELMA O'NEAL, EUGENE PALLETTE, JOAN PEERS, WILLIAM POWELL, CHARLES "BUDDY" ROGERS, LILLIAN ROTH, STANLEY SMITH, FAY WRAY *and* JACKIE SEARLE, MISCHA AUER, CECIL CUNNINGHAM, HENRY FINK, JACK LUDEN, JACK PENNICK, ROLFE SEDAN, ROBERT GREIG, IRIS ADRIAN.

CREDITS:

DOROTHY ARZNER, OTTO BROWER, EDMUND GOULDING, VICTOR HEERMAN, EDWIN H. KNOPF, ROWLAND V. LEE, ERNST LUBITSCH, LOTHAR MENDES, VICTOR SCHERTZINGER, EDWARD SUTHERLAND, FRANK TUTTLE *(Directors)*; ALBERT A. KAUFMAN *(Producer)*; ELSIE JANIS *(Production Supervisor)*; HARRY FISCHBECK, VICTOR MILNER *(Photographers)*; JOHN WENGER *(Production Designer)*; MERRILL WHITE *(Editor)*; DAVID BENNETT *(Choreographer)*. SONGS: *"Paramount on Parade," "Any Time's the Time to Fall in Love," "What Did Cleopatra Say?," "We're the Show Girls," "I'm True to the Navy Now"* by ELSIE JANIS *and* JACK KING; *"Sweepin' the Clouds Away"* by SAM COSLOW; *"I'm in Training for You," "Let Us Drink to the Girl of My Dreams," "Dancing to Save Your Sole"* by L. WOLFE GILBERT *and* ABEL BAER; *"My Marine"* by RICHARD A. WHITING *and* RAYMOND EAGEN; *"All I Want is Just One Girl"* by RICHARD A. WHITING *and* LEO ROBIN; *"We're the Masters of Ceremony"* by BALLARD MC DONALD *and* DAVE DREYER; *"Nichavo"* by MANA-ZUCCA; *"Song of the Gondolier—Torno a*

Sorrento" by LEO ROBIN *and* ERNESTO DE CURTIS; *"I'm Isador the Toreador" by* DAVID FRANKLIN, *with the music of Bizet's "Carmen." Color sequences by* TECHNICOLOR.

NOTES:

Advertised as "the singing-dancing festival of the stars, *Paramount on Parade* was Paramount's big extravaganza, utilizing the talents of no fewer than thirty-five of its stars and top featured players, eleven directors, innumerable writers, composers, lyrists, etc. in a series of sketches and production numbers under the general supervision of Elsie Janis.

Cooper was in the "Let Us Drink to the Girl of My Dreams" sketch. After a brief modern-day introduction, with Mary Brian and Jack Oakie, the scene led into a sentimental costume interlude filmed in the then two-color Technicolor process. This is actually the first time Cooper appeared in color, for his first full-length feature in the perfected three-color Technicolor was a decade away in DeMille's *North West Mounted Police*.

Highlights of this hodge-podge included the wildest—and funniest—apache dance ever filmed—between Evelyn Brent and Maurice Chevalier; delicious Nancy Carroll stepping out of a giant shoe and dancing to the tune "Dancing to Save Your Sole;" Ruth Chatterton's torchy rendition of "My Marine," sung to four marines, one of whom was Fredric March; Helen Kane's delightful "What Did Cleopatra Say?;" and Maurice Chevalier doing "Sweepin' the Clouds Away" with a bevy of girls, one of whom was Iris Adrian. Mordaunt Hall in *The New York Times* found the sequences, as a general rule, "of such excellence."

With Fay Wray, Richard Arlen, James Hall (partially hidden), Jean Arthur, Phillips Holmes, Joan Peers, Mary Brian, David Newell and Virginia Bruce

THE TEXAN

A Paramount Picture   1930

CAST:

GARY COOPER *(Enrique ["Quico"], The Llano Kid)*; FAY WRAY *(Consuelo)*; EMMA DUNN *(Señora Ibarra)*; OSCAR APFEL *(Thacker)*; JAMES MARCUS *(John Brown)*; DONALD REED *(Nick Ibarra)*; SOLEDAD JIMINEZ *(The Duenna)*; VEDA BUCKLAND *(Mary, the nurse)*; CESAR VANONI *(Pasquale)*; EDWIN J. BRADY *(Henry)*; ENRIQUE ACOSTA *(Sixto)*; ROMUALDO TIRADO *(Cabman)*; RUSSELL (RUSS) COLUMBO *(Singing cowboy at campfire)*.

CREDITS:

JOHN CROMWELL *(Director)*; DANIEL N. RUBIN *(Scenarist)*; OLIVER H. P. GARRETT *(Adaptation)*; VICTOR MILNER *(Photographer)*; VERNA WILLIS *(Editor)*; HENRY HATHAWAY *(Assistant Director)*; HECTOR TURNBULL *(Associate Producer)*; HARRY M. LINDGREN *(Sound Recorder)*. *From "A Double-Dyed Deceiver" by* O. HENRY.

SYNOPSIS:

In the Texas of 1885, Enrique ("Quico"), the Llano Kid, a swaggering bandit with a price on his head, rides into the town of scripture-quoting sheriff, John Brown. He soon plays poker with a swarthy young gambler and catches him cheating, shooting him in self-defense. On a train heading for Galveston, the Kid meets a man called Thacker who offers him a sure-fire proposition, since he has a glib knowledge of Spanish. He tells the Kid of a wealthy aristocrat, Señora Ibarra, whose only son ran away when he was ten. She has offered Thacker a handsome reward if he can find her boy and has told him of a strange design tattooed on the boy's wrist.

Thacker persuades the Llano Kid to pose as her son and coaches him. He easily deceives the old woman, and also captures the heart of his lovely "cousin" Consuelo. Soon the plot becomes distasteful to him and, when he discovers the lady's real son was the man he killed in the saloon brawl, he

75

calls the deal off. Thacker, therefore, hires desperadoes to do his bidding.

At the ranch, the Kid discovers Sheriff Brown,
who has been trailing him. He asks the lawman to
wait until night before arresting him, but, meanwhile, Thacker's men attack the ranch. The Kid
is wounded and Thacker killed. The sheriff, realizing that the Kid has gone straight, agrees to let
the dead Thacker assume the identity of the Llano
Kid.

NOTES:

This well-mounted filmization of the O. Henry short
story was directed by John Cromwell, who had
assisted Richard Wallace on the directorial chores
of *Seven Days Leave*, which wasn't released until
after *The Texan*. This was the third picture for
Cooper and Fay Wray, and, while the picture was a
success, the team didn't create a stampede.

Mordaunt Hall in *The New York Times* noted
that "The lean, lanky Mr. Cooper elicits a great
deal of sympathy as the double-dyed deceiver, so
much so that one is quite relieved at the final
decision of Sheriff Brown." *Variety* stated, "There
is plenty of action and good photography, including
some splendid and picturesque settings. Cooper
gives a performance that is neither better nor worse
than his earlier ones, and whether or not that is
enough—or more than enough—depends on whether
or not you are a Cooper fan. Emma Dunn, as the
mother, handled her role with some distinction.
Fay Wray is decorative. Oscar Apfel and James
Marcus are Chesterfieldian—they satisfy." *Screenland*, with its tongue in its cheek, wrote, "*The
Texan* will please the Cooper addicts, win new
friends for Fay, and pass a pleasant, if not too
exciting evening. Gary steps and speaks out, spouting
Spanish most acceptably and cutting a dashing
figure as a bold hombre. This big boy is becoming
a real actor." *New Movie* said, "You will like
Gary, who has never been more sincere, and you will
like the picture, too."

Paramount remade *The Texan* in 1939 as *The
Llano Kid*, with Tito Guizar stepping into Gary's
boots.

With Fay Wray

With Emma Dunn

On the set with director John Cromwell

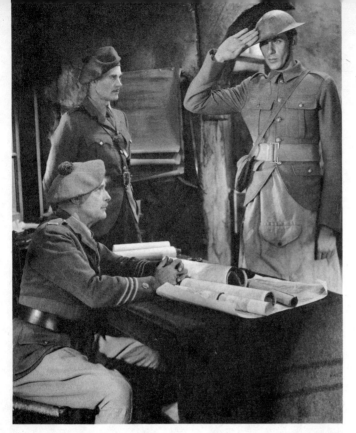

With Arthur Metcalfe and Larry Steers

SEVEN DAYS LEAVE

A Paramount Picture   1930

CAST:

GARY COOPER (*Kenneth Dowey*); BERYL MERCER (*Sarah Ann Dowey*); DAISY BELMORE (*Emma Mickelham*); NORA CECIL (*Amelia Twymley*); TEMPE PIGGOTT (*Mrs. Haggerty*); ARTHUR HOYT (*Mr. Willings*); ARTHUR METCALFE (*Colonel*); BASIL RADFORD (*Corporal*); LARRY STEERS (*Aide de Camp*).

CREDITS:

RICHARD WALLACE (*Director*); LOUIS D. LIGHTON (*Producer*); JOHN FARROW, DON TOTHEROH (*Scenarists*); CHARLES LANG (*Photographer*); GEORGE NICHOLLS, JR. (*Editor*); JOHN CROMWELL (*Assistant Director*); EUGENE MERRITT (*Sound Recorder*); RICHARD DIGGES, JR. (*Titler*). *Based on the play "The Old Lady Shows Her Medals"* by SIR JAMES M. BARRIE.

SYNOPSIS:

Sarah Ann Dowey, an old widowed Scotch scrub woman, frets because everyone in London except her is making a sacrifice for England during the war. Her three friends constantly boast of their sons at the front, while she had none. One day, while reading about the exploits of a young Canadian soldier in the famous "Black Watch" regiment, whose name is the same as hers, she decides to "adopt" him. Purchasing a "Black Watch" badge she boasts of her "son."

The "kiltie," Kenneth Dowey, is slightly wounded and sent to London on leave. A Y.M.C.A. worker tells him he has met his mother, which surprises the young man, since his mother is dead. He does, however, allow himself to be presented to the quaint old woman. Alone with her he chides her for the deception. She explains why she did it and

With Daisy Belmore, Tempe Piggott, Nora Cecil and Beryl Mercer

With Arthur Hoyt

With Beryl Mercer

offers her home to him during his leave. He accepts and explains that she is only his *mother* "on probation."

He takes her to fine restaurants and she proudly walks everywhere with him. One day he gets into a fight with three British sailors, who have jibed at him about his kilts. Angry, he threatens to desert, but Sarah convinces him not to. Now he realizes his great fondness for her and, before returning to duty, accepts Sarah as his mother. Later, in Flanders, he is sent behind enemy lines and never returns. Sarah receives his medals for bravery and puts them away carefully. With scrub bucket in hand, she proudly marches off to work.

NOTES:

Although Cooper thought this filmization of Barrie's play to be a "woman's picture," he gave one of his best performances as the ne'er-do-well kiltie. Beryl Mercer, who originated the role in the 1920 Broadway version, recreated her role with the right touches of humor and pathos. Richard Wallace, fresh from his success with *The Shopworn Angel*, was assisted on *Seven Days Leave* by John Cromwell, who later directed Cooper in *The Texan*.

Mordaunt Hall in *The New York Times* noted, "Miss Mercer's performance is faultless. And there is no failing to find with Mr. Cooper's impersonation, for, as in his other films, he lends a lifelike quality to the role." Richard Watts, Jr., in the *New York Herald Tribune*, wrote, "The portrayal of Gary Cooper is a bit puzzling. He constantly underplays his roles, with the result that you frequently feel that he is injuring the production, and yet he is so attractive a player and, in his later emotional scenes, so enormously real and honest, that you realize in the end how helpful he has been." Martin Dickstein in the *Brooklyn Daily Eagle* told his readers, "Gary Cooper's characterization of the soldier is a faultless exhibition, which, coming so soon after his magnificent performance in *The Virginian*, must establish this player as one of the most satisfying actors on the audible screen."

Seven Days Leave was one of the earliest of Paramount's "all-taking" films, and during production was called *Medals*. It was completed in the early months of 1929 but was not, however, released to the public until January of 1930.

With June Collyer

A MAN FROM WYOMING

A Paramount Picture   1930

CAST:

GARY COOPER *(Jim Baker);* JUNE COLLYER *(Patricia Hunter);* REGIS TOOMEY *(Jersey);* MORGAN FARLEY *(Lieutenant Lee);* E. H. CALVERT *(Major-General Hunter);* MARY FOY *(Inspector);* EMILE CHAUTARD *(French Mayor);* ED DEERING *(Sergeant);* WILLIAM B. DAVIDSON *(Major);* BEN HALL *(Orderly); and* HALL PARKER.

CREDITS:

ROWLAND V. LEE *(Director);* JOHN V. A. WEAVER, ALBERT SHELBY LE VINO *(Scenarists);* HARRY FISCH-BECK *(Photographer);* ROBERT BASSLER *(Editor);* EUGENE MERRITT *(Sound Recorder). From a story by* JOSEPH MONCURE MARCH *and* LEW LIPTON.

SYNOPSIS:

When war is declared, Jim Baker and his buddy Jersey, who work on a bridge construction in Wyoming, join the Army and are sent to France with the Engineer Corps. Jim is a Captain; Jersey, his lieutenant. Patrica Hunter, a former American society girl, is an ambulance driver there, a job she got through her uncle, Major-General Hunter. Bored with it all, Pat goes A.W.O.L. and wanders into Jim's company area. She draws enemy shell fire and Jim is forced to arrest her. When the company is relieved, Jim marches his group back and treats Pat as roughly as his men, yet admires her stamina. Impetuously, he marries her and they spend a three-day honeymoon in a French village.

Jim is sent back to the front and Pat returns to her unit to face a court-martial. Meanwhile, Jim's company runs into heavy fire and he is reported killed in action. The News reaches Pat and, embittered, she retires to a villa in Nice and "forgets" by becoming a hostess of wild parties for officers in "blighty."

Jim, not dead, but badly wounded, is sent to the

80

With June Collyer

With Regis Toomey

villa and is shocked to find the notorious woman he's heard much about is actually his wife Pat. Misconstruing her gaiety, Jim doesn't believe she has grieved for him. When he asks her to accompany him back to Wyoming, she refuses. Dejected, Jim returns to the front. Pat, now aroused, hurries after him. After the Armistice, the lovers meet in the town in which they were married—and stay together.

NOTES:

A Man From Wyoming was just another film on Gary Cooper's roster. No care was taken with the script and less on the effectiveness of the outcome. The public and critics booed. The *New York*

Evening Post wrote "Bad enough to be good entertainment if taken as farce. The word 'preposterous,' applied here to *The Dawn Patrol*, should have been saved for this film, which presents Gary Cooper as the gallant Captain Baker, and makes him marry June Collyer as the outlandish Patricia Hunter."

Screenland opined "It's never very convincing, but if you like Gary, rehashing the war, and June's dimples, you may be pleased." *Motion Picture News* replied, "Gary Cooper gives a fine performance. Toomey and Miss Collyer handle their parts well, but it is Cooper's work that carries the talker over many rough spots in the story."

82

With Betty Compson

THE SPOILERS

A Paramount Picture   1930

CAST:

GARY COOPER *(Glenister);* KAY JOHNSON *(Helen Chester);* BETTY COMPSON *(Cherry Malotte);* WILLIAM "STAGE" BOYD *(McNamara);* HARRY GREEN *(Herman);* SLIM SUMMERVILLE *(Slapjack Slims);* JAMES KIRKWOOD *(Dextry);* LLOYD INGRAHAM *(Judge Stillman);* OSCAR APFEL *(Voorhees);* GEORGE IRVING *(William Wheaton);* KNUTE ERICSON *(Ship Captain);* MERRILL MC CORMICK *(Miner);* CHARLES K. FRENCH *(Man in bar).*

CREDITS:

EDWARD CAREWE *(Director);* BARTLETT CORMACK, AGNES BRAND LEAHY *(Scenarists);* HARRY FISCHBECK *(Photographer);* WILLIAM SHEA *(Editor);* HARRY M. LINDGREN *(Sound Recorder). Based on the book by* REX BEACH.

SYNOPSIS:

Glenister and Dextry, partners of the rich Midas mine, befriend Helen Chester on the voyage to Nome, enabling her to escape pursuers with valuable papers. During this period, Glenister becomes infatuated with her. Government officials arrive in Nome, headed by McNamara, an unscrupulous politician (in love with Helen) and Judge Stillman, Helen's uncle, These crooked "officials" begin despoiling the richest claims.

Cherry Malotte, a faro dealer, greets Glenister affectionately, but he tells her that Helen has won his heart. Cherry is bitterly jealous. The conspiring McNamara and Judge Stillman then present a title to Midas and serve ejection papers on Glenister and Dextry. Instead of shooting it out, they listen to Glenister, who believes Helen to be sincere in her defense of the law and they agree to let the courts settle the dispute.

83

With Kay Johnson
and James Kirkwood

They eventually send for a lawyer after Cherry lies, telling Glenister that Helen is involved in the conspiracy. Meanwhile, McNamara and the judge try to gain entrance to the mine and Glenister and McNamara have a terrific fist-fight. Glenister wins and Cherry confesses she lied about the judge's niece, thus re-uniting Glenister and Helen.

NOTES:

Rex Beach's great Alaskan saga of the early 1900's has received five screen treatments. This was the third and one of the best. Director Edward Carewe gave his production tremendous physical action and kept a quick pace throughout, although the script remained faithful to the original, while utilizing the mobility of the camera. Despite the lovely heroine of Kay Johnson and the tinsel tart of Betty Compson, the emphasis again was on the conflicts between man and man. Cooper's fight with William "Stage" Boyd was, without doubt, the film's highlight.

Said *Motion Picture News*: "Cooper does perhaps the finest work of his career under the experienced direction of Edwin Carewe. James Kirkwood is most convincing, as is Betty Compson in a small but important role. Kay Johnson's acting is above reproach. She is excellent as the love interest."

Selig first filmed *The Spoilers* in 1913-14, with Tom Santschi, William Farnum and Kathlyn Williams, Goldwyn's version in 1923 had Milton Sills, Noah Beery and Anna Q. Nilsson. In 1942, Universal used Marlene Dietrich, John Wayne and Randolph Scott. The 1955 Universal-International cast featured Rory Calhoun, Anne Baxter and Jeff Chandler.

With William "Stage" Boyd

With William "Stage" Boyd
and Kay Johnson

On the set with Tom Santschi
and William Farnum,
the original men of *The Spoilers*

With Eve Southern

MOROCCO

A Paramount Picture   1930

CAST:

GARY COOPER (*Tom Brown*); MARLENE DIETRICH
(*Amy Jolly*); ADOLPHE MENJOU (*Kennington*); ULL-
RICH HAUPT (*Adjutant Caesar*); JULIETTE COMPTON
(*Anna Dolores*); FRANCIS MC DONALD (*Corporal
Tatoche*); ALBERT CONTI (*Colonel Quinnevieres*);
EVE SOUTHERN (*Madame Caesar*); MICHAEL VISAROFF
(*Barratire*); PAUL PORCASI (*Lo Tinto*); THERESA
HARRIS (*Camp Follower*); *with* EMILE CHAUTARD.

CREDITS:

JOSEF VON STERNBERG (*Director*); JULES FURTHMAN
(*Scenarist*); LEE GARMES (*Photographer*); HANS
DREIER (*Art Director*); TRAVIS BANTON (*Costumer*);
SAM WINSTON (*Editor*); HARRY D. MILLS (*Sound Re-
corder*); KARL HAJOS (*Musical Score*). SONGS: "*Give
Me the Man*" *and* "*What am I Bid*" *by* LEO ROBIN
and KARL HAJOS; "*Quand L'Amour Meurt*" *by*
CREMIEUX. *Based on the novel* "*Amy Jolly*" *by*
BENNO VIGNY.

SYNOPSIS:

Tom Brown, a devil-may-care American private in
the French Foreign Legion, is ruthless with women,
taking them as they come and leaving them. His
latest affair, with the wife of a Legion officer, has
begun to wane when he first sees Amy Jolly, a
cabaret singer newly arrived in the desert city. Amy
plays up to the handsome Tom during one of her
musical numbers, despite other suitors, among them
the debonaire Kennington, and arranges a rendezvous with the legionnaire in her apartment. He
finds her embittered by life, scorning men, yet he is
strangely attracted to her.

Fearing that she is gaining power over him,
Tom abruptly leaves and runs into Mme. Caesar,
who has followed him. Amy, intrigued, follows
him and interrupts the pair. Mme. Caesar is
enraged and tries to get street beggars to molest
Amy, Tom tries to defend her, but is arrested and
later assigned a dangerous mission by Mme. Caesar's
husband. Before leaving he goes to Amy, but after

85

With Marlene Dietrich

With Marlene Dietrich and Adolphe Menjou

overhearing Kennington proposing to her—he decides to leave.

The mission completed, Tom decides to stay on at the desert outpost. Amy hears he has been wounded and Kennington drives her to him. She finds Tom in a local dive with saucy Anna Dolores. Amy and Tom realize their mutual love, but his regiment leaves the following morning for another desert encampment. After some deliberation, Amy follows along with the other legion of women.

NOTES:

Morocco was Josef von Sternberg's introduction to American audiences of Marlene Dietrich, as seen through the eyes and lens of Josef von Sternberg. The effect on the public was dazzling—the rest is history. *Morocco* also provided Gary Cooper with a rare chance of being a heel of the first order, the love 'em and leave 'em kind of guy who fascinates throughout. A new brand of hero, he was marvelously effective in the role of Legionnaire Tom Brown.

It is all the more amazing when one realizes that the time von Sternberg spent on Dietrich and camera set-ups left little time for his male star. However, Cooper liked Dietrich from the first (although he disliked working with her mentor) and gave more of himself in this role.

Richard Watts, Jr. in the *New York Herald Tribune* noticed, "The understandably popular Gary Cooper, who underacts more completely than any other player within memory, never has been as effective and certainly never as expert an actor as he is in the role of the hero." Thornton Delehanty in the *New York Evening Post* told his readers, ". . . the scenes between these three (Dietrich, Cooper, Menjou), and between any combination of them, throb with portents. . . . Gary Cooper gives one of his best performances in this picture, a restrained and telling piece of work."

Said *Motion Picture:* "With all of the star's apparent subtlety, the picture is compounded of old familiar movie elements of unrequited love and revenge, with Menjou as an elegant continental and Gary Cooper, still in uniform, as the lover of many ladies! The scene where he quells the jeering mob at the vaudeville theater is the most spontaneous of the picture." *Picture Play* opined, "The success of Miss Dietrich is vastly aided by Gary Cooper, as the American, perhaps his best performance so far."

On the set with director
Josef von Sternberg

With Ullrich Haupt and Emile Chautard

88

Between "takes," measuring
himself against wagon wheel

FIGHTING CARAVANS

A Paramount Picture   1931

CAST:

GARY COOPER *(Clint Belmet)*; LILY DAMITA *(Felice)*; ERNEST TORRENCE *(Bill Jackson)*; FRED KOHLER *(Lee Murdock)*; TULLY MARSHALL *(Jim Bridger)*; EUGENE PALLETTE *(Seth Higgins)*; ROY STEWART *(Couch)*; MAY BOLEY *(Jane)*; JAMES FARLEY *(Amos)*; JAMES MARCUS *(The Blacksmith)*; EVE SOUTHERN *(Faith)*; DONALD MACKENZIE *(Gus)*; SYD SAYLOR *(Charlie)*; E. ALYN WARREN *(Barlow)*; FRANK CAMPEAU *(Jeff Moffitt)*; CHARLES WINNINGER *(Marshal)*; FRANK HAGNEY *(The Renegade)*; JANE DARWELL *(Pioneer Woman)*; IRVING BACON *(Barfly)*; HARRY SEMELS *(Brawler)*; IRON EYES CODY *(Indian after firewater)*; MERRILL MCCORMICK *(Townsman)*; TINY SANDFORD *(Man of the wagon train)*; CHIEF BIG TREE *(Indian during title credits)*.

CREDITS:

OTTO BROWER, DAVID BURTON *(Directors)*; EDWARD G. PARAMORE, JR., KEENE THOMPSON, AGNES BRAND LEAHY *(Scenarists)*; LEE GARMES, HENRY GERRARD *(Photographers)*; WILLIAM SHEA *(Editor)*; ROBERT ODELL *(Art Director)*; EARLE S. HAYMAN *(Sound Recorder)*; JOHN LEIPOLD, OSCAR POTOKER, EMIL BIERMAN, MAX BERGUNKER, EMIL HILB, HERMAN HAND, KARL HAJOS, SIGMUND KRUMGOLD, A. COUSMINER *(Musical Score)*. *Based on the novel by* ZANE GREY.

SYNOPSIS:

Before leaving Missouri as a guide for a cross-country caravan, Clint Belmet is arrested for disturbing the peace. His older partners, Bill and Jim, persuade Felice, an orphaned French girl whose wagon has just arrived to join the caravan, to pose as Clint's wife so the marshal will let him go. She agrees, because she thinks she's saving his life, but later finds out about the ruse when Clint tells her he has certain rights as a "bridegroom."

Another member of the caravan is Lee Murdock, an unscrupulous frontiersman in league with the Indians, who plans to betray the members of the caravan for his own gain. Meanwhile, Clint, intrigued by Felice's anger, apologizes and they become friends. The old guides now fear that their young friend, whom they raised, will want to marry and settle down. Their efforts to break up the romance are effective for a time.

A big Indian attack comes as the caravan is attempting to cross a river. Clint swims to a wagon loaded with kerosene and, after dumping the oil into the water, sets it afire. This action demoralizes the Indians' attack, but not before his two pals are killed, along with Lee Murdock. The remnants of the caravan push Westward with Clint as their sole guide and Felice beside him.

NOTES:

Although *Fighting Caravans* was based on the 1929 novel by Zane Grey, it bore a strong resemblance to the 1923 silent western *The Covered Wagon.* Paramount, like the other studios, put a great deal of effort into producing westerns, which were always good box-office.

This particular production warranted, among others: two directors, two photographers and no fewer than nine composers to assemble the musical score (not an uncommon practice in the early days of sound). It was, therefore, a western adventure of epic proportions. In fact, so much footage was shot for *Fighting Caravans* that, when William Shea completed his editing chores, there was enough background for another film. The film was *Wagon Wheels* and its star was Randolph Scott. Paramount released it in 1934.

Said the London *Times* "It is pleasant to see Mr. Gary Cooper back once again in the open spaces of the West where he belongs . . . Once more Mr. Cooper is denied the chance to show how he can act—all he has to do is to lounge about and look boyishly handsome and mischievous." Don Ashbaugh in the *Motion Picture Herald* commented, "The role of the hero, a young scout, is designed to fit Gary Cooper perfectly. No great demands are made upon him but he gives an interesting characterization, something more than the stereotyped western hero. And he looks and acts like a frontiersman rather than a Hollywood actor trying to resemble a cowman."

Whenever this film is shown on television, which isn't often enough, the title has been changed to *Blazing Arrows.*

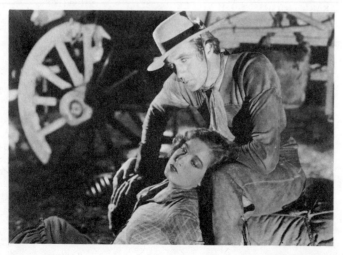

90   With Lily Damita

With Lily Damita

CITY STREETS

A Paramount Picture   1931

CAST:

GARY COOPER *(The Kid);* SYLVIA SIDNEY *(Nan);* PAUL LUKAS *(Big Boy Maskal);* WILLIAM "STAGE" BOYD *(McCoy);* GUY KIBBEE *(Pop Cooley);* STANLEY FIELDS *(Blackie);* WYNNE GIBSON *(Agnes);* BETTY SINCLAIR *(Pansy);* BARBARA LEONARD *(Girl);* TERRY CARROLL *(Esther March);* EDWARD LE SAINT *(Shooting gallery patron);* ROBERT HOMANS *(Inspector);* WILLARD ROBERTSON *(Detective);* HAL PRICE *(Shooting gallery onlooker);* ETHAN LAIDLAW *(Killer at prison);* GEORGE REGAS *(Machine-gunner);* BOB KORTMAN *(Servant);* LEO WILLIS *(Henchman);* BILL ELLIOTT *(Dance Extra);* ALLAN CAVAN *(Cop);* BERT HANLON *(Baldy);* MATTY KEMP *(Man stabbed with fork);* and KATE DRAIN LAWSON.

CREDITS:

ROUBEN MAMOULIAN *(Director);* E. LLOYD SHELDON *(Producer);* OLIVER H. P. GARRETT *(Scenarist);* MAX MARCIN *(Adaptation);* LEE GARMES *(Photographer);* WILLIAM SHEA *(Editor);* J. A. GOODRICH, M. M. PAGGIE *(Sound Recorders). Based on an original screenplay by* DASHIELL HAMMETT.

SYNOPSIS:

Nan, whose stepfather, Pop Cooley, is a henchman of the beer-running racketeer Big Boy Maskal, falls in love with a lanky Westerner employed in a carnival. Nan urges the Kid to join the racketeers, for the easy money, but he refuses. Pop Cooley is assigned to "bump off" Blackie, another aid of the suave racketeer, because Maskal wants Field's girl Agnes. Pop takes Blackie for a "ride" and is later freed on an alibi supplied by Agnes.

Nan refuses to "squeal" and is railroaded to prison. She sends Pop to tell the Kid what has happened and he is impressed with the young fellow's shooting. The Kid soon joins the racketeers, in hopes of saving Nan. Meanwhile, in prison, a disillusioned Nan becomes furious when she learns The Kid has joined the rackets. Finally released, Nan tries to convince the Kid to leave the gangsters, but he refuses. Soon, however, he crosses the racketeer and then outwits his henchmen, who are plotting to "get" him, and pretends he's out to get Maskal.

To prevent this, Nan meets Maskal in his apartment and begs him to throw the Kid out of the gang. Agnes enters and shoots Maskal for two-timing her, then throws the gun into the room and locks Nan inside. Nan is found with Maskal's body and is taken for a ride. The Kid (also doomed by orders) drives at breakneck speed and, thus, foils the gangster's plot. He eventually lets the men out and drives away with Nan.

NOTES:

After the critically-applauded, box office failure *Applause* (one of 1929's greatest films), Paramount didn't know what to do with their newest director, Rouben Mamoulian. They finally brought Mamoulian to the West Coast, in 1930, and gave him an original screenplay by Dashiell Hammett (his only one!). What evolved into *City Streets* remains one of the most sophisticated treatments of the gangster milieu ever filmed. Said Mamoulian: "You know, there are ten killings in this film, and you don't actually *see* one of them."

So unique were his innovations that studio executives began challenging him at every turn. One of the most beautiful scenes in the movie almost didn't stay in: Sylvia Sidney's prison soliloquy permitted the thoughts of the character to be heard and the brass thought the public wouldn't get the message. However, Mamoulian fought for his right to create, and won.

Clara Bow was originally set for the role of Nan, but, when she became involved in a court suit, Paramount swiftly substituted Sylvia Sidney. This was Sidney's first starring role in pictures, although she had appeared as a chorine in First National's *Broadway Nights* (1927) and Fox's *Thru Different Eyes* (1929). With her great eyes and soulful face, she soon became film's Depression Child.

Cooper was quite wonderful in a challenging role, which was unlike any he had previously been given. *Screenland* wrote, "Sylvia is a smash hit in her screen debut (*sic*), by far the finest actress of the new ingenue crop. Gary was never better."

Mordaunt Hall in *The New York Times* thought, "It is all melodramatic and incredible. Mr. Cooper gives a satisfactory showing as the Kid. Sylvia Sidney is excellent as Nan." *Motion Picture News* praised: "Gary Cooper, in the main role, handles a part different from his usual type, in a highly competent manner. Sylvia Sidney in her film debut (*sic*) makes a pleasing heroine and her dramatic moments are most praiseworthy."

With Sylvia Sidney

With Bob Kortman (left),
William "Stage" Boyd
and Wynne Gibson

Wynne Gibson

94

With Paul Lukas and Sylvia Sidney

I TAKE THIS WOMAN

A Paramount Picture   1931

CAST:

GARY COOPER *(Tom McNair);* CAROLE LOMBARD *(Kay Dowling);* HELEN WARE *(Aunt Bessie);* LESTER VAIL *(Herbert Forrest);* CHARLES TROWBRIDGE *(Mr. Dowling);* CLARA BLANDICK *(Sue Barnes);* GERALD FIELDING *(Bill Wentworth);* ALBERT HART *(Jake Mallory);* GUY OLIVER *(Sid);* SYD SAYLOR *(Shorty);* MILDRED VAN DORN *(Clara Hammell);* LESLIE PALMER *(Phillips);* ARA HASWELL *(Nora);* FRANK DARIEN *(the station agent);* DAVID LANDAU *(the circus boss); and* LEW KELLY.

CREDITS:

MARION GERING *(Director);* VINCENT LAWRENCE *(Scenarist);* VICTOR MILNER *(Photographer);* SLAVKO VORKAPICH *(Assistant Director);* TRAVIS BANTON *(Costumer);* EARLE S. HAYMAN *(Sound Recorder). Based on the novel "Lost Ecstasy" by* MARY ROBERTS RINEHART.

SYNOPSIS:

Beauty and her father's wealth have spoiled Kay Dowling, who thinks she can get away with anything and delights in shocking everyone. Mr. Dowling is furious with her escapades and, to tame her a bit, gives her the choice of three months on his Wyoming ranch or marrying Herbert Forrest, a devoted, but bland, suitor. Kay chooses the ranch.

Bitter about the whole thing, and missing her New York friends, Kay flirts with cowhand Tom McNair, pretending to love him. He believes her advances and, finally asks her to marry him. At first, she laughs, but soon sees it as a new thrill and rushes into the marriage. Her father disinherits her. To stick to her bargain—to spite her father—Kay tries to make a go of the ramshackle house Tom offers her. She works hard and sticks a year, but finally returns to her father. Tom follows her to New York to dissuade her from getting a divorce, but, once he becomes aware of her luxuri-

With Carole Lombard

With Carole Lombard and Lester Vail

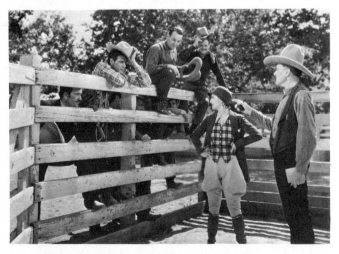

With Syd Saylor, Guy Oliver,
Carole Lombard and Lew Kelly

96

With Carole Lombard

ous surroundings, he scorns her and agrees to give her the divorce.

Now assured of her freedom, Kay isn't so sure she wants it, and follows him to the circus where he headlines in a cowboy act. He refuses to take her back, but Kay is watching when he is thrown from his horse and removed to the circus train. When he awakens, she is with him.

NOTES:

I Take This Woman was to have been another Gary Cooper-Fay Wray opus, but studio executives finally realized that the public just wasn't getting this team's message. They had the good sense to give the role of Kay Dowling, the spoiled heiress, to that marvelous zany Carole Lombard. Cooper and Lombard worked well together, but the flimsy storyline gave them little support.

Mordaunt Hall, in *The New York Times,* said, "This production was directed by Marion Gering and Slavko Vorkapich, who so far as the direction of the photography is concerned, have done their task well, but there are moments when the microphone is too much for them. . . . Be that as it may, Miss Lombard gives a capable performance. The gaunt Mr. Cooper also makes the most of his part."

The London *Times* noted, "Tom, who, since he is played by Mr. Gary Cooper, is both a cowboy and the soul of reticent and masculine honour . . . but . . . not even the personality of Mr. Cooper, nor the spirited Miss Lombard, save the obvious and laborious script."

HIS WOMAN

A Paramount Picture   1931

CAST:

GARY COOPER *(Captain Sam Whalan)*; CLAUDETTE COLBERT *(Sally Clark)*; AVERILL HARRIS *(Mate Gatson)*; RICHARD SPIRO *(Sammy)*; DOUGLASS DUMBRILLE *(Alisandroe)*; RAQUEL DAVIDA *(Maria Estella)*; HAMTREE HARRINGTON *(Aloysius)*; SIDNEY EASTON *(Mark)*; JOAN BLAIR *(Gertrude)*; CHARLOTTE WYNTERS *(Flo)*; HERSCHELL MAYALL *(Mr. Morrisey)*; JOE SPURIN CALLEIA *(The agent)*; LON HASCHAL *(Captain of Schooner)*; HARRY DAVENPORT *(Customs Inspector)*; JOHN T. DOYLE *(Doctor)*; EDWARD KEANE *(Boatswain)*; BARTON MACLANE, DONALD MCBRIDE, PRESTON FOSTER *(Crewmen)*.

CREDITS:

EDWARD SLOMAN *(Director)*; ADELAIDE HEILBRON, MELVILLE BAKER *(Scenarists)*; WILLIAM STEINER *(Photographer)*; ARTHUR ELLIS *(Editor)*; C. V. TUTHILL *(Sound Recorder)*. Based on the novel *"The Sentimentalist"* by DALE COLLINS.

SYNOPSIS:

Sam Whalan, a tramp-freighter captain, is going ashore in a tropical port when his crew rescues a drifting Navy boat containing a baby. Sam doesn't turn the kid over to authorities, keeping him in his cabin. The baby proves to be a handful, so Sam details his mate to help him find a sea-going "mother" for the infant. Sally Clark, a witness in a blackmailing case, who has been hiding away as a dancehall girl, has learned the case has been dropped and is eager to go home. She overhears Sam interviewing a few applicants and, knowing the type of girl he wants, quickly changes her makeup, assumes a prim mien, tells a fantastic story, landing the position—and a free trip back to the States.

They set sail and all is bliss until Sam's mate, Gatson recognizes Sally and threatens to expose her unless she yields to him. She refuses and an ensuing fight with Sam ends with Gatson falling overboard. Sally, meanwhile, has fallen for the skipper, while he too conceals tender feelings. When they dock in New York, Sam is arrested for attempted murder (another ship picked up Gatson). To save Sam, Sally becomes his witness, but, at the same time, loses Sam's respect. She then returns to jazzy nightlife, while he goes on a spree. They torture each other until the baby's serious illness brings them together again. Once the baby is out of danger, all is well.

NOTES:

This was the second film version of Dale Collins' novel *The Sentimentalist,* and neither one was particularly good. Pathé first filmed it as *Sal of Singapore,* in 1929, with Phyllis Haver. In fact, the working-title for this film was also *Sal of Singapore.* All exteriors were filmed along the Eastern seaboard; interiors, in Paramount's Astoria studios.

His Woman has a few effective moments, but it wallows in tedium and not even the presence of Claudette Colbert improved the feeble script. The baby, Richard Spiro, all but stole the show—along with two zippy Black comedians named Hamtree Harrington and Sidney Easton, who played a pair of stereotype Amos 'n' Andy-esque sailors—the chief reason why this picture has never been aired on television to date. This is a pity, since they were quite funny and such an integral part of the plot, that they couldn't be edited out without ruining the entire storyline.

The New York Times observed, "The most effective member of the cast is the baby, a rather remarkable infant, who is complete master of his limited emotional equipment. Gary Cooper and Claudette Colbert give their usual competent performances." Said the London *Times:* "Mr. Gary Cooper, youthful and debonair in white ducks, . . . has been miscast before in his career, but never quite so outrageously as in *His Woman.*"

With Joe Spurin Calleia
and Raquel Davida

With Claudette Colbert
and director Edward Sloman

With Claudette Colbert

Stuart Erwin gets a glimpse of Tallulah Bankhead and Gary Cooper in the talkie-about-the-talkies "Make Me a Star."

With Stuart Erwin
and Tallulah Bankhead

MAKE ME A STAR

A Paramount Picture   1932

CAST:

STUART ERWIN (*Merton Gill*); JOAN BLONDELL (*"Flips" Montague*); ZASU PITTS (*Mrs. Scudder*); BEN TURPIN (*Ben*); CHARLES SELLON (*Mr. Gashwiler*); FLORENCE ROBERTS (*Mrs. Gashwiler*); HELEN JEROME EDDY (*Tessie Kearns*); ARTHUR HOYT (*Hardy Powell*); DINK TEMPLETON (*Buck Benson*); RUTH DONNELLY (*The Countess*); SAM HARDY (*Jeff Baird*); OSCAR APFEL (*Henshaw*); FRANK MILLS (*Chuck Collins*); POLLY WALTERS (*Doris Randall*); VICTOR POTEL, BOBBY VERNON, SNUB POLLARD, BILLY BLETCHER, BUD JAMISON, NICK THOMPSON (*Fellow Actors*).

GUEST STARS (AS THEMSELVES):

TALLULAH BANKHEAD; CLIVE BROOK; MAURICE CHEVALIER; CLAUDETTE COLBERT; GARY COOPER; PHILLIPS HOLMES; FREDRIC MARCH; JACK OAKIE; CHARLIE RUGGLES; SYLVIA SIDNEY.

CREDITS:

WILLIAM BEAUDINE (*Director*); SAM WINTZ, WALTER DE LEON, ARTHUR KOBER (*Adaptation*); ALLEN SIEGLER (*Photographer*); LEROY STONE (*Editor*); EARLE S. HAYMAN (*Sound Recorder*). Based on the book *"Merton of the Movies"* by HARRY LEON WILSON *and the subsequent play by* GEORGE S. KAUFMAN *and* MOSS HART.

SYNOPSIS:

Merton Gill, a grocery clerk, longs to be a film star. He goes off to Hollywood and gets into a big studio, by telling a casting director that he has a diploma from a correspondence school of acting. After getting nowhere fast, he is befriended by a movie "extra" named "Flips" Montague and, through her, he is given a job in a "burlesque" western, as the hero. He plays his role in earnest.

Later, Merton is completely disillusioned when, at the preview, he realizes that he has performed like a buffoon. Thinking he has failed, he decides to return home but is stopped by Flips, who convinces him that he has become a great success as a comic.

NOTES:

Harry Leon Wilson's 1922 novel *Merton of the Movies* also became Broadway's biggest comedy hit of the 1922-23 season, with Glenn Hunter essaying the title role. Hunter repeated his comic portrayal in the 1924 silent made by Paramount. The studio decided to dust it off and remake it under another title as the first starring vehicle for Stuart Erwin, then one of Paramount's most popular supporting players.

Director William Beaudine went out of his way to achieve authenticity and shot his people in the studio restaurant, the various cutting rooms, and the entrance to the music building, which provided some funny business between Erwin and Ben Tur-pin. Sets from *Dr. Jekyll and Mr. Hyde* and *Madame Racketeer* were utilized, as well as several stars themselves. Gary Cooper and Tallulah Bankhead, in costume from *Devil and the Deep,* then filming, were among those who met Merton in the script.

Time commented, "Better than any other actor in Hollywood, Stuart Erwin has mastered the expression of befuddlement. . . . He makes Merton's grand gesture of presenting the extra girl with a wrist watch hilarious by the way he says: 'It's a little token of my esteem and . . . it's guaranteed.' Director William Beaudine had fine dialog to work with and he put in a few sharp touches of his own."

This film has never been exhibited on television, since rights to its distribution and/or screening were purchased by Metro-Goldwyn-Mayer, in 1947, when they re-vamped the script as a Red Skelton vehicle under its original title.

With Tallulah Bankhead

DEVIL AND THE DEEP

A Paramount Picture   1932

CAST:

TALLULAH BANKHEAD (*Pauline Sturm*); GARY COOPER (*Lieutenant Sempter*); CHARLES LAUGHTON (*Commander Charles Sturm*); CARY GRANT (*Lieutenant Jaeckel*); PAUL PORCASI (*Hassan*); JULIETTE COMPTON (*Mrs. Planet*); HENRY KOLKER (*Hutton*); DOROTHY CHRISTY (*Mrs. Crimp*); ARTHUR HOYT (*Mr. Planet*); GORDON WESTCOTT (*Lieutenant Toll*); JIMMIE DUGAN (*Condover*); KENT TAYLOR (*A Friend*); LUCIEN LITTLEFIELD (*Shopkeeper*); PETER BROCCO (*Wireless Operator*); WILFRED LUCAS (*Court Martial Judge*); DAVE O'BRIEN, HARRY GUTTMAN, GEORGE MAGRILL (*Submarine Crewmen*).

CREDITS:

MARION GERING (*Director*); BENN LEVY (*Scenarist*); CHARLES LANG (*Photographer*); J. A. GOODRICH (*Sound Recorder*); TRAVIS BANTON (*Costumer*); BERNARD HERZBRUN (*Art Director*); OTHO LOVERING (*Editor*). *Based on a story by* HARRY HERVEY.

SYNOPSIS:

Commander Charles Sturm, in charge of a submarine based in a small port on the north coast of Africa, has just transferred one of his young lieutenants for negligence of duty. His young wife Pauline, however, knows the real reason is jealousy. Confronted, he accuses her of infidelity and flies into a rage, driving her from the house. Pauline goes into town, where natives are celebrating the Moslem Feast of Beiram. Just as she is almost crushed by the crowd, a tall young man appears and guides her to a nearby store. To pacify the shopkeeper, he buys a bottle of cheap perfume.

Later, they drive into the desert. As they lie on the sand, Pauline spills the perfume on her dress and wipes it off with his handkerchief. They stay together that evening. The next morning, in town, she tells him they must not see one another again. Sturm, already suspicious of his wife, is even more so when he smells the perfume. His spirits are picked up temporarily, however, with the arrival of Sempter, his new lieutenant—until, during the

With Gordon Westcott, Peter Brocco,
Harry Guttman, Tallulah Bankhead,
George Magrill, and Charles Laughton

course of the conversation, Sempter drops his handkerchief and Sturm smells the same fragrance. Pauline comes in, discovering the identity of her husband's new lieutenant.

Pauline then rushes to the submarine, for she fears Sturm will do something drastic. When he discovers his wife aboard, he gives orders to submerge. Heading directly for a freighter, he turns the controls over to Sempter just as they hit it. The badly damaged vessel then sinks and the crewmen believe the lieutenant is to blame. At the height of the crisis, Pauline pulls a revolver from her handbag and holds everyone off, explaining that her husband was at fault. One by one, the crew rush to safety through the escape hatch, but Sturm dashes to the rear of the submarine, opens a hatchway, and drowns in the flood of water that ensues.

With Tallulah Bankhead

With Charles Laughton and Tallulah Bankhead

NOTES:

The stars of *Devil and the Deep* made a routine script work and provide the only reasons for seeing it today. The dialogue was awful; at one point, Cooper says to Tallulah "You look to me very lovely." It was a tour-de-force for Charles Laughton, whose vibrant personality took most of the reviews. One critic found Cooper "satisfactory as the lover," while another felt "he achieves a simple directness that goes most engagingly with his stalwart masculinity."

The London *Times,* after praising Mr. Laughton, said, "Miss Bankhead and Mr. Gary Cooper go through their less interesting parts with the precision and skilled display of their own characters that we expect of them." Mordaunt Hall in *The New York Times* found Mr. Laughton "forceful," Miss Bankhead "at her best" and felt Mr. Cooper "gives a sympathetic and vigorous interpretation as Lieutenant Sempter." *The New Yorker* thought Cooper "a little vague."

With
Tallulah Bankhead
and Charles Laughton

IF I HAD A MILLION

A Paramount Picture   1932

CAST:

GARY COOPER *(Gallagher);* GEORGE RAFT *(Eddie Jackson);* WYNNE GIBSON *(Violet);* CHARLES LAUGHTON *(The Clerk);* JACK OAKIE *(Mulligan);* FRANCES DEE *(Mary Wallace);* CHARLES RUGGLES *(Henry Peabody);* ALISON SKIPWORTH *(Emily);* W. C. FIELDS *(Rollo);* MARY BOLAND *(Mrs. Peabody);* ROSCOE KARNS *(O'Brien);* MAY ROBSON *(Mrs. Walker);* GENE RAYMOND *(John Wallace);* LUCIEN LITTLEFIELD *(Zeb);* RICHARD BENNETT *(John Glidden);* GRANT MITCHELL *(The Prison Priest);* JOYCE COMPTON *(Marie);* CECIL CUNNINGHAM *(Agnes);* IRVING BACON *(Chinaware Salesman);* BLANCHE FREDERICI *(Head Nurse, Old Ladies' Home);* DEWEY ROBINSON *(Cook, Old Ladies' Home);* GAIL PATRICK *(Secretary);* FRED KELSEY, WILLARD ROBERTSON *(Doctors);* KENT TAYLOR *(Bank Clerk);* JACK PENNICK *(Sailor);* BERTON CHURCHILL *(Warden);* JAMES BURTIS *(Jailer).*

CREDITS:

ERNST LUBITSCH, NORMAN TAUROG, STEPHEN ROBERTS, NORMAN MC LEOD, JAMES CRUZE, WILLIAM A. SEITER, H. BRUCE HUMBERSTONE *(Directors);* CLAUDE BINYON, WHITNEY BOLTON, MALCOLM STUART BOYLAN, JOHN BRIGHT, SIDNEY BUCHANAN, LESTER COLE, ISABEL DAWN, BOYCE DE GAW, WALTER DE LEON, OLIVER H. P. GARRETT, HARVEY GATES, GROVER JONES, ERNST LUBITSCH, LAWTON MACKALL, JOSEPH L. MANKIEWICZ, WILLIAM SLAVENS MC NUTT, SETON I. MILLER, TIFFANY THAYER *(Scenarists);* LOUIS D. LIGHTON *(Producer);* FRANK GRENZBACH, PHIL S. WISDOM *(Sound Recorders). Based on a story by* ROBERT D. ANDREWS.

SYNOPSIS:

Wealthy John Glidden is dying and his relatives have gathered around him like vultures. Enraged, he has a brainstorm and grabs the telephone directory. With a medicine dropper, he selects eight names—each to receive $1,000,000. His beneficiaries are: 1) Henry Peabody, a butter-fingered clerk in a china store, always docked for his breakage, who goes on a rampage smashing everything in sight. 2) Violet, a waterfront prostitute, who rents an expensive suite in a plush hotel and sleeps *alone* in a satin-sheeted bed, without her stockings. 3) Eddie Jackson, a forger who can't get anyone to cash his check and trades it for a night's shelter and the flophouse proprietor, thinking him crazy, lights his cigar with it. 4) A fat little clerk in a large, dreary office, who goes straight to the president of the company, knocks politely on his door, and then proceeds to give him the greatest raspberry ever heard. 5) Gallagher, a rough 'n' tough marine who gets his check on April 1st and, thinking it a gag from one of his two buddies, gives it away to a lunch stand owner. 6) Emily, an old vaudevillian, who, with her husband Rollo, whose new car has just been smashed to bits, sets about, with a string of secondhand cars, to clear the highways of all "road hogs." 7) John Wallace, a condemned murderer, a few hours before he faces the electric chair, who finds the check too late to get himself the lawyer he couldn't previously afford, and 8) Mrs. Walker, a grandmother wasting away in a hateful old ladies' home, who turns it into a resort hotel.

NOTES:

Cooper received top billing in this eight-episode story, although his segment was the weakest—and silliest—of the bunch. Norman McLeod directed this chapter, however, with verve, despite the script. Originally there were eight directors, one for each episode, however, in the final screen credits, director Lothar Mendes, who directed one of the segments, was deleted.

The special highlight of the film was Charles Laughton's bit as the fat, meek bookkeeper, which was written and directed by Ernst Lubitsch. The next-best was the delightful episode with W. C. Fields and Alison Skipworth: seeking vengeance on "road hogs." Wynne Gibson's episode was sheer bliss.

Said *Time* magazine: "*If I Had a Million* develops an obvious idea in an obvious way. Since the obvious idea is one which cinema producers have overlooked, and since it is handled with skill and enthusiasm, *If I Had a Million* gives the impression of being a startlingly original picture as well as clever and interesting." William Boehnel in the *New York World-Telegram* felt "It is a pity that with so much in it that is good, it can only be recommended for various chapters rather than as a whole."

With Richard Bennett
and James Burtis

With Joyce Compton,
Jack Oakie
and Roscoe Karns

With Helen Hayes

A FAREWELL TO ARMS

A Paramount Picture   1932

CAST:

HELEN HAYES (*Catherine Barkley*); GARY COOPER (*Lieutenant Frederic Henry*); ADOLPHE MENJOU (*Major Rinaldi*); MARY PHILIPS (*Helen Ferguson*); JACK LA RUE (*The Priest*); BLANCHE FREDERICI (*Head Nurse*); HENRY ARMETTA (*Bonello*); GEORGE HUMBERT (*Piani*); FRED MALATESTA (*Manera*); MARY FORBES (*Miss Van Campen*); TOM RICKETTS (*Count Greffi*); ROBERT COUTERIO (*Gordoni*); GILBERT EMERY (*British Major*); PEGGY CUNNINGHAM (*Molly*); AGUSTINO BORGATO (*Giulio*); PAUL PORCASI (*Inn Keeper*); ALICE ADAIR (*Cafe Girl*).

CREDITS:

FRANK BORZAGE (*Director*); BENJAMIN GLAZER, OLIVER H. P. GARRETT (*Scenarists*); CHARLES LANG (*Photographer*); OTHO LOVERING (*Editor*); HANS DREIER, ROLAND ANDERSON (*Art Directors*); HAROLD C. LEWIS (*Sound Recorder*); TRAVIS BANTON (*Costumer*); ARTHUR JACOBSON, LOU BORZAGE (*Assistant Directors*); RALPH RAINGER, JOHN LEIPOLD, BERNHARD (BERNARD) KAUN, PAUL MARQUARDT, HERMAN HAND, W. FRANKE HARLING (*Musical Score*); CHARLES GRIFFIN (*Technical Adviser—War Sequences*); DR. JARDINI (*Technical Adviser—Hospital Sequences*); EDWARD A. BLATT (*Associate Producer*). Based on the novel by ERNEST HEMINGWAY.

SYNOPSIS:

Back from the front, Lieutenant Frederic Henry finds his close friend Major Rinaldi excited about the arrival of some English nurses, especially Catherine Barkley. That evening, Frederic goes to a local dive. He is drunk when the Austrians begin bombing the village and everyone rushes to safety. Concealed in an areaway, Frederic discovers that he is with a woman and, thinking she is from

106

With Helen Hayes and Adolphe Menjou

the dive, talks to her in a frank manner—until he sees that she is a nurse from the nearby hospital.

The next night, the Major introduces Frederic to Catherine Barkley and both laugh over the previous night's misadventure. The two become inseparable, and soon they are hopelessly in love. However, Frederic goes back to the front, and the Major, jealous of the relationship, has Catherine transferred to Milan. Frederic is seriously wounded and is rushed to the hospital, where Major Rinaldi performs an operation. Regretting his jealous actions, the Major then sends his young friend to Milan to be with Catherine.

All is bliss for the couple until he is well enough to return to the front. Quietly, Catherine crosses into Switzerland to await the birth of their child; she sends him many letters, but they never get past the Major, whose jealousy is alive again. Meanwhile, the lieutenant's letters are returned and, because he has not heard from Catherine, he finally goes to Milan and tries to locate her. He learns she is in Switzerland and gets to her soon after their baby has been born dead. She, too, is near death—but they are together as news comes that the war is over.

NOTES:

A Farewell to Arms, from his 1930 novel, was the first Hemingway opus to reach the screen. The scenarists pretty much ignored the war, building up the romance between Lt. Henry and Catherine Barkley, and made the whole affair quite legitimate in the bargain.

Paramount filmed two endings; one, like the book, had Catherine die giving birth to the Lieutenent's dead child, and the other had her live. In true Hollywood tradition, the latter was preferred and ultimately used. Hemingway was displeased and, at the time of the picture's release,

With Helen Hayes, Mary Philips
and Robert Couterio

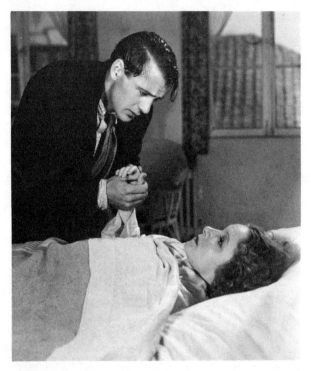

With Helen Hayes

With director Frank Borzage
and photographer Charles Lang

told a reporter for the *Arkansas Democrat* "I did not intend a happy ending."

Hemingway wasn't filmed again until 1943, also at Paramount and also starring Gary Cooper (*For Whom the Bell Tolls*). However, *A Farewell to Arms* was to have two more film versions. In a revamped, but thoroughly engrossing, version it appeared in 1950 as *Force of Arms* with William Holden, Nancy Olsen, and Frank Lovejoy. In 1957, producer David O. Selznick ended an otherwise brilliant career on a sour note with his own over-blown version of *A Farewell to Arms*. Rock Hudson was Lieutenant Henry, Jennifer Jones was Catherine Barkley and Vittorio de Sica was Major Rinaldi. This $4,000,000-disaster had only one major virtue, the superb color photography of Piero Portalupi and Oswald Morris.

Of the first *A Farewell to Arms,* critics said "The performances of Helen Hayes and Adolphe Menjou are among the outstanding of the year, while Cooper probably does the best work of his career. Jack LaRue and Mary Philips contribute splendid performances. And cinematographer Lang must not be forgotten." (*Photoplay*); "Gary Cooper, particularly in the closing scenes, is revealed as an actor with a greater emotional depth than he has ever displayed before." (Martin Dickstein in the *Brooklyn Daily Eagle*).

The *New York Daily News* found Cooper "as natural and convincing an actor as might have had years of stage training—which isn't the case. Gary is a true product of the celluloid. His performance as carefree Lt. Henry is thoroughly ingratiating."

A Farewell to Arms was nationally re-issued in 1938, but, since the rights were purchased by Selznick International Pictures, television rights are uncertain. It is quite possible it may never be seen again.

The film was nominated for four Academy Awards: including Best Picture; Hans Dreier and Roland Anderson for the Art Direction; Charles Lang for cinematography; and Harold C. Lewis for Sound Recording. Mr. Lewis won for his contribution.

With Joan Crawford

TODAY WE LIVE

A Metro-Goldwyn-Mayer Picture   1933

CAST:

JOAN CRAWFORD *(Diana Boyce-Smith);* GARY COOPER *(Bogard);* ROBERT YOUNG *(Claude);* FRANCHOT TONE *(Ronnie);* ROSCOE KARNS *(McGinnis);* LOUISE CLOSSER HALE *(Applegate);* ROLLO LLOYD *(Major);* HILDA VAUGHN *(Eleanor).*

CREDITS:

HOWARD HAWKS *(Director and Producer);* EDITH FITZGERALD, DWIGHT TAYLOR *(Adaptation);* OLIVER T. MARSH *(Photographer);* EDWARD CURTIS *(Editor);* WILLIAM FAULKNER *(Dialogue);* CEDRIC GIBBONS *(Art Director);* ADRIAN *(Costumer);* DOUGLAS SHEARER *(Sound Recorder). From the story "Turnabout" by* WILLIAM FAULKNER.

SYNOPSIS:

Diana Boyce-Smith, an aristocratic English girl, tries to do her part at home while her father fights at the front during the early years of the World War. She rents the family home to Bogard, a young American studying in England, just before she receives news of her father's death. On the same day Ronnie, her brother, and Claude, a childhood sweetheart, get orders to report to the front. Bogard consoles her and wins her affection. By the time she realizes she loves him, she has joined an ambulance unit to be near Ronnie and Claude. Later, when America enters the war, Bogard joins the American Flying Corp.

Diana and her three men are now at the front. Ronnie and Claude are operating a torpedo boat in the "skipper fleet," in the North Sea, while Bogard flies over the lines in a bomber. Bogard's plane is wrecked and Diana believes him dead, so she gives herself to Claude after he and Ronnie return from a raid. Shortly, after, Bogard returns to find Diana living with Claude. Shock is great for both and he soon accepts a "death order,"

William Cotton's
caricature used
for advertisement

In "Today We Live" the stellar honors
are shared by Joan Crawford and Gary
Cooper. Directed by Howard Hawks it i:
a picture of which M-G-M is justly proud

★ The above painting of Joan Crawford by William Cotton is the first

from which there will be no return, to blow up a ship. Claude is blinded during another raid and, not wanting to be a burden to Diana, he has Ronnie send a note to Bogard saying that they will blow up the ship with their torpedo boat. The boys go to their death before Bogard gets the note.

NOTES:

This was William Faulkner's first literary effort to reach the screen—from his short story "Turnabout." He handled the dialogue, which sounded like short urgent telegrams, instead of dialogue between people, himself. Cooper was loaned to Metro-Goldwyn-Mayer and his role involved him only in the love story with Joan Crawford, whose part was totally a figment in the scenarist's

imagination (Faulkner's story contained no women).

Said *The New York Times,* "Gary Cooper is restrained, sympathetic and quite believable as Bogard." John S. Cohen, Jr., in the *New York Sun* lauded, ". . . Gary Cooper, who has really learned to act in the talkies, almost equals his performance in *A Farewell to Arms. Today We Live* is a first-rate program film . . ." The *New York Evening Post* wrote, "As it is, Gary Cooper and Roscoe Karns . . . are the only genuine touches." The *New York American* noted, "Aside from the affectingly romantic and stirring story, director Howard Hawks has endowed his picture with a host of thrilling detail. Air shots are superb, and those at sea run a close second. . . ."

110

With Joan Crawford

With Roscoe Karns and Robert Young

112

With Frances Fuller

ONE SUNDAY AFTERNOON

A Paramount Picture   1933

CAST:

GARY COOPER *(Biff Grimes);* FAY WRAY *(Virginia Brush);* NEIL HAMILTON *(Hugo Barnstead);* FRANCES FULLER *(Amy Lind);* ROSCOE KARNS *(Snappy Downer);* JANE DARWELL *(Mrs. Lind);* CLARA BLANDICK *(Mrs. Brush);* SAM HARDY *(Dr. Startzman);* HARRY SCHULTZ *(Schneider);* JAMES BURTIS *(Dink Hoops);* A. S. BYRON *(Foreman);* JACK CLIFFORD *(Watchman); and* JOHNNY ST. CLAIR.

CREDITS:

STEPHEN ROBERTS *(Director);* LOUIS D. LIGHTON *(Producer);* WILLIAM SLAVENS MC NUTT, GROVER JONES *(Scenarists);* VICTOR MILNER *(Photographer);* ELLSWORTH HOAGLAND *(Editor);* HANS DREIER, W. B. IHNEN *(Art Directors);* HARRY D. MILLS *(Sound Recorder);* TRAVIS BANTON *(Costumer). Based on the stage play by* JAMES HAGAN.

SYNOPSIS:

Biff Grimes, a dentist, has always felt that he married the wrong girl, Amy Lind, although he suddenly discovers how wise his selection was. Through the years, Biff has always longed for vengeance on Hugo Barnstead, the man who married Biff's girl Virginia. However, when he finally sees how his dream princess turned out, he quickly decides that Hugo has really done him the greatest possible favor.

NOTES:

This was the first version of James Hagan's *One Sunday Afternoon* to be done on the screen. Since there have been two succeeding versions, it is unlikely that this picture will ever again see the light of day. Warner Bros. purchased the rights to re-film it in 1941 and called their version *The Strawberry Blonde,* casting James Cagney, Olivia de Havilland and Rita Hayworth. Warners re-made

it again in 1948 under its original title—but added songs—which permitted them to cast Dennis Morgan, Jack Carson and Janis Paige.

This *One Sunday Afternoon* was one of the finest films that director Stephen Roberts ever turned out; it was loaded with charm, and period (1910) authenticity. It also re-united Cooper with Fay Wray and introduced lovely Frances Fuller—repeating her stage role—to movie audiences.

Richard Watts, Jr., in the *New York Herald Tribune,* remarked that "Gary Cooper, who possesses a certain hick quality which fits in well with the Biff Grimes part, is better than usual, if hardly as helpful to the proceedings as was Mr. Nolan [Note: Lloyd Nolan starred in the Broadway stage version as Biff Grimes]. Miss Fay Wray, now safely escaped from both King Kong and Lionel Atwill, is satisfactory enough as the girl Biff is foolish enough to believe he should have married."

Mordaunt Hall in *The New York Times* noted "Gary Cooper, whose performance, like the picture as a whole, is praiseworthy in many respects, fails to impress one with the character's aggressive personality. The author's Biff Grimes went around with a chip on his shoulder, but Mr. Cooper portrays him in a milder fashion, which does not help the story."

Variety, however, felt "Its substance is delicate character humor and elusive sentimental appeal and these are qualities that are difficult to translate from footlights to celluloid . . . its faults cannot be laid at the door of the players who give the story engaging interpretation, particularly the performances of the two central characters . . . Cooper makes a departure playing a character role that calls for nice judgment, embodying a composite of that shade of humor that verges close to pathos and needs a nice balance.

"It seems a little astonishing to find this player of many formal leading-man roles suddenly blossoming into a very human character, as though he had been playing home-spun people all his life. Cooper has for years been playing a procession of stuffed-shirt polite roles and somehow giving them a human touch, that they didn't intrinsically have, by virtue of some subtlety, awkward masculinity, suppressed in polite roles, but vaguely sensed."

With Frances Fuller, Fay Wray
and Neil Hamilton

With Fay Wray

With Miriam Hopkins

DESIGN FOR LIVING

A Paramount Picture   1933

CAST:

FREDRIC MARCH *(Tom Chambers);* GARY COOPER *(George Curtis);* MIRIAM HOPKINS *(Gilda Farrell);* EDWARD EVERETT HORTON *(Max Plunkett);* FRANKLIN PANGBORN *(Mr. Douglas);* ISABEL JEWELL *(Lisping Stenographer);* HARRY DUNKINSON *(Mr. Egelbauer);* HELENA PHILLIPS *(Mrs. Egelbauer);* JAMES DONLIN *(Fat Man);* VERNON STEELE *(First Manager);* THOMAS BRAIDON *(Second Manager);* JANE DARWELL *(Housekeeper);* ARMAND KALIZ *(Mr. Burton);* ADRIENNE D'AMBRICOURT *(Proprietress of Café);* WYNDHAM STANDING *(Max's Butler);* NORA CECIL *(Tom's Secretary);* GRACE HAYLE *(Woman on staircase);* OLAF HYTTEN *(Englishman at train);* MARY GORDON *(Theatre Chambermaid);* LIONEL BELMORE, CHARLES K. FRENCH *(Theatre Patrons);* ROLFE SEDAN *(Bed Salesman); and* MATHILDE COMONT.

CREDITS:

ERNST LUBITSCH *(Director and Producer);* BEN HECHT *(Scenarist);* VICTOR MILNER *(Photographer);* FRANCIS MARSH *(Editor);* HANS DREIER *(Art Director);* TRAVIS BANTON *(Costumer);* M. M. PAGGIE *(Sound Recorder). Based on the play by* NOËL COWARD.

SYNOPSIS:

When Tom Chambers, a budding playwright, and George Curtis, a budding painter, fall asleep on a train to Paris, they are sketched by Gilda Farrell, who sits across from them, and they become an inseparable trio. Gilda is a commercial artist and both young men are in love with her—and she loves them. Gilda, sensing the rivalry between them, suggests they all live together, on a strictly platonic basis. She becomes their critic and spurs them on

115

to greater heights. Soon, Tom is off to London to have his play produced, but he gets a letter from George saying that the "gentlemen's agreement" has broken down. Tom's play is a hit and he quickly returns to Paris, only to find that George, also becoming known for his work, is in Nice painting a portrait.

Gilda confesses her love for Tom, but George returns next morning and is furious with them. She leaves the men arguing, departs for America with her boss Max Plunkett and marries him. For a year, Gilda entertains Max's boring clients at parties. She's on the verge of revolt when Tom and George suddenly appear at an important gathering, and behave so outlandishly that guests leave in disgust. Max is furious, but relieved, when Gilda declares that she's leaving him. Together, the happy trio return to Paris and a new "gentlemen's agreement."

NOTES:

The film version of Noël Coward's delicate comedy was given a top-notch cast, good production values, and an agile script, but it wasn't successful at the box office, nor did it please the critics. Richard Watts, Jr., in his *New York Herald Tribune* review, said, "The filmed *Design for Living,* if anything, [is] even more superficial than the original. . . . You could hardly expect Mr. Cooper to be properly at home as a witty sophisticate, and I fear that he isn't."

The prime reason for the film's failure was best summed up by Andrew Sarris, in his 1963 review in The *Village Voice,* ". . . the trouble with Cooper and March was that they were too masculine for the effete implications of the plot . . . Where Coward took the sex lightly for laughs, Lubitsch took it seriously for pathos, and Coward's wit thereby dissolved on the screen."

With Miriam Hopkins and Fredric March

With Fredric March and Grace Hayle

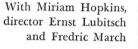
With Miriam Hopkins,
director Ernst Lubitsch
and Fredric March

116

With Charlotte Henry

ALICE IN WONDERLAND

A Paramount Picture   1933

CAST:

CHARLOTTE HENRY *(Alice) and (in alphabetical order)* RICHARD ARLEN *(The Cheshire Cat);* ROSCOE ATES *(The Fish);* WILLIAM AUSTIN *(The Gryphon);* BILLY BARTY *(The White Pawn and The Baby);* BILLY BEVAN *(The Two of Spades);* COLIN CAMPBELL *(Garden Frog);* HARVEY CLARK *(Father William);* GARY COOPER *(The White Knight);* JACK DUFFY *(Leg of Mutton);* HARRY EKEZIAN *(First Executioner);* LEON ERROL *(Uncle Gilbert);* LOUISE FAZENDA *(The White Queen);* W. C. FIELDS *(Humpty-Dumpty);* ALEC B. FRANCIS *(The King of Hearts);* SKEETS GALLAGHER *(The White Rabbit);* MEYER GRACE *(Third Executioner);* CARY GRANT *(The Mock Turtle);* ETHEL GRIFFIES *(Governess);* LILLIAN HARMER *(The Cook);* RAYMOND HATTON *(The Mouse);* STERLING HOLLOWAY *(The Frog);* EDWARD EVERETT HORTON *(The Mad Hatter);* ROSCOE KARNS *(Tweedledee);* COLIN KENNY *(The Clock);* BABY LE ROY *(Joker);* LUCIEN LITTLEFIELD *(Father William's Son);* MAE MARSH *(The Sheep);* CHARLES MC NAUGHTON *(Five of Spades);* POLLY MORAN *(The Dodo Bird);* JACK OAKIE *(Tweedledum);* PATSY O'BYRNE *(The Aunt);* EDNA MAY OLIVER *(The Red Queen);* GEORGE OVEY *(Plum Pudding);* MAY ROBSON *(The Queen of Hearts);* CHARLIE RUGGLES *(The March Hare);* JACKIE SEARL *(Dormouse);* ALISON SKIPWORTH *(The Duchess);* NED SPARKS *(The Caterpillar);* WILL STANTON *(Seven of Spades);* FORD STERLING *(The White King);* JOE TORRILLO *(Second Executioner);* JACQUELINE WELLS [*later* JULIE BISHOP] *(Alice's Sister).*

CREDITS:

NORMAN MC LEOD *(Director);* LOUIS D. LIGHTON *(Producer);* JOSEPH L. MANKIEWICZ, WILLIAM CAMERON

117

Adventures in Wonderland, the fantasy Lewis Carroll (Charles Lutwidge Dodgson) wrote in 1865, but borrowed slightly from his 1871 sequel *Alice Through the Looking-Glass.*

In Alice's wonderful dream, she comes into a marvelous land of adventure. After drinking a magic potion and eating a magic cake, she grows alternately tall and short and runs into a generous assortment of odd characters. She philosophizes with the Caterpillar; takes advise from a vanishing Cheshire Cat; has a wild tea-party with the March Hare, the Mad Hatter and the Dormouse; plays croquet with the King and Queen of Hearts; watches the Mock Turtle dance; and, eventually, meets the handsome White Knight, Tweedledum and Tweedledee, and many others.

This imaginative production, while closely following the text and spirit of Carroll's original stories, and characters, was ahead of its time, but did not do well at the box office. Audiences were not amused to find their screen favorites submerged in strange costumes and ill-fitting makeup— although that was the charm of the overall concept. Some of the most creative talent ever assembled on the Paramount lot slaved to bring this fantasy a freshness and uniqueness. Perhaps they all worked a little *too* hard.

Cooper was one of the few of the top stars who was fairly recognizable—as the White Knight. Originally, Paramount imported young Ida Lupino from England for the role of Alice but, after testing her, they changed to Brooklyn-born Charlotte Henry, who gave a delightful characterization in the difficult role of Alice. She was to make more film appearances, including Laurel and Hardy's *March of the Wooden Soldiers*, but later faded away, while Lupino went on to a progressive acting and directing career in movies and, later, television.

Howard Barnes in the *New York Herald Tribune* stated, "The most unfortunate aspect of the screen version is in its generous but ill-advised assembling of film notables. You may be amused at Gary Cooper's make-up as the White Knight . . . For Miss Henry in the role of Alice, there can be nothing but praise." Mordaunt Hall, *The New York Times'* critic, felt "It is a marvel of camera magic and staging, but there are times when several of the players appear to be giving more thought to their grotesque appearances than to the reflection of their lines. Gary Cooper makes a very poor White Knight."

MENZIES *(Scenarists);* HENRY SHARP, BERT GLENNON *(Photographers);* ELLSWORTH HOAGLAND *(Editor);* DIMITRI TIOMKIN *(Musical Score);* EUGENE MERRITT *(Sound Recorder);* ROBERT ODELL *(Set Decorator);* GORDON JENNINGS, FARCIOT EDOUART *(Technical Effects);* WALLY WESTMORE, NEWT JONES *(Masks and Costumes);* LE ROY PRINZ *(Pageantry);* NATHANIEL FINSTEN *(Musical Supervision). From "Alice's Adventures in Wonderland" and "Alice Through the Looking-Glass" by* LEWIS CARROLL.

NOTES:

This filmed version was based primarily on *Alice's*

With Marion Davies

OPERATOR 13

A Cosmopolitan Production
A Metro-Goldwyn-Mayer Picture   *1933*

CAST:

MARION DAVIES (*Gail Loveless*); GARY COOPER (*Captain Jack Gailliard*); JEAN PARKER (*Eleanor*); KATHARINE ALEXANDER (*Pauline*); TED HEALY (*Doctor Hitchcock*); RUSSELL HARDIE (*Littledale*); HENRY WADSWORTH (*John Pelham*); DOUGLASS DUMBRILLE (*General Stuart*); WILLARD ROBERTSON (*Captain Channing*); FUZZY KNIGHT (*Sweeney*); SIDNEY TOLER (*Major Allen*); ROBERT MC WADE (*Colonel Sharpe*); MARJORIE GATESON (*Mrs. Shackleford*); WADE BOTELER (*Gaston*); WALTER LONG (*Operator 55*); HATTIE MC DANIEL (*Cook*); FRANCIS MC DONALD (*Denton*); WILLIAM H. GRIFFITH (*Mac*); JAMES MARCUS (*Staff Colonel*); THE FOUR MILLS BROTHERS; SAM MC DANIEL (*Old Bob*); BUDDY ROOSEVELT (*Civilian*); FRANK MCGLYNN, JR., WHEELER OAKMAN (*Scouts*); DON DOUGLAS (*Confederate Officer*); SI JENKS (*White Trash*); REGINALD BARLOW (*Colonel Storm*); ERNIE ALEXANDER, RICHARD POWELL (*Confederate Sentries*); BELLE DAUBE (*Mrs. Dandridge*); WILFRED LUCAS (*Judge*); BOB STEVENSON (*Guard*); MARTIN TURNER (*Wickman*); FRANK BURT (*Confederate Lieutenant*); WALLIE HOWE (*Clergyman*); WILLIAM HENRY (*Young Lieutenant*); RICHARD TUCKER (*Execution Officer*); ARTHUR GRANT (*Chaplain*); SHERRY TANSEY (*Officer*); LIA LANCE (*Witch Woman*); CHARLES LLOYD (*Union Private*); DE WITT C. JENNINGS (*Artillery Man*); SAM ASH (*Lieutenant*); ERNIE ADAMS (*Orderly*); CLARENCE HUMMEL WILSON (*Claybourne*); FRANKLIN PARKER (*John Hay*); CLAUDIA COLEMAN (*Nurse*); STERLING HOLLOWAY (*Wounded Soldier*); SHERRY HALL (*Army Officer*); DOUGLAS FOWLEY (*Union Officer*); FRANK MARLOWE (*Confederate Officer*); FRED WARREN (*Grant*); JOHN ELLIOTT (*Lee*); FRANK LEIGHTON (*Union Major*); JAMES C. MORTON (*Secret Service Man*); HATTIE HILL, JOHN KIRKLEY (*Slaves*); JOHN LARKIN; POPPY WILDE (*Party Guests*).

119

With Katharine Alexander and Marion Davies

CREDITS:

RICHARD BOLESLAVSKY *(Director)*; LUCIEN HUBBARD *(Producer)*; HARRY THEW, ZELDA SEARS, EVE GREENE *(Scenarists)*; GEORGE FOLSEY *(Photographer)*; CEDRIC GIBBONS *(Art Director)*; ARNOLD GILLESPIE, EDWIN B. WILLIS *(Associate Art Directors)*; ADRIAN *(Costumer)*; FRANK SULLIVAN *(Editor)*; DR. WILLIAM AXT *(Musical Score)*; GILMORE BEHMER *(Research Director)*; SONGS: *"Sleepy Head," "Jungle Fever,"* and *"Once in a Lifetime" by* WALTER DONALDSON *and* GUS KAHN. *Based on the story by* ROBERT W. CHAMBERS.

SYNOPSIS:

During the Civil War, Gail Loveless, an actress, is urged by Allan Pinkerton to become a Union spy. Disguised as an octoroon servant, she accompanies Pauline Cushman, a noted spy, into Confederate lines. Pauline becomes a guest in the Dandridge mansion, headquarters of Confederate General "Jeb" Stuart, while Gail is employed as the officers' washwoman. In this capacity, Gail meets Captain Jack Gailliard, a scout on the General's staff. Soon Pauline's spy activities are uncovered and she is sentenced to death, but, with the aid of Gail, escapes to Northern lines.

Meanwhile, it is learned that Gailliard is organizing Southern sympathizers in the north and, subsequently, the lovely Gail masquerades as a Southern belle, under the name Ann Claibourne, at the Shackleford mansion in Richmond. When Gailliard meets her this time, he falls in love with her. However, both have their duty in mind, and Gail does not hesitate to send her secret information, even though it spells grief for those with whom she is living.

Gail is discovered and flees with another Union spy, disguised as a groom, and Gailliard gives chase. He catches up with the pair and the groom wants to kill Gailliard, but Gail handcuffs herself to him. When a Union column approaches their hide-out, a spring-house, the groom, still dressed in Confederate clothes, is shot. However, no trace is found of Gail and Gailliard, who are hiding in the well. In a blacksmith shop, Jack files off the cuffs and kissing Gail goodbye, heads back for Confederate lines.

With Marion Davies

With Henry Wadsworth,
Jean Parker,
Marjorie Gateson
and Marion Davies

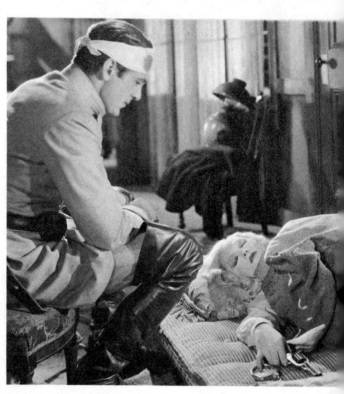

With Marion Davies

NOTES:

Operator 13 was Gary Cooper's third loan-out film of his Paramount contract and his second picture at Metro-Goldwyn-Mayer. Like all Marion Davies' films, *Operator 13*, or *Spy 13,* as it was called in England, was given a lavish treatment. George Folsey was nominated for an Academy Award for his beautiful photography. Although Richard Boleslavsky's direction was imaginative, there were too many instances of abrupt changes of scene, which caused confusion in the storyline.

This was clearly Marion Davies' picture, from start to finish, despite the fact that Cooper gave her fine support. The *London Daily Telegraph*
noted "The best part of the film is Miss Marion Davies. For some time she is disguised as a mulatto lady's maid and has a chance, as a rule denied Hollywood stars, to prove that she can act. She takes the chance with enthusiasm. Later, undisguised, little is required of her but charm and beauty enough to justify the infatuation of the Southern officer, who is entirely adequately played by Mr. Gary Cooper."

Variety added "Miss Davies is highly amusing as the girl who is constantly carrying laundry in baskets, but who is really Operator 13."

With Carole Lombard

NOW AND FOREVER

A Paramount Picture   1934

CAST:

GARY COOPER *(Jerry Day)*; CAROLE LOMBARD *(Toni Carstairs)*; SHIRLEY TEMPLE *(Penelope Day)*; SIR GUY STANDING *(Felix Evans)*; CHARLOTTE GRANVILLE *(Mrs. J. H. P. Crane)*; GILBERT EMERY *(James Higginson)*; HENRY KOLKER *(Mr. Clark)*; TETSU KOMAI *(Mr. Ling)*; JAMESON THOMAS *(Chris Carstairs)*; HARRY STUBBS *(Mr. O'Neill)*; EGON BRECHER *(Doctor)*; ANDRE CHARON *(Inspector)*; AGOSTINO BORGATO *(Fisherman)*; RICHARD LOO *(Hotel Clerk)*; LOOK CHAN *(Assistant Manager)*; AKIM TAMIROFF *(French Jeweller)*; BUSTER PHELPS *(Boy with skates)*; ROLFE SEDAN *(Hotel Manager)*; YNEZ SEABURY *(Girl)*; SAM HARRIS *(Man at pool)*; GRACE HALE *(Lady in store)*; RONNIE COSBY *(Little Boy)*.

CREDITS:

HENRY HATHAWAY *(Director)*; LOUIS D. LIGHTON *(Producer)*; VINCENT LAWRENCE, SYLVIA THALBERG *(Scenarists)*; HARRY FISCHBECK *(Photographer)*; ELLSWORTH HOAGLAND *(Editor)*; HANS DREIER, ROBERT USHER *(Art Directors)*; HAROLD C. LEWIS *(Sound Recorder)*; TRAVIS BANTON *(Costumer)*. SONG: *"The World Owes Me a Living"* by LARRY MOREY and LEIGH HARLINE. *Based on an original story, "Honor Bright,"* by JACK KIRKLAND and MELVILLE BAKER.

SYNOPSIS:

Jerry Day plans to extract $75,000 from his aristocratic brother-in-law, in return for full custody of his little daughter, Penny, whose mother is long dead. Jerry's travelling companion, Toni Carstairs, balks at the idea of selling his own child, even for $75,000. They separate, and she goes to Paris. Jerry meets Penny and finds her a charming child, who has been held down by stultifying atmosphere of his brother-in-law's home. He changes his mind and takes her with him to Paris, on funds he obtains by selling fictitious gold mine stock to elderly Felix Evans.

Jerry and Toni are happy being together again, and he decides to go straight selling real estate.

123

With Sir Guy Standing

With **Charlotte Granville**

With Carole Lombard,
Shirley Temple
and Andre Charon

Soon, however, he meets Evans, who discloses that he is a jewel thief and that he permitted Jerry to defraud him so that he could force him to become his accomplice. Jerry refuses. A wealthy widow, Mrs. Crane, loves Penny and offers to adopt her. Jerry, now broke, steals her necklace, hoping to dispose of it through Evans. Penny discovers the necklace in her teddy bear and thinks her father a thief until Toni takes the blame, so the little girl won't hate her father.

Determined to set things right, Jerry demands that Evans return the necklace, but is forced to kill him in a gun battle, during which he is severely injured himself. Concealing his injury, he makes a full confession to Mrs. Crane and asks her to adopt Penny, which she does. Jerry and Toni bid farewell to Penny at the train station, then Toni rushes Jerry to the nearest hospital to get medical care.

NOTES:

This comedy-drama originally had a tragic ending, with Cooper dying in the car with Lombard and he driving over the cliff. However, Paramount felt it didn't fit the mold of the light-heartedness that preceded it, so it was changed. This was not one of Cooper's better films, but it did re-team him with lovely Carole Lombard and the upcoming star Shirley Temple.

REVIEWS:

Said the *New York American:* "Mr. Cooper does excellently in a role that is much improved by the underplaying which is his habit." Thornton Delehanty in the *New York Evening Post* observed, *"Now and Forever* may not be a great story—it has its loopholes—but it is expertly contrived to furnish first-rate entertainment."

The *New York Sun* declared, ". . . Gary Cooper plays with quiet sympathy and humor . . . it is by far his best bit of acting," while the London *Times* thought, ". . . it is only because Mr. Gary Cooper is able to look so romantic in the part of a lost soul that one can believe even at rare moments in the uplifting effects of the company of Shirley Temple . . . It is also fortunate that Mr. Cooper is one of the few actors who can carry off a martyrdom with dignity, since after his reformation he is crushed by every possible misfortune."

On the Paramount lot
with Carole Lombard
and Shirley Temple

With Helen Vinson

THE WEDDING NIGHT

A Samuel Goldwyn Production
Released Thru United Artists   1935

CAST:

GARY COOPER *(Tony Barrett)*; ANNA STEN *(Manya)*; RALPH BELLAMY *(Fredrik)*; HELEN VINSON *(Dora Barrett)*; SIEGFRIED RUMANN *(Nowak)*; ESTHER DALE *(Kaise)*; LEONID SNEGOFF *(Sobieski)*; ELEANOR WESSELHOEFT *(Mrs. Sobieski)*; MILLA DAVENPORT *(Grandmother)*; AGNES ANDERSON *(Helena)*; HILDA VAUGHN *(Hezzie)*; WALTER BRENNAN *(Jenkins)*; DOUGLAS WOOD *(Heywood)*; GEORGE MEEKER *(Gilly)*; HEDI SHOPE *(Anna)*; OTTO YAMAOKA *(Taka)*; VIOLET AXZELLE *(Frederica)*; ED EBELE *(Uncle)*; ROBERT LOUIS STEVENSON, 2ND, AUGUSTE TOLLAIRE, DAVE WENGREN, GEORGE MAGRILLE, BERNARD SIEGEL, HARRY SEMELS *(Men at Wedding)*; ROBERT BOLDER *(Doctor)*; ALPHONSE MANTELL *(Waiter)*; MIAMI ALVAREZ, CONSTANCE HOWARD, JAY EATON, JAY BELASCO *(Guests at Party)*; RICHARD POWELL *(Truck Driver)*.

CREDITS:

KING VIDOR *(Director)*; SAMUEL GOLDWYN *(Producer)*; EDITH FITZGERALD *(Scenarist)*; GREGG TOLAND *(Photographer)*; RICHARD DAY *(Art Director)*; ALFRED NEWMAN *(Musical Director)*; OMAR KIAM *(Costumer)*; STUART HEISLER *(Editor)*; FRANK MAKER *(Sound Recorder)*; WALTER MAYO *(Assistant Director)*. Based on an original story by EDWIN KNOPF.

SYNOPSIS:

Author Tony Barrett, losing his grip, takes his publisher's advice that he and his wife Dora move into the quiet old Connecticut farmhouse that he inherited from his grandfather. Almost broke, Tony gladly sells an untilled field to Jan Nowak, a neighboring Polish farmer. Tony calls at the Nowak home and learns that the field is a wedding

126

gift for Nowak's beautiful daughter Manya and Fredrik, a young Polish farmer, who is her father's choice, not hers.

Tony decides to write a new novel around these colorful people, with Manya as the heroine. Dora, tiring of the country, quarrels with Tony and returns to New York. Soon Manya is helping the awkward *bachelor* with household chores and, although love blooms, both remain silent. After a fearful blizzard, which forces Manya to stay at Tony's home, Nowak suspects the worst and commands Manya to marry Fredrik within two days. Fearing a loveless marriage, she returns to Tony's home, only to find Dora has returned and has read the completed novel and recognizes Manya as the heroine. She talks to Manya and convinces her to leave without seeing her husband. Tony learns that the wedding has taken place and rushes to the Nowak house, insists on dancing with Manya and then leaves drunk.

Later, Fredrik staggers to the bridal chamber, but is repulsed by Manya. He blames Tony and sets out to kill him. Manya rushes to warn Tony. Fred arrives and, during the ensuing struggle, Manya falls down a staircase and dies. Tony and Dora eventually return to New York. The novel is a huge success.

NOTES:

The Wedding Night was Cooper's 39th film appearance since *The Winning of Barbara Worth*,

and marked his return to the Goldwyn Studio, as a star.

Goldwyn had Edwin Knopf write a story to utilize the special talents of Anna Sten, whose *Nana* the year before had brought nothing but cheerless reviews and dismal box office receipts. The result was a sensitive story of a peasant girl from one world meeting and falling in love with a stranger from another and it was produced and directed with great taste and care. This time Miss Sten won deservedly fine reviews, but the public still ignored her. Her career as a star was over—one of the great mysteries of the 1930's.

Cooper and Sten worked beautifully together; the chemistry was perfection itself. Helen Vinson, as Cooper's wife, gave one of her finest performances, as a possessive woman and, in direct contrast to Miss Sten's, hers was a more vibrant personality.

Thornton Delehanty in the *New York Evening News* said "*The Wedding Night* is neither spectacular nor hair-raising. Its situations are not trumped up for dramatic effect. The incidents are welded by the logic of a quietly tragic love story which Mr. Cooper and Miss Sten make eminently believable and in which the directorial hand of King Vidor is unerringly present." Eileen Creelman in the *New York Sun* opined "Mr. Cooper, by well-timed understatement and quiet humor, has made the man real."

With Helen Vinson

127

With Anna Sten

With Anna Sten

With Anna Sten and Ralph Bellamy

THE LIVES OF A BENGAL LANCER

A Paramount Picture   1935

CAST:

GARY COOPER *(Lieutenant McGregor)*; FRANCHOT TONE *(Lieutenant Fortesque)*; RICHARD CROMWELL *(Lieutenant Stone)*; SIR GUY STANDING *(Colonel Stone)*; C. AUBREY SMITH *(Major Hamilton)*; MONTE BLUE *(Hamzulia Khan)*; KATHLEEN BURKE *(Tania Volkanskaya)*; COLIN TAPLEY *(Lieutenant Barrett)*; DOUGLASS DUMBRILLE *(Mohammed Khan)*; AKIM TAMIROFF *(Emir)*; JAMESON THOMAS *(Hendrickson)*; NOBLE JOHNSON *(Ram Singh)*; LUMSDEN HARE *(Major General Woodley)*; J. CARROL NAISH *(Grand Vizier)*; ROLLO LLOYD *(The Ghazi (Prisoner))*; CHARLES STEVENS *(McGregor's Servant)*; BOSWHAN SINGH *(Nuim Shah)*; ABDUL HASSAN *(Ali Hamdi)*; MISCHA AUER *(Afridi)*; CLIVE MORGAN *(Lieutenant Norton)*; EDDIE DAS *(Servant)*; LEONID KINSKEY *(Snake Charmer)*; HUSSAIN HASRI *(Muezzin)*; JAMES WARWICK *(Lieutenant Gilhooley)*; GEORGE REGAS *(Kushal Khan)*; MAJOR SAM HARRIS, CARLI TAYLOR *(British Officers)*; RAM SINGH, JAMIEL HASSON, JAMES BELL, GENERAL IKONNIKOFF, F. A. ARMENTA *(Indian Officers)*; CLAUDE KING *(Experienced Clerk)*; REGINALD SHEFFIELD *(Novice)*; RAY COOPER *(Assistant to Grand Vizier)*; MYRA KINCH *(Solo Dancer)*; LYA LYS *(Girl on Train)*.

CREDITS:

HENRY HATHAWAY *(Director)*; LOUIS D. LIGHTON *(Producer)*; WALDEMAR YOUNG, JOHN L. BALDERSTON, ACHMED ABDULLAH *(Scenarists)*; GROVER JONES, WILLIAM SLAVENS MC NUTT *(Adaptation)*; CHARLES LANG *(Photographer)*; HANS DREIER, ROLAND ANDERSON *(Art Directors)*; ELLSWORTH HOAGLAND *(Editor)*; HAROLD C. LEWIS *(Sound Recorder)*; MILAN RODER *(Musical Score)*; CLEM BEAUCHAMP, PAUL WINZ *(Assistant Directors)*; LE ROY PRINZ *(Pageantry/Choreography)*. *Based on the novel by* MAJOR FRANCIS YEATS-BROWN.

With Akim Tamiroff and Franchot Tone

With Richard Cromwell,
Franchot Tone and C. Aubrey Smith

SYNOPSIS:

Two new officers, Lieutenants Forsythe and Stone, are assigned to the 41st Regiment of Bengal Lancers, located in the dangerous open country of Northwest India. The latter is the son of the Commanding Officer, Colonel Stone, and both men are placed in the charge of Lieutenant McGregor, an experienced frontier fighter. Young Stone thinks he'll be greeted as a son, but winces when the colonel greets him as coldly as the other officers, soon becoming bitter.

McGregor is given the order to lead a small detail in search of Lieutenant Barrett, a spy who has not been heard from in weeks. The unit makes contact with Barrett and learns that Mohammed Khan is effecting a coalition of the tribes, promising them 2,000,000 rounds of ammunition. McGregor reports to the colonel, who tells him that that amount of ammunition has just been consigned to the friendly Emir of Gopal. The Lancers find an "excuse" for visiting the Emir's palace which enables them to be there for a week of "pig-sticking," hunting wild boar with lances.

The following day, the colonel is slightly wounded during the hunt, while protecting his son, and McGregor and Forsythe soon discover that young Stone has been kidnapped by the alluring Russian spy Tania and taken to the Khan's mountain fort. Colonel Stone refuses to send aid, but the lieutenants, disguised as pilgrims, gain entry to the fort. Discovered and taken prisoner, they find Stone and all three are tortured. Stone finally gives the Khan the information he seeks, and, four days later, the men see the munitions arrive in the Khan's city. The Khan taunts them about the 300 Lancers who are planning to attack his fort. They break loose, and young Stone proves himself courageous in a mad frenzy by killing the Khan and McGregor dies as he blows up the arsenal. Weeks later, the colonel pins the D.S.O. on Forsythe and his son and the Victoria Cross on the saddle of McGregor's horse.

NOTES:

This is one of the all-time great adventures of the screen. Seldom has any producer matched its mounting; any director its spirit and pace and excitement; any cast its performances. It was a genuine hit when initially released, in 1935, has since had several re-issues and is continually shown on television, although seldom complete.

It won six Academy Award nominations. It was nominated for Best Picture; Henry Hathaway for his direction; Ellsworth Hoagland for his editing; Waldemar Young, John L. Balderston, Achmed Abdullah, Grover Jones and William Slavens McNutt for their splendid scenario; Harold Lewis for his sound recording; and Clem Beauchamp and Paul Winz for their chores as assistant directors, which, of course, included all of the second unit work. The latter two gentlemen won.

Said the *New York American:* "A robust thriller. . . . Gangling Gary Cooper, every long inch an officer, stalks strikingly through both comic and tragic sequences." The *New York Evening Post* thought, "The acting throughout is exceptionally good. Gary Cooper and Franchot Tone handle their badinage with humor and restraint."

The *London Daily Telegraph* added, *"Bengal Lancer* is terrific . . . the best army picture ever made. There is no love story. The theme is the conflict between duty and sentiment. . . . Gary Cooper and Franchot Tone are magnificent as the two subalterns. Henry Hathaway has directed brilliantly." The *New York World-Telegram* said, "The acting is of a superior quality. Gary Cooper has seldom had a more sympathetic or effective part than McGregor, and he performs the task imposed upon him expertly and effectively . . . the direction is of a high quality and the photography is splendid."

The fantastic settings devised by Hans Dreier and Roland Anderson were so noteworthy that they were later slightly revamped for Cecil B. DeMille's *The Crusades.*

With Kathleen Burke, Douglass Dumbrille, Franchot Tone and Richard Cromwell

With Kathleen Burke and Franchot Tone

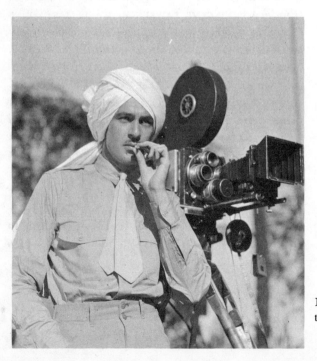

Dashing Bengal Lancer taking a break

131

With Ann Harding

PETER IBBETSON

A Paramount Picture   1935

CAST:

GARY COOPER *(Peter Ibbetson);* ANN HARDING *(Mary, Duchess of Towers);* JOHN HALLIDAY *(Duke of Towers);* IDA LUPINO *(Agnes);* DOUGLASS DUMBRILLE *(Colonel Forsythe);* VIRGINIA WEIDLER *(Mimsey);* DICKIE MOORE *(Gogo);* DORIS LLOYD *(Mrs. Dorian);* ELSA BUCHANAN *(Madame Pasquier);* CHRISTIAN RUB *(Major Duquesnoit);* DONALD MEEK *(Mr. Slade);* GILBERT EMERY *(Wilkins);* MARGUERITE NAMARA *(Madame Ginghi);* ELSA PRESCOTT *(Katherine);* MARCELLE CORDAY *(Maid);* ADRIENNE D'AMBRICOURT *(Nun);* THERESA MAXWELL CONOVER *(Sister of Mercy);* COLIN TAPLEY *(First Clerk);* CLIVE MORGAN *(Second Clerk);* AMBROSE BARKER *(Third Clerk);* THOMAS MONK *(Fourth Clerk);* BLANCHE CRAIG *(The Countess).*

CREDITS:

HENRY HATHAWAY *(Director);* LOUIS D. LIGHTON *(Producer);* VINCENT LAWRENCE, WALDEMAR YOUNG *(Scenarists);* CONSTANCE COLLIER *(Adaptation);* JOHN MEEHAN, EDWIN JUSTUS MAYER *(Additional Scenes);* CHARLES LANG *(Photographer);* ERNST TOCH *(Musical Score);* STUART HEISLER *(Editor);* HARRY D. MILLS *(Sound Recorder);* HANS DREIER, ROBERT USHER *(Art Directors);* GORDON JENNINGS *(Special Effects);* NAT W. FINSTON *(Musical Director). Based on the novel by* GEORGE DU MAURIER *and subsequent play by* JOHN NATHANIEL RAPHAEL.

SYNOPSIS:

Architect Peter Ibbetson visits Paris and returns to an enormous garden where he, then called Gogo,

With Ann Harding

133

used to play as a child with a girl named Mimsey. The garden now is overgrown and ruined. Meanwhile, the Duke of Towers commissions the firm young Ibbetson works for to build new stables on the Duke's country estate. Peter is sent, but soon fired by Mary, the Duchess, for not following her orders. She soon relents, however, and he is given a free hand and they become close friends. Then the Duke believes Peter is in love with his wife, and asks him to leave. During the heated argument which follows, Ibbetson reverts to a peculiar mannerism and Mary recognizes him as the beloved Gogo of her childhood and, when he realizes that the duchess is really his Mimsey, they embrace each other—to the Duke's consternation.

Mary explains to her husband that they were childhood sweethearts, which seems to satisfy him. Later, knowing that they'll soon be parted forever, the couple embrace just as the Duke enters the room with pistol in hand. As he fires, Peter hurls a chair and kills him. Ibbetson is then sentenced to life imprisonment. In his cell, he dreams of his childhood and cries out and the guards—thinking he is a rebellious prisoner—beat him, which does serious damage to his spine. In a semi-conscious state, he sees Mary enter his cell. She tells him that they will always be together—in their dreams—their real escape from the harsh realities of life. Peter disbelieves, but Mary says that she will send him a ring the next day as proof that their dreaming *is* real. The ring arrives, as she said it would.

Over the years, Peter remains happy and, although he and Mary are getting old, they remain young in their dreams. When Mary dies, she tells him she will wait for him in their garden. Soon, Peter dies and they are together again.

NOTES:

George du Maurier's 1891 novel was the basis of the silent film called *Forever* (1922), with Elsie Ferguson and Wallace Reid, which was also produced on the stage, with the Barrymores (John and Lionel) and Constance Collier. *Peter Ibbetson* has also been adapted to the operatic stage by Deems Taylor.

Henry Hathaway again directed Cooper in what many consider the most perfectly-filmed fantasy. The production values were top-notch (Ernst Toch's touching musical score won an Academy Award nomination) and the acting was laudable.

The *New York Daily News* reported that "Gary Cooper is miscast. He isn't the type to spend his adult life mooning over a love he'd lost in childhood, as Peter Ibbetson did." However, the *New York World-Telegram* felt, ". . . His performance in the title role is by far the best he has done on the screen to date. It is, in every way, a fine piece of work."

Ida Lupino, who almost was Alice to Cooper's White Knight in *Alice in Wonderland*, played, with relish, the role of Agnes, the woman who lost him to his childhood sweetheart, beautifully realized by Ann Harding.

With Ida Lupino

On the set with director
Henry Hathaway
(looking at film strip),
Ann Harding
and John Halliday

With Elsa Prescott
and Blanche Craig

With Marlene Dietrich

DESIRE

A Paramount Picture   1936

CAST:

MARLENE DIETRICH *(Madeleine de Beaupré);* GARY COOPER *(Tom Bradley);* JOHN HALLIDAY *(Carlos Margoli);* WILLIAM FRAWLEY *(Mr. Gibson);* ERNEST COSSART *(Aristide Duval);* AKIM TAMIROFF *(Police Official);* ALAN MOWBRAY *(Dr. Edouard Pauquet);* ZEFFIE TILBURY *(Aunt Olga);* HARRY DEPP *(Clerk);* MARC LAWRENCE *(Valet);* HENRY ANTRIM *(Chauffeur);* ARMAND KALIZ *(Jewelry Clerk);* GASTON GLASS *(Jewelry Clerk);* ALBERT POLLET *(French Policeman);* GEORGE DAVIS *(Garage Man);* CONSTANT FRANKE *(Border Official);* ROBERT O'CONNOR *(Customs Official);* STANLEY ANDREWS *(Customs Inspector);* RAFAEL BLANCO *(Driver of haywagon);* ALDEN CHASE *(Clerk in Hotel);* TONY MERLO *(Waiter);* ANNA DELINSKY *(Servant);* ALICE FELIZ *(Pepi);* ENRIQUE ACOSTA *(Pedro);* GEORGE MAC QUARRIE *(Clerk with gun);* ISABEL LA MAL *(Nurse);* OLIVER ECKHARDT *(Husband);* BLANCHE CRAIG *(Wife);* ROLLO LLOYD *(Clerk in Mayor's Office);* ALFONSO PEDROSA *(Oxcart Driver).*

CREDITS:

FRANK BORZAGE *(Director);* ERNST LUBITSCH *(Producer);* EDWIN JUSTUS MAYER, WALDEMAR YOUNG, SAMUEL HOFFENSTEIN *(Scenarists);* CHARLES LANG *(Photographer);* HANS DREIER, ROBERT USHER *(Art Directors);* FREDERICK HOLLANDER *(Musical Score).* SONG: *"Awake in a Dream"* by FREDERICK HOLLANDER *and* LEO RUBIN; TRAVIS BANTON *(Costumer);* WILLIAM SHEA *(Editor);* HARRY D. MILLS *(Sound Recorder). From a comedy by* HANS SZEKELY *and* R. A. STEMMLE.

SYNOPSIS:

Madeleine du Beaupré steals a pearl necklace from a Paris jewelry firm and rushes by car for the

Spanish border. On the road, she zooms past Tom Bradley, a young American engineer on vacation, who is also heading for Spain. At the border, going through customs, Madeleine drops the pearls into Tom's coat pocket and he gets safely through. After a series of attempts to get the pearls back, she meets him again in San Sebastian, where Tom is introduced to Madeleine's confederate, "Prince" Margoli. The pair invite Tom to the country and he accepts, for he's already fallen in love with Madeleine.

At dinner, Tom wears the coat which contains the pearls. Pretending to do magic tricks, Margoli calmly takes the necklace from Tom's pocket and is soon off to Madrid. Then, another confederate, "Aunt Olga," arrives to order Madeleine to Madrid, where there's a good chance to sell the gems. When

Madeleine refuses, Olga, realizing her beautiful young cohort is in love, points out the futility of marriage and reminds her of her past record. In despair, Madeleine tells Tom she is married and, later, reveals the fact that she is a thief. Tom is overjoyed that she really isn't married and convinces her to return the pearls to the jeweler, who is so touched by the situation that he doesn't press charges. Tom and Madeleine then take off for America.

NOTES:

Cooper had stated after *Morocco* was released that he would not make another picture with Dietrich, meaning that he would not do so under von Sternberg's direction. In fact, Paramount had been

With Marlene Dietrich

With John Halliday

eager to team them immediately after *Morocco* in *Dishonored*, but Cooper balked. By 1935, Dietrich and von Sternberg had parted and, when asked about co-starring with her in *The Pearl Necklace*, the film's original title, Cooper readily agreed. Cooper and Dietrich were a good pair; his quiet, well-mannered countenance complemented her sophisticated style perfectly. *Desire*'s story was really nothing special, but the special attention paid its two stars, and the way they handle their roles, is well worth several viewings.

The *New York World-Telegram* thought Cooper "as the young engineer contributes a buoyant performance in light comedy that could scarcely be improved upon." *The New York Times* wrote, ". . . Mr. Cooper displays a talent for light comedy that is not altogether unexpected but still gratifying." And, Thornton Delehanty in the *New York Evening Post,* said Cooper was "a subtle and sure player who knows the value of restraint and is artist enough to employ it."

Said the *Illustrated London News:* ". . . The altogether delightful performance of Mr. Gary Cooper brings a freshness and humour to its fundamental convention which make it excellent entertainment." The *New York Sun* summed things up pretty well, declaring, "Gary Cooper, never more charming, plays the naive lad from Detroit . . . it's the kind of character Americans like to think typically American, and Mr. Cooper has a grand time with it."

With John Gilbert
and Marlene Dietrich on the set

With Jean Arthur

MR. DEEDS
GOES TO TOWN

A Columbia Picture   1936

CAST:

GARY COOPER (*Longfellow Deeds*); JEAN ARTHUR (*Babe Bennett*); GEORGE BANCROFT (*MacWade*); LIONEL STANDER (*Cornelius Cobb*); DOUGLASS DUM-BRILLE (*John Cedar*); RAYMOND WALBURN (*Walter*); MARGARET MATZENAUER (*Madame Pomponi*); H. B. WARNER (*Judge Walker*); WARREN HYMER (*Bodyguard*); MURIEL EVANS (*Theresa*); RUTH DONNELLY (*Mabel Dawson*); SPENCER CHARTERS (*Mal*); EMMA DUNN (*Mrs. Meredith*); WYRLEY BIRCH (*Psychiatrist*); ARTHUR HOYT (*Budington*); STANLEY ANDREWS (*James Cedar*); PIERRE WATKIN (*Arthur Cedar*); JOHN WRAY (*Farmer*); CHRISTIAN RUB (*Swenson*); JAMESON THOMAS (*Mr. Semple*); MAYO METHOT (*Mrs. Semple*); MARGARET SEDDON (*Jane Faulkner*); MARGARET MC WADE (*Amy Faulkner*); RUSSELL HICKS (*Dr. Malcolm*); GUSTAV VON SEYFFERTITZ (*Dr. Frazier*); EDWARD LE SAINT (*Dr. Fosdick*); CHARLES (LEVISON) LANE (*Hallor*); IRVING BACON (*Frank*); GEORGE COOPER (*Bob*); GENE MORGAN (*Waiter*);

WALTER CATLETT (*Morrow*); EDWARD GARGAN (*Second Bodyguard*); PAUL HURST (*First Deputy*); PAUL PORCASI (*Italian*); FRANKLIN PANGBORN (*Tailor*); GEORGE F. ("GABBY") HAYES (*Farmers' Spokesman*); MARY LOU DIX (*Shop Girl*); GEORGE MEEKER (*Brookfield*); BARNETT PARKER (*Butler*); PATRICIA MONROE, LILLIAN ROSS (*Hat Check Girls*); PEGGY PAGE (*Cigarette Girl*); JANET EASTMAN (*Shop Girl*); BUD FLANNIGAN [*later* DENNIS O'KEEFE] (*Reporter*); DALE VAN SICKEL (*Lawyer*); *and* CECIL CUNNINGHAM, BESS FLOWERS, ANN DORAN, BILLY BEVAN, BEATRICE CURTIS, BEATRICE BLINN, PAULINE WAGNER, FRANK HAMMOND, CHARLES SULLIVAN, FLO WIX, HAL BUDLONG, ETHEL PALMER, JUANITA CROSLAND, VACEY O'DAVOREN.

CREDITS:

FRANK CAPRA (*Director and Producer*); ROBERT RISKIN (*Scenarist*); JOSEPH WALKER (*Photographer*);

With Margaret McWade
and Margaret Seddon

With Irving Bacon, Douglass Dumbrille,
Muriel Evans, Lionel Stander,
Margaret Matzenauer and Raymond Walburn

With Vacey O'Davoren
and Barnett Parker

GENE HAVLICK (*Editor*); HOWARD JACKSON (*Musical Director*); STEPHEN GOOSSON (*Art Director*); E. ROY DAVIDSON (*Special Photographic Effects*); SAMUEL LANGE (*Costumer*); EDWARD BERNDS (*Sound Recorder*); D. D. COLEMAN (*Assistant Director*). *Based on the story "Opera Hat" by* CLARENCE BUDINGTON KELLAND.

SYNOPSIS:

Longfellow Deeds, a quiet young man from Mandrake Falls who has just inherited $20,000,000, arrives in New York and manages to elude reporters. MacWade, editor of a big newspaper, assigns sob-sister Babe Bennett to get an exclusive story on the millionaire hick. Escaping from his bodyguards, Longfellow takes a walk, during which he comes upon a young girl who has fainted. It's Babe Bennett. She gives her name as Mary Dawson, an unemployed stenographer, and, later, they dine together. Deeds' simplicity provides her with the beginnings of a swell yarn. She christens him "Cinderella Man" and he never suspects Mary is responsible for the headlines.

Longfellow and "Mary" find themselves in love, but Babe is a reporter first, and continues to send her stories in. When he discovers she is a reporter, he experiences his biggest disappointment in the big city. Because of Babe's articles, a tremendous crowd descends upon his residence and accuses him of squandering millions while they starve.

Deeds decides to give his money away, since it has only brought him unhappiness. He promises each of his accusers a small self-sustaining sum. His attorney, who believes his client insane and sees a fortune slipping through his fingers, has Deeds arrested. At the trial, Deeds makes no effort to defend his sanity until Babe speaks in his behalf. He then convinces everyone in the courtroom that if he is crazy, so is everyone else!

NOTES:

Take a simple story, inject it with literately funny dialogue and credible situations—with a pinch of screwy, or "pixilated," humor—assemble a first-rate cast and you end up with *Mr. Deeds Goes to Town.* That's what Frank Capra and Robert Riskin did. The happy result was one of the 1930's best pictures. This was Cooper's first time at Columbia and, under the astute direction of Capra and the chemistry of this association, he was pure bliss. Never was Cooper more natural or refreshing than as Longfellow Deeds—a truly great screen portrayal.

Henry T. Murdock in the *Philadelphia Evening Public Ledger* said, "As the verse-scribbling Longfellow Deeds, innocent amateur both in tuba playing and the art of spending millions, Gary Cooper turns another corner in a career which has slowly developed him from a wooden-faced hero of horse-operas into a sensitive player with a reticent but wholly American wit." Thornton Delehanty, in the *New York Evening Post*, thought, "For deftness and sheer likeability there is no actor on the screen today who can turn in a more satisfying performance." Critic Frank S. Nugent was moved to say, "Longfellow Deeds is the hero of the occasion and Longfellow Deeds becomes one of our favorite characters under the attentive handling of Mr. Cooper, who is proving himself one of the best light comedians in Hollywood."

Mr. Deeds Goes to Town won the New York Film Critics award for Best Picture. Frank Capra won an Oscar for his direction, while Cooper received his first Academy Award nomination. Also nominated were: Robert Riskin's screenplay; the film itself; and the Columbia Sound Department, under the supervision of John Livadary.

Mr. Deeds arrived on television in the fall of 1969 as a weekly 30-minute programmer.

On the set with director Frank Capra

With Jean Arthur

On the set with
Jack Mulhall, John Halliday
and director
Robert Florey (dark shirt)

HOLLYWOOD BOULEVARD

A Paramount Picture   1936

CAST:

JOHN HALLIDAY (*John Blakeford*); MARSHA HUNT (*Patricia Blakeford*); ROBERT CUMMINGS (*Jay Wallace*); C. HENRY GORDON (*Jordan Winslow*); FRIEDA INESCORT (*Alice Winslow*); ESTHER RALSTON (*Flora*); ESTHER DALE (*Martha*); BETTY COMPSON (*Betty*); ALBERT CONTI (*Sanford*); RICHARD POWELL (*Moran*); RITA LA ROY (*Nella*); OSCAR APFEL (*Dr. Inslow*); PURNELL PRATT (*Mr. Steinman*); IRVING BACON (*Gus the Bartender*); LOIS KENT (*Little Girl*); GREGORY GAY (*Russian Writer*); ELEANORE WHITNEY (*Herself*); TOM KENNEDY (*Bouncer*); GERTRUDE SIMPSON (*Gossipy Woman*); and HYMAN FINK, THOMAS JACKSON, ED CECIL, PHIL TEAD, EDDIE DUNN, MONTY VANDEGRIFT, FRANCES MORRIS, RUTH CLIFFORD, JO-ANNE DUDLEY.

And the following stars from the silent screen: FRANCIS X. BUSHMAN (*Director, Desert Scene*); MAURICE COSTELLO (*Director*); MAE MARSH (*Carlotta Blakeford*); CHARLES RAY (*Assistant Director*); HERBERT RAWLINSON (*Manager, Grauman's Chinese Theatre*); JANE NOVAK (*Mrs. Steinman*); KATHRYN "KITTY" MC HUGH (*Secretary*); BRYANT WASHBURN (*Robert Martin*); WILLIAM DESMOND (*Guest*); JACK MULHALL (*Man at Bar*); ROY D'ARCY (*The Sheik*); CREIGHTON HALE (*Man at Bar*); MABEL FORREST (*Mother*); BERT ROACH (*Scenario Writer*); HARRY MYERS, JACK MOWER, FRANK MAYO and PAT O'MALLEY (*Themselves*).

Unbilled guest at bar: GARY COOPER.

CREDITS:

ROBERT FLOREY (*Director*); A. M. BOTSFORD (*Producer*); MARGUERITE ROBERTS (*Scenarist*); GEORGE CLEMENS (*Photographer*); KARL STRUSS (*Cameraman*); GREGORY STONE (*Musical Score*); HARVEY JOHNSTON (*Editor*); WALTER H. OBERST (*Sound Re-*

With John Halliday

corder); HANS DREIER, EARL HEDRICK (*Art Directors*); EDWARD F. CLINE (*Production Supervisor*). *Based on a story by* FAITH THOMAS.

SYNOPSIS:

Old-time actor John Blakeford is through in Hollywood and can't get work. His family have deserted him, and he feels the end is near. However, an unscrupulous magazine publisher, Jordan Winslow, offers $25,000 to publish Blakeford's memoirs and the actor accepts. The story is given the "treatment" and becomes a sensation, scandalizing his estranged family. His daughter Patricia pleads with him and he finally goes to the publisher, who refuses to cancel the forthcoming installments of the serialization. The publisher warns him to finish the memoirs or he'll see that Blakeford is fired from a comeback picture which has just come his way.

Later, the two quarrel and Jordan shoots Blakeford. The blame falls on Patricia, but her clever fiance, Jay Wallace, clears her by playing a dictaphone recording which contains the conversation that led to her father's death.

NOTES:

This story of Hollywood was typical "B" stuff, but *Hollywood Boulevard* is interesting today, largely because of the silent stars who appear in various capacities in the script. Cooper's bit was probably done as a favor to John Halliday and naturally, went unbilled.

The *Brooklyn Daily Eagle* found it "a swift-paced and entertaining melodrama. . . ," while *The New York Times* called it ". . . a pretty hoary melodrama and slight enough excuse for a whole series of homilies upon the uncertainty of fame and fortune in the glamour city."

With Madeleine Carroll

THE GENERAL DIED AT DAWN

A Paramount Picture   1936

CAST:

GARY COOPER *(O'Hara);* MADELEINE CARROLL *(Judy Perrie);* AKIM TAMIROFF *(General Yang);* DUDLEY DIGGES *(Mr. Wu);* PORTER HALL *(Peter Perrie);* WILLIAM FRAWLEY *(Brighton);* J. M. KERRIGAN *(Leach);* PHILIP AHN *(Oxford);* LEE TUNG FOO *(Mr. Chen);* LEONID KINSKEY *(Stewart);* VAL DURAN *(Wong);* WILLIE FUNG *(Bartender);* HANS FUERBERG *(Yang's Military Advisor);* SARAH EDWARDS, PAUL HARVEY *(American couple);* SPENCER CHAN *(Killer);* HAROLD TONG, CHARLES LEONG, THOMAS CHAN, HARRY YIP, SWAN YEE, KAM TONG *(House Boys);* FRANK YOUNG *(Clerk);* WALTER WONG *(Bartender);* CAROL DE CASTRO *(Clerk);* BARNETT PARKER *(Englishman);* HANS VON MORHART *(Mandarin);* DUDLEY LEE, WALTER LEM, THOMAS LEE, GEORGE WONG WAH *(Waiters on Train);* TOM UNG *(Steward on Train);* TAFT JUNG, SAM LABORADOR, RICHARD YOUNG, JUNG KAI, HARRY LEONG, CHAN SUEY, PAUL TOM, LOO LOY, QUON GONG, WONG FONG, LEO ABBEY, BOB JOWE *(Guards);* GEORGE CHAN *(Porter); and* CLIFFORD ODETS, JOHN O'HARA, SIDNEY SKOLSKY *and* LEWIS MILESTONE *(Reporters).*

CREDITS:

LEWIS MILESTONE *(Director);* WILLIAM LE BARON *(Producer);* CLIFFORD ODETS *(Scenarist);* VICTOR MILNER *(Photographer);* WERNER JANSSEN *(Musical Score);* HANS DREIER, ERNST FEGTO *(Art Directors);* EDA WARREN *(Editor);* TRAVIS BANTON *(Costumer);* HARRY D. MILLS *(Sound Recorder). Based on a novel by* CHARLES G. BOOTH.

SYNOPSIS:

The Northern districts of China are being terrorized by the ruthless Chinese bandit chief General Yang.

144

He and his twelve aides hope one day to rule the twelve provinces and subjugate China's millions. O'Hara, an American soldier of fortune, sides with the suppressed peasants, accepting the job of carrying a large sum of money to Shanghai to buy guns for their defense. He is to go to Pengwa, then fly to Shanghai where he is to meet with the loyal Mr. Wu and Mr. Chen, who are in contact with an American gun-runner named Brighton.

Oxford, General Yang's chief aide, makes an attempt on O'Hara's life at Pengwa, but fails. He enlists the services of a cowardly American, Peter Perrie, to help him. Perrie plays on the sympathy of his daughter Judy, enducing her to lure O'Hara aboard a train, which is later intercepted by Yang's troups. O'Hara is captured and the money is given to Perrie to carry to Shanghai. Perrie tries to double-cross the General and is about to leave when O'Hara, escaped from Yang, appears and kills him in self-defense. All are again captured by Yang's men and taken aboard his junk to be tortured until they reveal the location of the money, which Perrie hid in a false lining of a suitcase. The money is found, but, at the same time, Yang is fatally stabbed. As he dies, O'Hara uses the General's love of publicity to persuade him to set them free. He agrees, ordering his twelve aides to kill each other as he dies.

NOTES:

Paramount acquired the services of Broadway's fair-haired boy, Clifford Odets, to handle the screen treatment of Charles G. Booth's adventurous novel. Odets may have thought he was writing an inflammatory piece about oppression, although, actually, he was preparing a new anti-hero for Gary Cooper and another adventure film for his already impressive roster. During production, the title was called *Chinese Gold* but, when released, the title became *The General Died at Dawn*. The production was top-notch in all departments, and Odets, along with novelist John O'Hara, columnist Sidney Skolsky and director Milestone, became extras—as reporters—in the railroad car sequence at a salary of $5.00 per day.

Said the London *Times:* "Mr. Akim Tamiroff is both alarming and subtle in the part of General Yang. It is more difficult to make a hero interesting, but as Mr. Cooper always manages to suggest that his innocence conceals both intelligence and sincerity, so he contrives to give to this innocent

With Akim Tamiroff
and Madeleine Carroll

With Akim Tamiroff

part a touch of more reasonable and genuine heroism than it would normally have. The director, Mr. Lewis Milestone, makes the film move at an excellent pace and the settings are both elaborate and picturesque."

The *Brooklyn Daily Eagle* called the film "a slick and handsome melodrama. It moves. In direction and photography it has undeniable class and the acting is up to the demands of the script. But like most movies, it is empty of any ideas or characters that remain with you longer than it takes to reach the nearest subway entrance."

Merle Oberon was originally cast as Judy Perrie but was too busy with other commitments to start shooting, and was replaced by Madeleine Carroll.

Akim Tamiroff was nominated for the first Academy Award for a performance "by an actor in a supporting role." Werner Janssen's musical score and Victor Milner's photography also received Academy nominations.

On the set with Madeleine Carroll,
Clifford Odets,
director Lewis Milestone
and novelist John O'Hara

With Lee Tung Foo
and Dudley Digges

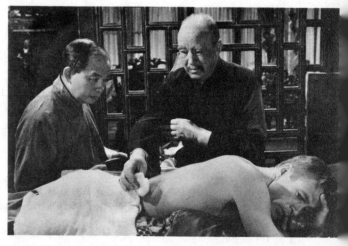

146

With Jean Arthur

THE PLAINSMAN

A Paramount Picture   1936

CAST:

GARY COOPER *(Wild Bill Hickok)*; JEAN ARTHUR *(Calamity Jane)*; JAMES ELLISON *(Buffalo Bill Cody)*; CHARLES BICKFORD *(John Latimer)*; PORTER HALL *(Jack McCall)*; HELEN BURGESS *(Louisa Cody)*; JOHN MILJAN *(General George Armstrong Custer)*; VICTOR VARCONI *(Painted Horse)*; PAUL HARVEY *(Chief Yellow Hand)*; FRANK MC GLYNN, SR. *(Abraham Lincoln)*; GRANVILLE BATES *(Van Ellyn)*; PURNELL PRATT *(Captain Wood)*; PAT MORIARTY *(Sgt. McGinnis)*; CHARLES JUDELS *(Tony the Barber)*; ANTHONY QUINN *(A Cheyenne Warrior)*; GEORGE MAC QUARRIE *(General Merritt)*; GEORGE "GABBY" HAYES *(Breezy)*; FUZZY KNIGHT *(Dave)*; GEORGE ERNEST *(An Urchin)*; FRED KOHLER *(Jack)*; FRANK ALBERTSON *(A Young Soldier)*; HARRY WOODS *(Quartermaster Sgt.)*; FRANCIS MC DONALD *(Gambler on Boat)*; FRANCIS FORD *(Veteran)*; IRVING BACON *(Soldier)*; EDGAR DEARING *(Custer's Messenger)*; EDWIN MAXWELL *(Stanton)*; JOHN HYAMS *(Schuyler Colfax)*; BRUCE WARREN *(Captain of the "Lizzie Gill")*; MARK STRONG *(Wells Fargo Agent)*; CHARLIE STEVENS *(Injun Charlie)*; ARTHUR AYLESWORTH, DOUGLAS WOOD, GEORGE CLEVELAND *(Van Ellyn's Associates)*; LONA ANDRE *(Southern Belle)*; LEILA MC INTYRE *(Mary Todd Lincoln)*; HARRY STUBBS *(John F. Usher)*; DAVISON CLARK *(James Speed)*; C. W. HERZINGER *(William H. Seward)*; WILLIAM HUMPHRIES *(Hugh McCulloch)*; SIDNEY JARVIS *(Gideon Welles)*; WADSWORTH HARRIS *(William Dennison)*; and STANHOPE WHEATCROFT, NOBLE JOHNSON, TED OLIVER, JAMES MASON, BUD OSBORNE, FRANKLYN FARNUM, LANE CHANDLER, HANK BELL, LOUISE STUART, GAIL SHERIDAN, BUD FLANNIGAN [later DENNIS O'KEEFE], BLACKJACK WARD, JANE KECKLEY, CORA SHUMWAY, TEX DRISCOLL, WILBUR MACK, FRANCIS SAYLES.

With Victor Varconi and Jean Arthur

With Ted Oliver and Fred Kohler

CREDITS:

CECIL B. DE MILLE (*Director and Producer*); WALDE-MAR YOUNG, HAROLD LAMB, LYNN RIGGS (*Scenarists*); JEANIE MAC PHERSON (*Adaptation*); VICTOR MILNER, GEORGE ROBINSON (*Photographers*); GEORGE ANTHEIL (*Musical Score*); ANNE BAUCHENS (*Editor*); WILLIAM H. PINE (*Associate Producer*); HARRY M. LINDGREN (*Sound Recorder*); HANS DREIER, ROLAND ANDERSON (*Art Directors*); BORIS MORROS (*Musical Director*); ARTHUR ROSSON (*Second Unit Director*); RICHARD HARLAN (*Assistant Director*); GORDON JENNINGS, FARCIOT EDOUART, DEWEY WRIGLEY (*Special Camera Effects*); A. E. FREUDEMAN (*Set Decorator*); NATALIE VISART, DWIGHT FRANKLIN, JOE DE YONG (*Costumers*). *Based on data from the stories "Wild Bill Hickok" by* FRANK J. WILSTACH *and "The Prince of Pistoleers" by* COURTNEY RYLEY COOPER *and* GROVER JONES.

SYNOPSIS:

After the Civil War, arms dealers plan to sell repeating rifles to the Indians through the unscrupulous John Lattimer. Meanwhile, Wild Bill Hickok learns from a wounded scout that Indians have attacked a nearby garrison and reports his findings to General Custer, who promptly sends Buffalo Bill Cody with a wagon train of arms to the garrison. Hickok is sent to talk with Yellow Hand, Chief of the Cheyenne, but, on his way, he sees Calamity Jane being captured by Indians and rides to her rescue.

At Yellow Hand's camp, Hickok is tortured because he won't give information about the wagon train, but Calamity, unable to witness any more torture, divulges the secret and both are released. Hickok and Calamity then go their separate ways, each trying to right the wrong created by Calamity's weakness. Eventually, Hickok faces Lattimer and kills him. However, before the cavalry arrives, Hickok is shot in the back by Lattimer's accomplice McCall. Cody, riding to aid Hickok with General Merritt's men, arrives too late.

NOTES:

This was Cooper's first film under the direction of the great showman Cecil B. DeMille. Whatever liberty DeMille took with history was surely compensated for by the enthusiasm, detail and larger-than-life finished film. His productions

With Anthony Quinn and James Ellison

Wiith James Ellison and Helen Burgess

pleased audiences of every type, the world over, which is really what movies are all about.

Cooper was a fine choice for the role of Wild Bill Hickok. His own personality, combined with the basic ingredients supplied by the scenarists, etched a splendid portrait of one of America's greatest frontiersman. Jean Arthur, Cooper's delightful co-star of *Mr. Deeds Goes to Town*, gave a vigorous performance as Calamity Jane. The supporting cast, as in all DeMille pictures, was first-rate, down to the last squaw.

Said the London *Times:* "Mr. Cooper is sardonic, cynical, and immensely impressive, whether he is being tortured by Indians, leading forlorn hopes, or pretending that he does not love Calamity Jane. . . . If the West in its pioneer days is to be opened up again, Mr. Cooper and Miss Arthur, with the lavish assistance of Mr. Cecil DeMille, are certainly the people to do it." The critic in the *New York World-Telegram* noted that "The performances are excellent. Gary Cooper acts Wild Bill Hickok with considerable force, humor and salty flavor, and Jean Arthur makes the high-spirited Calamity Jane a genuine character by the authenticity of her playing." The *New York American* added that "By the simple expedient of being himself and not acting at all, he [Gary Cooper] remains winning and effective."

During its production, *The Plainsman* had two working-titles: *Buffalo Bill* and *This Breed of Men*.

With Charles Bickford

SOULS AT SEA

A Paramount Picture   1937

CAST:

GARY COOPER *("Nuggin" Taylor)*; GEORGE RAFT *(Powdah)*; FRANCES DEE *(Margaret Tarryton)*; HENRY WILCOXON *(Lt. Stanley Tarryton)*; HARRY CAREY *(Captain of "William Brown")*; OLYMPE BRADNA *(Babsie)*; ROBERT CUMMINGS *(George Martin)*; PORTER HALL *(Court Prosecutor)*; GEORGE ZUCCO *(Barton Woodley)*; VIRGINIA WEIDLER *(Tina)*; JOSEPH SCHILDKRAUT *(Gaston de Bastonet)*; GILBERT EMERY *(Captain Martisel)*; LUCIEN LITTLEFIELD *(Toymaker-Tina's father)*; PAUL FIX *(Violinist)*; TULLY MARSHALL *(Pecora)*; MONTE BLUE *(Mate of "William Brown")*; STANLEY FIELDS *(Capt. Paul M. Granley)*; FAY HOLDEN *(Mrs. Martin)*; CLYDE COOK *(Hendry)*; ROLLO LLOYD *(Parchy)*; WILSON BENGE *(Doctor)*; ROLFE SEDAN, EUGENE BORDEN *(Friends of de Bastonet)*; LEE SHUMWAY *(Mate)*; ETHEL CLAYTON *(Passenger)*; HARVEY CLARK *(Court Clerk)*; FORBES MURRAY *(Associate Justice)*; DAVISON CLARK *(Bailiff)*; WILLIAM STACK *(Judge)*; CHARLES MIDDLETON *(Foreman of Jury)*; OLAF HYTTEN *(Proprietor)*; FORRESTER HARVEY *(Proprietor of Pub)*; JANE WEIR *(Barmaid)*; LINA BASQUETTE *(Brunette in saloon)*; PAULINE HADDON *(Blonde)*; LOWELL DREW *(Jury Foreman)*; PAUL STANTON *(Defense Attorney)*; LESLIE FRANCIS *(Woodley's Secretary)*; ROBERT BARRAT *(The Reverend)*; CONSTANTINE ROMANOFF *(Drinker in Pub)*; and AGNES AYRES, MARGARET DAGGETT, BETTY LORRAINE, LILLIAN DEAN.

CAST IN CUT-SEQUENCES:

JAMESON THOMAS, CECIL CUNNINGHAM, COLIN TAPLEY, STANLEY ANDREWS, ROBERT WARWICK, MARY GORDON, WARD BOND, VIVA TATTERSALL, BELLE MITCHELL, *and* EDWARD VAN SLOAN, *among others.*

With Porter Hall

With George Raft

With Henry Wilcoxon

CREDITS:

HENRY HATHAWAY (*Director*); GROVER JONES, DALE VAN EVERY (*Scenarists*); CHARLES LANG, JR. (*Photographer*); GORDON JENNINGS (*Special Photographic Effects*); ELLSWORTH HOAGLAND (*Editor*); HANS DREIER, ROLAND ANDERSON (*Art Directors*); A. E. FREUDEMANN (*Interior Decorations*); HARRY MILLS, JOHN COPE (*Sound Recorders*); EDITH HEAD (*Costumer*); W. FRANKE HARLING, MILAN RODER, BERNHARD (BERNARD) KAUN, JOHN LEIPOLD (*Musical Score*); BORRIS MORROS (*Musical Director*); HAL WALKER (*Assistant Director*). SONGS: *"Susie Sapple" and "Hang Boys Hang"* by RALPH RAINGER *and* LEO ROBIN. *Based on a story by* TED LESSER.

SYNOPSIS:

"Nuggin" Taylor and his friend Powdah are mates on a slave ship. The captain is killed during an uprising and Taylor assumes command. Being an abolitionist at heart, he deliberately lets the slaves escape and, later, lets the ship be captured by a British cruiser. Both men are taken to Liverpool, but charges are dismissed for lack of evidence. A Naval Intelligence Service Officer offers Taylor a secret assignment to gather evidence to help break up the powerful slave syndicate, which he accepts.

He sails for America on the "William Brown" with Powdah and, during the trip, falls in love with Margaret, the sister of Lieutenant Tarryton, who is in league with the slavers. Tarryton suspects Taylor of being a spy and searches his cabin. Taylor enters and a fight ensues, during which a little girl in an adjoining cabin becomes frightened and knocks over a lamp. Soon the ship is ablaze and an explosion shatters the hull. There is only one lifeboat left intact and the scramble for it is stopped by Taylor, who explains that only a few can go. Tarryton fights with him again and is thrown overboard. Taylor puts Margaret in the lifeboat, intending to remain behind, but Powdah knocks him out and loads his friend in the boat too. Powdah goes below, looking for Babsie, Margaret's maid, with whom he is in love, but finds her fatally wounded and remains with her as the ship goes down.

Taylor awakens in the overcrowded lifeboat and puts several people out, to save the rest, and assumes full command. Margaret is horrified at this action and, once they are rescued, she brings manslaughter charges against him. At his trial, in Philadelphia,

151

With Harry Carey, Frances Dee,
George Raft and Olympe Bradna

the Intelligence officer relates how Taylor had to save himself in order to complete his important secret mission. He goes free—into the arms of Margaret.

NOTES:

Souls at Sea was originally planned on a massive scale and it was thought that it would indeed rival MGM's beautiful *Mutiny on the Bounty*. Once it was completed, plans were underway to release in at road-show prices at select theatres throughout the country. But someone must have had second thoughts, for, before *Souls at Sea* was released in September of 1937, it had undergone many major cuts, including Queen Victoria's court, cast enough to float another vessel, at least, and several other sequences.

The result was still a good sea-going adventure, but more routine than great. The *New York Daily News* felt "He [Cooper] invests the salty adventurer with a romantic glamour," while the *Brooklyn Daily Eagle* found that "the acting is pretty routine . . ." The *New York Sun* observed, "He [Cooper] plays his part with great restraint and subtlety and is always convincing."

George Raft was originally offered the part of Powdah but refused it because of the way the character dies. He was replaced by Lloyd Nolan, who, it was felt by some executives, resembled Cooper too much, and he was replaced by Anthony Quinn. Raft—fearing competition—then agreed to play the role. Frances Dee replaced Frances Farmer.

THE ADVENTURES OF MARCO POLO

A Samuel Goldwyn Production
Released Thru United Artists   1938

CAST:

GARY COOPER (*Marco Polo*); SIGRID GURIE (*Princess Kukachin*); BASIL RATHBONE (*Ahmed*); ERNEST TRUEX (*Binguccio*); ALAN HALE (*Kaidu*); GEORGE BARBIER (*Kublai Khan*); BINNIE BARNES (*Nazama*); LANA TURNER (*Nazama's maid*); STANLEY FIELDS (*Bayan*); HAROLD HUBER (*Toctai*); H. B. WARNER (*Chen Tsu*); EUGENE HOO (*Chen Tsu's Son*); HELEN QUAN (*Chen Tsu's Daughter*); SOO YONG (*Chen Tsu's Wife*); MRS. NG (*Chen Tsu's Mother*); LOTUS LIU (*Visahka*); FERDINAND GOTTSCHALK (*Persian Ambassador*); HENRY KOLKER (*Nicolo Polo*); HALE HAMILTON (*Maffeo Polo*); ROBERT GREIG (*Chamberlain*); REGINALD BARLOW (*Giuseppe*); WARD BOND (*Mongol Guard*); JAMES LEONG (*Tartar Warrior*); DICK ALEXANDER (*Ahmed's Aide*); JASON ROBARDS (*Messenger*); GLORIA YOUNGBLOOD, DIANA MONCARDO, DORA YOUNG, MIA SCHIOKA (*Court girls*).

CREDITS:

ARCHIE MAYO (*Director*); SAMUEL GOLDWYN (*Producer*); ROBERT E. SHERWOOD (*Scenarist*); RUDOLPH MATE (*Photographer*); HUGO FRIEDHOFER (*Musical Score*); ALFRED NEWMAN (*Musical Director*); RICHARD DAY (*Art Director*); JULIA HERON (*Set Decorator*); FRED ALLEN (*Editor*); THOMAS T. MOULTON (*Sound Recorder*); JAMES BASEVI (*Special Effects*); GEORGE HAIGHT (*Associate Producer*); WALTER MAYO (*Assistant Director*). Based on a story by N. A. POGSON.

SYNOPSIS:

Handsome Marco Polo, popular with the ladies of Venice's back canals, is the son of the leading merchant, who dispatches him and his bookkeeper, Binguccio, to the luxurious court of Kublai Khan in Pekin to discover oriental treasures

153

and complete trade agreements which will bring wealth to the Polo brothers. After an arduous journey, Marco Polo meets townsman Chen Tsu and learns much of the Chinese ways, especially the making of firecrackers, collecting samples for his father.

At the court, Marco Polo falls in love with Princess Kukachin, betrothed to the Persian King; arouses the hatred of the Babylonian, Ahmed, the scheming foreign-born minister of state; and mildly amuses the Emperor. Later, sent as a spy to the rebel camp of Kaidu, Marco saves the warrior's life and, in tribute, demands the support of the rebel army in saving the throne of Kublai Khan from the treacherous Ahmed, reserving the beautiful princess for himself.

With Sigrid Gurie

NOTES:

The Adventures of Marco Polo was Cooper's only film for Samuel Goldwyn that failed to win audience and critical approval. Although a great deal of money was spent on its production, the results were most unsatisfactory. The glossy sets were inferior to those constructed for Columbia's *Lost Horizon,* then playing movie houses around the world, and Goldwyn's "Norwegian" discovery, Sigrid Gurie, it was soon revealed, was from Flatbush.

John Cromwell, the original director, quit after five days of filming *Marco Polo* as serious drama, only to be replaced by Archie Mayo, who never quite knew what should be done with Robert E. Sherwood's tongue-in-cheek script.

The critics, as they usually are, were divided. Said the *Illustrated London News:* "Incredible and splendid, this super-production permits no subtleties of acting. Mr. Gary Cooper, striding through it with his customary ease, preserves his invincible sincerity against heavy odds." William Boehnel in the *New York World-Telegram* commented, "Anyway, *The Adventures of Marco Polo* is grand fun, the kind of entertainment the movies do so effectively. Gary Cooper . . . plays Polo with just the right romantic and adventurous spirit." The *New York Sun's* critic ended his review saying "In spite of its elaborate settings and the presence of Gary Cooper, *The Adventures of Marco Polo* never quite lives up to its promises."

With H. B. Warner

With Binnie Barnes

With Sigrid Gurie and Lotus Lui

With Claudette Colbert

BLUEBEARD'S EIGHTH WIFE

A Paramount Picture   1938

CAST:

CLAUDETTE COLBERT (*Nicole de Loiselle*); GARY COOPER (*Michael Brandon*); EDWARD EVERETT HORTON (*The Marquis de Loiselle*); DAVID NIVEN (*Albert de Regnier*); ELIZABETH PATTERSON (*Aunt Hedwige*); HERMAN BING (*Monsieur Pepinard*); WARREN HYMER (*Kid Mulligan*); FRANKLIN PANGBORN, ARMAND CORTES (*Assistant Hotel Managers*); ROLFE SEDAN (*Floorwalker*); LAWRENCE GRANT (*Professor Urganzeff*); LIONEL PAPE (*Monsieur Potin*); TYLER BROOKE (*Clerk*); TOM RICKETTS (*Uncle Andre*); BARLOW BORLAND (*Uncle Fernandel*); CHARLES HALTON (*Monsieur de la Coste—President*); PAULINE GARON (*Customer*); RAY DE RAVENNE (*Package Clerk*); SHEILA DARCY (*Maid*); BLANCHE FRANKE (*Cashier*); JOSEPH ROMANTINI (*Headwaiter*); ALPHONSE MARTELL (*Hotel Employee*); HAROLD MINJIR (*Photographer*); GINO CORRADO (*Waiter who carries Marquis*); TERRY RAY [*later* ELLEN DREW] (*Secretary*); LEON AMES (*Ex-Chauffeur*); OLAF HYTTEN (*Valet*); GRACE GOODALL (*Nurse*); JIMMIE DIME (*Prizefighter*); *and* ALEX WOLOSHIN, GEORGE DAVIS, ALBERT D'ARNO, MARISKA ALDRICH, PAUL GUSTIN, HOOPER ATCHLEY, JOHN PICORRI, ALBERT PETIT, JOSEPH CREHAN, WOLFGANG A. ZILZER, HENRY ROQUEMORE, SALLY MARTIN, EUGENE BORDEN, JEAN DE BRIAC, HARRY LAMONT, JACQUES VANAIRE, MICHAEL VISAROFF, PAUL BRYAR, GLORIA WILLIAMS, BARBARA JACKSON, MAINE BURTON, JOYCE MATHEWS, PAULA DE CARDO, GWEN KENYON, SUZANNE RIDGWAY, LOLA JENSON, CAROL PARKER, DOROTHY DAYTON, NORAH GALE, HARRIETTE HADDON, RUTH ROGERS *and* DOROTHY WHITE.

CREDITS:

ERNST LUBITSCH (*Director and Producer*); CHARLES BRACKETT, BILLY WILDER (*Scenarists*); CHARLTON ANDREWS (*Adaptation*); LEO TOVER (*Photographer*);

156

WILLIAM SHEA (*Editor*); HANS DREIER, ROBERT USHER (*Art Directors*); FREDERICK HOLLANDER, WERNER R. HEYMANN (*Musical Score*); HARRY D. MILLS (*Sound Recorder*); JOHN LEIPOLD (*Orchestrations*). *Based on a play by* ALFRED SAVOIR.

SYNOPSIS:

A wealthy American, Michael Brandon, who has many ex-wives and many millions, walks into a Riviera department store to buy pajamas and walks out with a girl he determines to make his eighth wife. She is Nicole de Loiselle, the beautiful daughter of an impoverished French aristocrat. Despite his enormous wealth, Nicole gives Michael the first runaround he's ever experienced, which, of course, only stimulates his interest, making him more aggressive.

He tries to win her by over-paying her father for some phony antiques, which only infuriates her. However, under great pressure from her father, Nicole accepts Michael's proposal of marriage, making it quite clear that his money is all she's after. During their honeymoon throughout Europe, Nicole tries to tame the American "Bluebeard," for fear she'll end up like his previous seven brides.

She wins these little battles, but loses the war. So successful are her plots that they backfire and he grants her a divorce. Nicole's victory is, indeed, a pyrrhic one, for, although she has gained a fortune, she has lost the man she has come to love. The tables now turned and Nicole becomes the pursuer, chasing "Bluebeard" all over France. He takes refuge in a secluded sanatorium near Paris, so Nicole buys the place and has him placed in a strait-jacket. Michael, realizing he has met his match, relents.

NOTES:

Again, director Ernst Lubitsch felt he could take Gary Cooper out of his realm and make him a sophisticated gentleman. Cooper may have been one off-screen, but he couldn't give such an illusion on screen. A Mr. Deeds yes, but not the hero of this piece. He and Claudette Colbert worked well together, despite this handicap and Lubitsch sprinkled fun throughout. However, the fans (could they have been wiser than we've ever thought?) turned thumbs down and it lost money.

The *New York World-Telegram* remarked "Gary

With Grace Goodall

With Armand Cortes and Franklin Pangborn

Cooper is capital as Michael, playing the part with ease, drollery and spirit . . . However, F. S. Nugent, in his *New York Times* reveiw, stated, "Although it's not a bad comedy by our current depressed standards, it has the dickens of a time trying to pass off Gary Cooper as a multi-marrying millionaire. Put seven divorced wives behind Mr. Deeds, each with a $50,000 a year settlement, and it becomes pretty hard to believe that he's just a small boy at heart—which is the principal charm of Paramount's gangling hero."

The *New York Sun* felt, *"Bluebeard's Eighth Wife* is slim but funny, with Mr. Cooper and Miss Colbert racing happily through each unexpected episode." Howard Barnes in the *New York Herald Tribune* said, "Mr. Cooper is not altogether at ease in the role of a cosmopolitan banker, but he saves the part from being a caricature, and when the action permits, he cuts loss with splendid comic results."

With Elizabeth Patterson,
Edward Everett Horton
and Claudette Colbert

With Merle Oberon

THE COWBOY AND THE LADY

A Samuel Goldwyn Production
Released Thru United Artists   1938

CAST:

GARY COOPER *(Stretch);* MERLE OBERON *(Mary Smith);* PATSY KELLY *(Katie Callahan);* WALTER BRENNAN *(Sugar);* FUZZY KNIGHT *(Buzz);* MABEL TODD *(Elly);* HENRY KOLKER *(Mr. Smith);* HARRY DAVENORT *(Uncle Hannibal Smith);* EMMA DUNN *(Ma Hawkins);* WALTER WALKER *(Ames);* BERTON CHURCHILL *(Henderson);* CHARLES RICHMAN *(Dillon);* FREDRIK VOGEDING *(Captain);* ARTHUR HOYT *(Valet);* MABEL COLCORD *(Old Woman);* BILLY WAYNE, ERNIE ADAMS, RUSS POWELL, JACK BAXLEY, JOHNNY JUDD *(Rodeo Riders).*

CREDITS:

H. C. POTTER *(Director);* SAMUEL GOLDWYN *(Producer);* S. N. BEHRMAN, SONYA LEVIEN *(Scenarists);* GREGG TOLAND *(Photographer);* RICHARD DAY *(Art Director);* ALFRED NEWMAN *(Musical Score);* SHERMAN TODD *(Editor);* OMAR KIAM *(Costumer);* JAMES BASEVI *(Associate Art Director);* JULIE HERON *(Set Director);* RAY BINGER *(Special Photographic Effects);* PAUL NEAL *(Sound Recorder);* EDDIE BERNOUDY *(Assistant Director).* SONGS: *by* LIONEL NEWMAN, ARTHUR QUENZER *and* L. WOLFE GILBERT, *"Er-ru-ti-tu-ti" and "The Cowboy and the Lady." From an original story by* LEO MCCAREY *and* FRANK R. ADAMS.

SYNOPSIS:

When fun-loving Mary Smith and her uncle Hannibal are picked up in a nightclub raid, her Senator father, who is running for President, whisks her off to his Florida estate. Completely bored, she joins her maid and the cook on a blind date with three cowboys appearing in a local rodeo show. Mary is paired with Stretch Willoughby and wins him over with the story that she is

159

With Merle Oberon

supporting four sisters and a drunken father. A kitchen party at the Smith mansion follows and soon the couple are in love.

Before sailing for Galveston the next morning, Stretch goes back to propose, but her nervous chatter disillusions him and he departs. Mary, realizing her love for him, turns up on the steamer, but Stretch ignores her. He later relents and they are married by the ship's captain. Rodeo-tent life doesn't agree with Mary, so Stretch sends her back to Florida with the understanding that she will join him later on his Montana ranch.

Plans for the nomination of Senator Smith for the presidency are hastened when the secret marriage is discovered by his aides. Stretch gets a telegram saying that Mary will be delayed, but ignores it and rushes to the Smith mansion during a gala dinner party. The obvious hits him when Mary evades his glances. Treated as a curiosity by the throng, he puts them down with a brittle speech before he leaves. When an annulment is proposed by the Senator's aide, Mary faints. Uncle Hannibal then explains to his brother how his political ambitions are ruining his daughter's chance for happiness and the Senator withdraws from the presidential race and escorts Mary out West to her cowboy husband.

NOTES:

This breezy little comedy made ample use of Cooper's screen personality, the shy, whimsical boy who's a pretty nice fella until he's being made fun of—then all Hell breaks loose. He and Merle Oberon worked well together and projected the fact that they were having a grand time with the script. *The Cowboy and the Lady* was nominated for three Academy Awards (for Best Song, the title tune, for Best Sound Recording; and for Alfred Newman's musical score). An Oscar was won by Thomas T. Moulton, head of the Samuel Goldwyn Sound Department.

The *Brooklyn Daily Eagle* critic told his readers, "Gary Cooper, the long-legged Montana boy who was ill at ease as Marco Polo and as a modern Bluebeard earlier this year, got back into chaps and Stetson to play *The Cowboy and the Lady* for Samuel Goldwyn. That gave all of us, including Mr. Goldwyn, something to be thankful for. Gary is natural again, and with the aid of Merle Oberon and Harry Davenport he makes an enticing picture out of an old fable."

Said the *New York Journal-American:* "Mr. Cooper's big moments are those when he whimsically furnishes a make-believe house and, later, when he sternly tells the effete Easterners what he thinks of them." The *New York Daily News* thought, "Gary Cooper is ideal in the role of the softspoken cowboy and Merle Oberon makes a lovely heroine and they both help disguise the weaknesses and lack of originality of the plot."

With Merle Oberon

BEAU GESTE

A Paramount Picture   1939

CAST:

GARY COOPER *(Beau Geste);* RAY MILLAND *(John Geste);* ROBERT PRESTON *(Digby Geste);* BRIAN DONLEVY *(Sergeant Markoff);* SUSAN HAYWARD *(Isobel Rivers);* J. CARROL NAISH *(Rasinoff);* ALBERT DEKKER *(Schwartz);* BRODERICK CRAWFORD *(Hank Miller);* CHARLES BARTON *(Buddy McMonigal);* JAMES STEPHENSON *(Major Henri de Beaujolais);* HEATHER THATCHER *(Lady Patricia Brandon);* G. P. HUNTLEY, JR. *(Augustus Brandon);* JAMES BURKE *(Lieutenant Dufour);* HENRY BRANDON *(Renouf);* ARTHUR AYLESWORTH *(Renault);* HARRY WOODS *(Renoir);* HAROLD HUBER *(Voisin);* STANLEY ANDREWS *(Maris);* DONALD O'CONNOR *(Beau at 12);* BILLY COOK *(John at 10);* MARTIN SPELLMAN *(Digby at 12);* DAVID HOLT *(Augustus at 12);* ANN GILLIS *(Isobel at 10);* HARVEY STEPHENS *(Lieutenant Martin);* BARRY MACOLLUM *(Krenke);* RONNIE RONDELL *(Bugler);* FRANK DAWSON *(Burdon, the Butler);* GEORGE CHANDLER *(Cordier);*

DUKE GREEN *(Glock);* THOMAS JACKSON *(Colonel in Recruiting Office);* JEROME STORM *(Sergeant-Major);* JOSEPH WHITEHEAD *(Sergeant);* HARRY WORTH, NESTOR PAIVA *(Corporals);* GEORGE REGAS, FRANCIS MC DONALD *(Arab Scouts);* CARL VOSS, JOE BERNARD, ROBERT PERRY, LARRY LAWSON, HENRY SYLVESTER, JOSEPH WILLIAM CODY *(Legionnaires);* JOE COLLING *(Trumpeter O. Leo);* GLADYS JEANS *(Girl in Port Said Cafe);* and BOB KORTMAN, GINO CORRADO.

CREDITS:

WILLIAM A. WELLMAN *(Director and Producer);* ROBERT CARSON *(Scenarist);* THEODOR SPARKUHL, ARCHIE STOUT *(Photographers);* THOMAS SCOTT *(Editor);* HANS DREIER, ROBERT ODELL *(Art Directors);* ALFRED NEWMAN *(Musical Score);* EDWARD POWELL *(Orchestrator);* HUGO GRENZBACH, WALTER OBERST

With Robert Preston and Ray Milland

(Sound Recorders); LOUIS VAN DER ECKER *(Technical Adviser). Based on the novel "Beau Geste" by* PERCIVAL CHRISTOPHER WREN.

SYNOPSIS:

The three Geste brothers join the French Foreign Legion in order that none of them should be thought guilty of stealing a valuable sapphire, the renowned "Blue Water," from their guardian, Lady Patricia Brandon. At the Legion training post, a sneak thief named Rasinoff overhears each brother boast that it was he who stole the gem and now has it in his possession. Cruel Sergeant Markoff wrings this information out of him and plots to get the jewel for himself.

He separates the brothers when he selects a group for duty at Fort Zinderneuf. Digby Geste is sent to Fort Tokotu. Beau and John go to Fort Zinderneuf, which soon becomes a living hell, with

Sergeant Markoff taking command after the death of an inexperienced young lieutenant. The result of his cruel dictatorship is a mass mutiny. Since the Geste brothers are not involved in it, Markoff orders Beau and John to shoot the leaders of the rebellion. When they refuse, he threatens to have them shot, but suddenly the fort is attacked by a wild desert tribe. Beau is shot and Markoff searches for the gem, when John, with the help of the dying Beau, rams a bayonet through the sergeant's chest.

Beau gives John two letters (one for Markoff and one for Lady Brandon) before he dies. John then sets fire to the Fort—giving Beau a hero's funeral—as a relief column appears on the horizon.

NOTES:

Cooper finally got his chance to play the hero of Percival Christopher Wren's marvelous adventure yarn, *Beau Geste*. He came to Paramount in 1926,

With Robert Preston
and Ray Milland

With Robert Preston,
Susan Hayward and Ray Milland

With G. P. Huntley, Jr.,
Robert Preston and Heather Thatcher

too late for the first filming (with Ronald Colman) but this 1939 version was given a fine production by director William A. Wellman and Cooper's personality fit the role of Beau to a "T."

Magnificent sets were constructed for this production and a splendid cast procured, with a superb performance from Brian Donlevy which almost stole the show. Alfred Newman composed a rousing musical score and the photography was on a high level. *Beau Geste* won Academy Award nominations for Brian Donlevy for Supporting Actor and Hans Dreier and Robert Odell for Art Direction.

This was Cooper's last film under his Paramount contract and, henceforth, he decided to "free-lance."

Bland Johaneson, in her *New York Daily Mirror* review, noted, "The men dote upon Mr. Cooper for his stature, his taciturnity, his gaunt countenance. The apotheosis of the manly, he is flawlessly fitted for the strong, silent, boyish heroics of *Beau Geste*. That he no longer looks quite boyish enough to play the grateful ward of a patrician lady is a captious criticism—and one the men will not tolerate. . . . Brian Donlevy as the horrendous Sgt. Markoff shines as the outstanding actor in the piece. . . . A suitable vehicle for such an aggressively he-man star as Mr. Cooper. His admirers will applaud his restraint, and the fans generally will approve Mr. William Wellman's handsome treatment of a well-loved adventure tale."

Howard Barnes in the *New York Herald Tribune* said "Gary Cooper plays the title role staunchly and stays properly restrained in the melodramatic and sentimental interludes . . ." The *New York Times* critic, however, felt "There is something a little nightmarish about the heroics of the Geste brothers with their somewhat stagey, 'Let me be the first to die' competition, something unreal about their eternal Britishness, which is not improved by the fact that Beau is now Gary Cooper. . . ."

Universal acquired the rights to *Beau Geste* in 1966, but had the nerve to make this classic adventure a witless, wearisome, and worthless essay at entertainment.

With J. Carrol Naish, Brian Donlevy
and Ray Milland (right)

165

THE REAL GLORY

A Samuel Goldwyn Production
Released Thru United Artists   1939

CAST:

GARY COOPER *(Doctor Bill Canavan);* ANDREA LEEDS *(Linda Hartley);* DAVID NIVEN *(Lieutenant McCool);* REGINALD OWEN *(Captain Hartley);* BRODERICK CRAWFORD *(Lieutenant Larson);* KAY JOHNSON *(Mabel Manning);* CHARLES WALDRON *(Padre Rafael);* RUSSELL HICKS *(Captain Manning);* ROY GORDON *(Colonel Hatch);* BENNY INOCENCIO *(Miguel);* VLADIMIR SOKOLOFF *(Datu);* RUDY ROBLES *(Lieutenant Yabo);* HENRY KOLKER *(The General);* TETSU KOMAI *(Alipang);* ELVIRA RIOS *(Mrs. Yabo);* LUKE CHAN *(Top Sergeant);* ELMO LINCOLN *(U.S. Captain);* JOHN VILLASIN *(Moro Priest);* CHARLES STEVENS *(Cholera Victim);* KAREN SORRELL *(Young Native Woman);* SOLEDAD JIMINEZ *(Old Native Woman);* LUCIO VILLEGAS, NICK SHAID *(Old Native Men);* KAM TONG *(Filipino Soldier);* MARTIN WILKINS, BOB NAIHE, SATINI PUAILOA, KALU SONKUR, SR., GEORGE KALUNA, CAIYU AMBOL *(Moro Warriors).*

CREDITS:

HENRY HATHAWAY *(Director);* SAMUEL GOLDWYN *(Producer);* JO SWERLING, ROBERT R. PRESNELL *(Scenarists);* RUDOLPH MATE *(Photographer);* ALFRED NEWMAN *(Musical Director);* DANIEL MANDELL *(Editor);* JAMES BASEVI *(Art Director);* JEANNE BEAKHURST *(Costumer);* JULIA HERON *(Set Decorator);* R. O. BINGER, PAUL EAGLER *(Special Photographic Effects);* JACK NOYES *(Sound Recorder);* RICHARD TALMADGE *(Associate Director);* EDDIE BERNOUDY *(Assistant Director);* COL. WILLIAM H. SHUTAN *(Technical Adviser).*

SYNOPSIS:

Doctor Canavan and two soldiers of fortune, Lieutenants McCool and Larson, endeavor to quell a terrorist uprising in the Philippine Islands just after the Spanish-American War. To add to the complications that already exist, two women arrive from the States: the Commanding Officer's wife, Mrs. Manning, comes to be with her husband and Linda Hartley, daughter of the Executive Officer, arrives unannounced.

Soon Captain Manning is hacked to death by one of the terrorists in front of his wife. Captain Hartley immediately assumes command. Canavan, despite orders to the contrary, takes a Moro boy he has befriended to reconnoiter in the hills. Here he witnesses the mystic rites of a holy war's inception. He is placed under arrest. Meanwhile, the terrorists dam the stream which is the fort's water supply. Shortly after, cholera breaks out and Doctor Canavan, released, sets about—with Linda as his nurse—to overcome this dread disease.

Once the spread of the disease has been curbed, Canavan goes out after Captain Hartley and his men to blow up the dam. Returning to the fort, they find a siege in progress. After much bloodshed

victory is theirs. Canavan then decides to return to Oklahoma with Linda and practice medicine.

NOTES:

Another rip-snorting adventure film again pleased audiences around the world, and the cash registers at the Goldwyn Studio were ringing loudly. Cooper was quite good as Dr. Canavan and the supporting cast was more than able. The screen's first Tarzan, Elmo Lincoln, had a small bit part in this production, which contained the usual Goldwyn technicians and results.

Life magazine noted, in part, "The picture however is less a personal triumph for Gary Cooper than for the professional stunt men, headless dummies and repaint experts. Though *The Real Glory* may seem gory to U.S. audiences, it is mild compared to a special version prepared for South

With Andrea Leeds

With Andrea Leeds

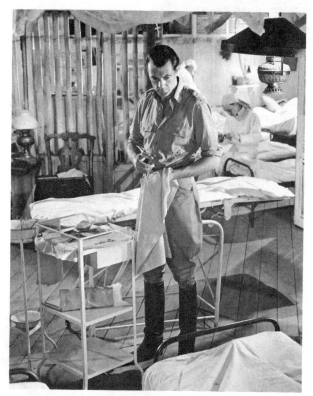

American audiences, which are much more bloodthirsty." Bland Johaneson in the *New York Daily Mirror* said, "Gallant Mr. Cooper, who has been a dashing ornament to the military outposts for so many years, takes up a station in the Philippines for *The Real Glory*. Mr. Cooper displays his usual calm valor, and he has a pleasant cast to support him."

It is interesting to note what the *Daily Worker* thought about all this. Said Howard Rushmore in that publication: "In times like these, we question the wisdom of rattling the bones in Yankee imperialism's closet. To show the Moros as bloodthirsty savages is neither fair to them nor to history."

With David Niven
and Broderick Crawford

THE WESTERNER

A Samuel Goldwyn Production
Released Thru United Artists 1940

CAST:

GARY COOPER (*Cole Hardin*); WALTER BRENNAN (*Judge Roy Bean*); DORIS DAVENPORT (*Jane-Ellen Mathews*); FRED STONE (*Caliphet Mathews*); PAUL HURST (*Chickenfoot*); CHILL WILLS (*Southeast*); CHARLES HALTON (*Mort Borrow*); FORREST TUCKER (*Wade Harper*); TOM TYLER (*King Evans*); ARTHUR AYLSWORTH (*Mr. Dixon*); LUPITA TOVAR (*Teresita*); JULIAN RIVERO (*Juan Gomez*); LILLIAN BOND (*Lily Langtry*) DANA ANDREWS (*Bart Cobble*); ROGER GRAY (*Eph Stringer*); JACK PENNICK (*Bantry*); TREVOR BARDETTE (*Shad Wilkins*); BILL STEELE (*Tex Cole*); BLACKJACK WARD (*Buck Harrigan*); JAMES "JIM" COREY (*Lee Webb*); BUCK MOULTON (*Charles Evans*); TED WELLS (*Joe Lawrence*); JOE DE LA CRUZ (*Mex*); FRANK CORDELL (*Man*); PHILIP CONNOR (*Johnyancy*); CAPT. C. E. ANDERSON (*Hezekiah Willever*); ARTHUR "ART" MIX (*Seth Tucker*); WILLIAM GILLIS (*Leon Beauregard*); BUCK CONNOR (*Abraham Wilson*); DAN BORZAGE (*Joe Yates*); SPEED HANSON (*Walt McGary*); GERTRUDE BENNETT (*Abigail*); MIRIAM SHERWIN (*Martha*); ANNABELLE ROUSSEAU (*Elizabeth*); HELEN FOSTER (*Janice*); CONNIE LEON (*Langtry's Maid*); CHARLES COLEMAN (*Langtry's Manager*); LEW KELLY (*Ticket Man*); HEINIE CONKLIN (*Man at Window*); LUCIEN LITTLEFIELD (*A Stranger*); CORBET MORRIS (*Orchestra Leader*); STANLEY ANDREWS (*Sheriff*); PHIL TEAD (*Prisoner*); HENRY ROQUEMORE (*Stage Manager*); BILL BAUMAN (*Man getting haircut*); HANK BELL (*Deputy*); *and* MARIE LAYTON, BOB FLEMING.

CREDITS:

WILLIAM WYLER (*Director*); SAMUEL GOLDWYN (*Producer*); JO SWERLING, NIVEN BUSCH (*Scenarists*); GREGG TOLAND (*Photographer*); JAMES BASEVI (*Art Director*); DMITRI TIOMKIN (*Musical Score*); DANIEL MANDELL (*Editor*); JULIA HERON (*Set Decorator*);

With Blackjack Ward
and Jim Corey

With Walter Brennan,
Forrest Tucker, Arthur Aylsworth and Bob Fleming

With Walter Brennan
and Lillian Bond

IRENE SALTERN (*Costumer*); FRED LAU (*Sound Recorder*); WALTER MAYO (*Assistant Director*); ARCHIE STOUT (*Assistant Photographer*). *Based on an original story by* STUART N. LAKE.

SYNOPSIS:

Drifter Cole Hardin, falsely accused of stealing a horse, is brought into the Vinegarroon saloon-court of Judge Roy Bean, the sole law "west of the Pecos." While the jury is deliberating, Cole discovers Bean's idolatry of Lily Langtry, the beauteous "Jersey Lily." Cole tells the judge that he knows Lily well. Bean is stunned and quickly maneuvers to have Cole reprieved, so that he can get him a lock of Lily's hair.

Cole spends the night with the judge and only gets away because he steals the old man's gun. Continuing on a journey toward California, Cole happens to stop at the farm of Caliphet Mathews, whose daughter, Jane-Ellen, convinces him that the homesteaders are right in their fight with the cattlemen. Cole decides to remain in the territory.

Cole goes back into town and declares himself on the side of the farmers. Judge Bean is about to arrest him when he remembers the lock of hair. He promises to help round up cattle on the range and they set out together. Afterwards, Cole gives Bean a lock of Lily's hair—cut from Jane-Ellen's head. A few nights later, the Judge's men start burning crops and homes of the farmers and Jane-Ellen's father is killed. Cole goes after Bean, but learns he has gone to nearby Fort Davis to see Lily Langtry, buying out the entire house for his sole pleasure.

After the overture, the curtain rises to expose Cole with both guns drawn. He and Bean shoot it out and Bean slumps to the floor. Cole picks him up and escorts him to "Jersey Lily," whose hand he kisses before he dies.

NOTES:

Producer Goldwyn and director Wyler decided to make a sophisticated Western drama and put the best talents at their disposal to work. Wyler directed in a slow, tense style, with just enough emphasis on "action" to keep the viewer interested. His main aim was characterization and Cooper and his old cohort Walter Brennan each had a field day, with the character role in the lead.

Brennan was excellent as Judge Roy Bean and for his work, he became the first actor in screen history to win a third Academy Award for Best Supporting Actor. Stuart N. Lake received a nomination for his Original Story and James Basevi's Art Direction also was cited for a nomination.

It is interesting to note that, although composer Dimitri Tiomkin got screen credit, Goldwyn did not like his musical score and had his friend Alfred Newman completely re-write it, a task which received no screen credit because of prior contractual agreements. *The Westerner* was the film debut of Forrest Tucker, then age 25, and Dana Andrews, age 29.

One critic felt, "Gary Cooper and Brennan make a grand team. Cooper's reserve and knowledge of human nature make a perfect dramatic foil for Brennan's garrulousness . . ." John Beaufort in the *Christian Science Monitor* admitted, "Notwithstanding an excellent performance by Gary Cooper, *The Westerner* is Walter Brennan's picture. . . . Mr. Cooper's Hardin is excellently done in this actor's easy, laconic style. Mr. Cooper is an economical player who can accomplish much with the flicker of an expression." The *Daily Worker* wrote, "As the Westerner Gary Cooper plays with his usual understatement. Gregg Toland's camerawork on the great outdoors deserves top mention. When nothing happens in the story, his shots are beautiful to see."

With Doris Davenport

With Madeleine Carroll

NORTH WEST MOUNTED POLICE

A Paramount Picture in Technicolor   1940

CAST:

GARY COOPER *(Dusty Rivers)*; MADELEINE CARROLL *(April Logan)*; PAULETTE GODDARD *(Louvette Corbeau)*; PRESTON FOSTER *(Sgt. Jim Brett)*; ROBERT PRESTON *(Constable Ronnie Logan)*; GEORGE BANCROFT *(Jacques Corbeau)*; LYNNE OVERMAN *(Tod McDuff)*; AKIM TAMIROFF *(Dan Duroc)*; WALTER HAMPDEN *(Chief Big Bear)*; LON CHANEY, JR. *(Shorty)*; MONTAGUE LOVE *(Inspector Cabot)*; FRANCIS MC DONALD *(Louis Riel)*; GEORGE E. STONE *(Johnny Pelang)*; WILLARD ROBERTSON *(Superintendent Harrington)*; REGIS TOOMEY *(Const. Jerry Moore)*; RICHARD DENNING *(Const. Thornton)*; ROBERT RYAN *(Const. Dumont)*; DOUGLAS KENNEDY *(Const. Carter)*; CLARA BLANDICK *(Mrs. Burns)*; RALPH BYRD *(Const. Ackroyd)*; LANE CHANDLER *(Const. Fyffe)*; JULIA FAYE *(Wapiskan)*; JACK PENNICK *(Sgt. Field)*; ROD CAMERON *(Corporal Underhill)*; JAMES SEAY *(Const. Fenton)*; JACK CHAPIN *(Bugler)*; ERIC ALDEN *(Const. Kent)*; WALLACE REID, JR. *(Const. Rankin)*; BUD GEARY *(Const. Herrick)*; EVAN THOMAS *(Capt. Gower)*; DAVIDSON CLARK *(Surgeon Roberts)*; CHIEF THUNDERCLOUD *(Wandering Spirit)*; HARRY BURNS *(The Crow)*; LOU MERRIL *(Lesure)*; YNEZ SEABURY *(Mrs. Shorty)*; PHILLIP TERRY *(Const. Judson)*; SOLEDAD JIMINEZ *(Grandmother)*; KERMIT MAYNARD *(Const. Porter)*; ANTHONY CARUSO, PAUL SUTTON *(Indians)*; *and* EVA PUIG, GEORGE REGAS, CHARLENE WYATT, JACK LUDEN, EMORY PARNELL, ED BRADY, CHIEF JOHN BIG TREE, TED OLIVER, WILLIAM HAADE, COLIN TAPLEY, JAMES FLAVIN, ARCHIE TWITCHELL, IRENE COLMAN, FRANK LACKTEEN, JANE KECKLEY, SAM ASH, HARRY SEMELS, NESTOR PAIVA, CONSTANTE FRANKE, NOBLE JOHNSON, RAY MALA, MONTE BLUE, CHIEF YOWLACHIE, NORMA NELSON, WELDON HEYBURN,

With Earl Askam and
Preston Foster

With Madeleine Carroll

DAVID DUNBAR, DICK BOTILLER, EDITH MILLS, CHARLES 'INJUN' STEVENS, JACK CLIFFORD, TEX RAND, DAVID NEWELL, EARL ASKAM.

CREDITS:

CECIL B. DE MILLE (*Director and Producer*); ALAN LE MAY, JESSIE LASKEY, JR., C. GARDNER SULLIVAN (*Scenarists*); VICTOR MILNER, W. HOWARD GREENE (*Photographers*); ANNE BAUCHENS (*Editor*); HANS DREIER, ROLAND ANDERSON (*Art Directors*); WILLIAM H. PINE (*Associate Producer*); VICTOR YOUNG (*Musical Score*); HARRY M. LINDGREN, JOHN COPE (*Sound Recorders*); GORDON JENNINGS, FARCIOT EDOUART (*Special Photographic Effects*); DAN SAYRE GROESBECK, JOE DE YONG (*Set Decorators*); ARTHUR ROSSON (*Assistant Director*); NATALIE VISART, JOE DE YONG (*Costumers*); WALLY WESTMORE (*Makeup Artist*); EDWIN

MAXWELL (*Dialogue Supervisor*); NATALIE KALMUS, HENRI JAFFA (*Technicolor Consultants*); MAJOR G. F. GRIFFIN, R.C.M.P., SERGEANT GEORGE A. PRINGLE, N.W.M.P. (*Technical Advisers*). Based on "*Royal Canadian Mounted Police*" by R. C. FETHERSTON-HAUGH.

SYNOPSIS:

In 1885, just fifteen years after the crushing of the Riel Rebellion, the Royal Canadian Mounted Police, aided by some Texas Rangers, put down a second revolt against British domination. Two love stories are interwoven into the exciting tapestry of the great Northwest at that time. Mountie Ronnie Logan loves Meti wildcat Louvette, who, it turns out, is in love with ranger Dusty Rivers. Rivers, however, has fallen for Ronnie's beautiful

With Walter Hampton, Monte Blue,
Ray Mala (partially hidden),
Preston Foster and George Bancroft

With Robert Preston

sister April, who is the sweetheart of Mountie Jim Brett.

Ronnie betrays the troup of Mounties, because of his infatuation with Louvette, leaving his post and going off with her, which makes it possible for Indians to ambush a police detail. Eventually, Louvette's father, Jacques Corbeau—Louis Riel's partner in crime—is slain and peace returns to the Canadian landscape, through the heroics of the Mounties and their comrades-in-arms, the Texas Rangers.

NOTES:

North West Mounted Police was not only Cecil B. DeMille's first film shot entirely in Technicolor, but it also was Gary Cooper's first color feature film. Previously, Cooper had only once appeared in a color sequence of a film—in *Paramount on Parade* (1930). Strangely enough, David Newell, who appeared with Cooper in that color sequence, appeared as an extra in this film.

Again, the lush DeMille spectacle took hold and audiences were devastated by the gorgeous color photography. Cooper was perfect as the independent man of action, Madeleine Carroll was beautifully photographed and Paulette Goddard gave a deliciously evil performance as the no-good half-breed Louvette. Preston Foster, who appeared as an extra in Cooper's *His Woman* nine years earlier, did fine work as his co-star.

The New York Times remarked, "Only Mr. Cooper preserves his cool, dry, congenial personality. He is himself, even in a DeMille film. And that it is—a big, sprawling, sometimes tedious picture in which the note of heroism is beaten like a drum to the accompanying clash of color symbols." The *Philadelphia Record* wrote, "Handsome, naive, and gory, the film gives DeMille an opportunity to pay tribute to the heroes who patrolled the wild Northwest during the violent 80's."

"Gary Cooper plays the Texas Ranger," said the *New York World-Telegram*, "with all the ease and charm and dry humor that have made him one of the cinema's outstanding leading men." Rose Pelswick, in her *New York Journal-American* review, simply noted, "Cecil B. DeMille's *North West Mounted Police* is bang-up entertainment, a large-scale outdoor melodrama packed with exciting soldier-and-Injun fights and boasting gorgeously Technicolored shots of Canada's mountains, lakes and forests as well as of the Canadian constabulary.

Producer-director DeMille has not forgotten that the first requisite of a moving picture is that it move, for, in addition to lavishness of production and cast, he has given his newest film generous helpings of adventure, romance and blood-and-thunder action. The principals acquit themselves ably."

North West Mounted Police received a total of five Academy Award nominations: Victor Milner and W. Howard Greene, for their splendid color photography; Anne Bauchens, for her astute editing; Victor Young, for his spirited and melodious musical score; Hans Dreier and Roland Anderson, for their art direction; and Loren Ryder, head of Paramount's Sound Department, for the sound recording. Anne Bauchens, who edited all of De-Mille's sound pictures, won the coveted Oscar for her work on this film.

With Robert Preston and Paulette Goddard

With Barbara Stanwyck

MEET JOHN DOE

A Warner Bros. Picture   1940

CAST:

GARY COOPER (*John Doe—Long John Willoughby*); BARBARA STANWYCK (*Ann Mitchell*); EDWARD ARNOLD (*D. B. Norton*); WALTER BRENNAN (*Colonel*); JAMES GLEASON (*Henry Connell*); SPRING BYINGTON (*Mrs. Mitchell*); GENE LOCKHART (*Mayor Lovett*); ROD LA ROCQUE (*Ted Sheldon*); IRVING BACON (*Beany*); REGIS TOOMEY (*Bert Hansen*); WARREN HYMER (*Angelface*); ALDRICH BOWKER (*Pop Dwyer*); ANN DORAN (*Mrs. Hansen*); STERLING HOLLOWAY (*Dan*); MRS. GARDNER CRANE (*Mrs. Brewster*); J. FARRELL MACDONALD (*Sourpuss Smithers*); PAT FLAHERTY (*Mike*); CARLOTTA JELM, TINA THAYER (*Ann's Sisters*); BENNIE BARTLETT (*Red the Office Boy*); SARAH EDWARDS (*Mrs. Hawkins*); STANLEY ANDREWS (*Weston*); ANDREW TOMBES (*Spencer*); PIERRE WATKIN (*Hammett*); GARRY OWEN (*Sign Painter*); CHARLIE WILSON (*Charlie Dawson*); GENE MORGAN (*Mug*); CYRIL THORNTON (*Butler*); EDWARD EARLE (*Radio M. C.*); MIKE FRANKOVICH (*Radio Announcer*); HARRY HOL-MAN (*Mayor Hawkins*); BESS FLOWERS (*Newspaper Secretary*); EMMA TANSEY (*Mrs. Delancy*); MITCHELL LEWIS (*Bennett*); BILLY CURTIS, JOHNNY FERN (*Midgets*); VERNON DENT (*Man*); SUZANNE CARNAHAN [*later* SUSAN PETERS], MARIS WRIXON (*Autograph Hounds*); VAUGHN GLASER (*Governor*); SELMER JACKSON, KNOX MANNING, JOHN B. HUGHES (*Radio Announcers at Convention*); THE HALL JOHNSON CHOIR *and* LUCIA CARROLL, ED STANLEY, ED HERNE, LAFE MC KEE, CHARLES K. FRENCH, CYRIL RING, EDWARD MC WADE, GAIL NEWBRAY, EDDIE COBB, INEZ GAY, FRANK MORAN.

CREDITS:

FRANK CAPRA (*Director and Producer*); ROBERT RISKIN (*Scenarist*); GEORGE BARNES (*Photographer*); DIMITRI TIOMKIN (*Musical Score*); DANIEL MANDELL (*Editor*); STEPHEN GOOSSON (*Art Director*); SLAVKO

VORKAPICH (*Montage Effects*); JACK COSGROVE (*Special Effects*); ARTHUR S. BLACK (*Assistant Director*); NATALIE VISART (*Costumer*); HALL JOHNSON (*Choral Arrangements*); LEO F. FORBSTEIN (*Musical Director*); C. A. RIGGS (*Sound Recorder*). *From an original story by* RICHARD CONNELL *and* ROBERT PRESNELL.

SYNOPSIS:

Angered because she has been fired, newspaper columnist, Ann Mitchell fabricates and has printed in her final column a phony letter signed by "John Doe," in which the writer announces that he is going to commit suicide on Christmas Eve as a protest against all the misery, hypocrisy and corruption which exist in the country. When rivals accuse the paper of cheap publicity, it becomes necessary to produce someone to impersonate the nonexistent letter writer.

The frantic editor and Ann, now back on the payroll with a substantial increase, find him in the person of a penniless, hungry bush-league pitcher, whose arm has gone back on him. What started out as a spiteful joke takes on unbelievable proportions, for letters flood the newspaper office. Ann writes love-thy-neighbor articles for him and his fan mail increases. Then he is put on the radio and, before long, John Doe Clubs are mushrooming everywhere.

Then powerful publisher, D. B. Norton, in true Fascist style, steps in and encourages the clubs and eventually holds a convention, at which he intends Doe to nominate him as a third party candidate for the presidency. When Doe refuses, Norton exposes him as a fake. However, John Doe can still commit suicide on Christmas Eve, as was threatened in the letter. And this he seriously plans to do, but as he is about to jump, he is stopped by Ann.

NOTES:

Ever since their successful *Mr. Deeds Goes to Town*, director Frank Capra and scenarist Robert Riskin wanted another script for Cooper. They found it at Warner Bros. and created another solid film entertainment that is still studied and discussed today. *Meet John Doe* contains one of Cooper's all-time great performances and one which certainly would have won him an Academy Award had not *Sergeant York* followed it and done just that.

Said the *New York World-Telegram:* "Mr. Capra's direction is brilliant. More than anyone else he

With Edward Arnold

With Walter Brennan and Barbara Stanwyck

179

knows how to take the little man and picture him in all his simplicity, with all his ambitions, desires, heartaches, and laughter. The acting, too, is brilliant. Gary Cooper has never been better . . . and Barbara Stanwyck is supremely good as the columnist, lovely and talented." Howard Barnes, in the *New York Herald Tribune,* wrote, "While Capra has never been more knowing and sincere in his direction, he has had invaluable support from Gary Cooper in the central role. The part was hand-tailored for the actor, but he does much more than just fit it. He gives a splendid and utterly persuasive portrayal. . . . Only Cooper, I believe, could have so completely fulfilled Capra's conception in *Meet John Doe.* I am not certain that he is a great actor, but he is great in this motion picture."

The *Baltimore Evening Sun*'s critic noted, "Certainly he [Gary Cooper] is so right in every respect as this country's Everyman that it is hard to imagine anyone else in Hollywood filling the bill. This rangy, engaging actor has that magic of personality that provides a lift for every scene in which he is involved."

180

With Barbara Stanwyck

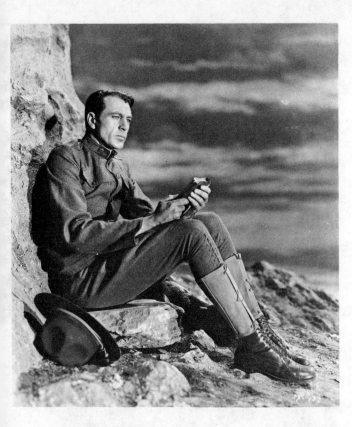

SERGEANT YORK

A Warner Bros. Picture   1941

CAST:

GARY COOPER (*Alvin C. York*); WALTER BRENNAN (*Pastor Rosier Pile*); JOAN LESLIE (*Gracie Williams*); GEORGE TOBIAS (*Michael T. "Pusher" Ross*); STANLEY RIDGES (*Major Buxton*); MARGARET WYCHERLY (*Mother York*); WARD BOND (*Ike Botkin*); NOAH BEERY, JR. (*Buck Lipscomb*); JUNE LOCKHART (*Rose (York)*); DICKIE MOORE (*George York*); CLEM BEVANS (*Zeke*); HOWARD DA SILVA (*Lem*); CHARLES TROWBRIDGE (*Cordell Hull*); HARVEY STEPHENS (*Captain Danforth*); DAVID BRUCE (*Bert Thomas*); CHARLES (CARL) ESMOND (*The German Major*); JOSEPH SAWYER (*Sergeant Early*); PAT FLAHERTY (*Sergeant Harry Parsons*); ROBERT PORTERFIELD (*Zeb Andrews*); ERVILLE ALDERSON (*Nate Tomkins*); JOSEPH GERARD (*General Pershing*); FRANK WILCOX (*Sergeant*); DONALD DOUGLAS (*Captain Tillman*); LANE CHANDLER (*Corporal Savage*); FRANK MARLOWE (*Beardsley*); JACK PENNICK (*Corporal Cutting*); JAMES ANDERSON (*Eb*); GUY WILKERSON (*Tom*); TULLY MARSHALL (*Uncle Lige*); LEE "LASSES" WHITE (*Luke, the Target Keeper*); JANE ISBELL (*Gracie's Sister*); FRANK ORTH (*Drummer*); ARTHUR AYLESWORTH (*Marter, Bartender*); RITA LA ROY, LUCIA CARROLL, KAY SUTTON (*Girls in saloon*); ELISHA COOK, JR. (*Piano Player*); WILLIAM HAADE (*Card Player*); JODY GILBERT (*Fat Woman*); VICTOR KILIAN (*Andrews*); FRANK FAYLEN, MURRAY ALPER (*Butt Boys*); GAYLORD (STEVE) PENDLETON, CHARLES DRAKE (*Scorers*); THEODORE VON ELTZ (*Prison Camp Commander*); ROLAND DREW (*Officer*); RUSSELL HICKS (*General*); JEAN DEL VAL (*Marshal Foch*); SELMER JACKSON (*General Duncan*); CREIGHTON HALE (*AP Man*); GEORGE IRVING (*Harrison*); ED KEANE (*Oscar of the Waldorf*); BYRON BARR [*later* GIG YOUNG] (*Soldier*); *and* SI JENKS, RAY TEAL, KIT GUARD, DICK SIMMONS.

CREDITS:

HOWARD HAWKS (*Director*); JESSE LASKY, HAL B. WAL-
LIS (*Producers*); ABEM FINKEL, HARRY CHANDLEE,
HOWARD KOCH, JOHN HUSTON (*Scenarists*); SOL
POLITO (*Photographer*); ARTHUR EDESON (*Battle
Sequences*); WILLIAM HOLMES (*Editor*); JOHN HUGHES
(*Art Director*); MAX STEINER (*Musical Score*); HUGO
FRIEDHOFER (*Orchestrator*); LEO F. FORBSTEIN (*Musi-
cal Director*); OLIVER S. GARRETSON (*Sound Re-
corder*); PERC WESTMORE (*Makeup Artist*); DONOHO
HALL, PAUL WALTERS, CAPT. F.A.R. WILLIAM YETTES
(*Technical Advisers*); FRED MAC LEAN (*Set Deco-
rator*). Based on the diary of Sergeant York as
edited by TOM SKEYHILL.

SYNOPSIS:

Alvin C. York is a rough and tough, sharp-shooting
farmer living in Tennessee's Valley of the Three
Forks, who gets "religion" in his own way. He hates
no one and, when drafted for service in World
War I, registers as a conscientious objector. Major
Buxton, an understanding officer in his company,
proves to York that violence is sometimes necessary
to insure freedom when he gives him an American
history book.

In the Argonne Forest, as a sergeant in the
American Expeditionary Forces, York sees his good
friend "Pusher" Ross, a Bronx Subway guard,
killed and, in anger, kills twenty-five of the enemy
and captures 132 prisoners single-handedly. This
act of valor causes General John J. Pershing to
acclaim York as "the greatest civilian soldier of
the war," for which he receives the Congressional
Medal of Honor, France's Croix de Guerre, the
Distinguished Service Cross and the Medaille
Militaire, among others.

NOTES:

Just after the New York *premiere* of *Sergeant York*,
the real Alvin C. York was besieged by reporters
for his reactions to the film and the way in which
he was portrayed on the screen by Gary Cooper.
World War I's most decorated hero thought a moment and slowly replied "Very natural."

"Sergeant York and I had quite a few things in
common even before I played him on the screen,"
Cooper once said. "We both were raised in the
mountains—Tennessee for him, Montana for me—
and learned to ride and shoot as a natural part of
growing up. *Sergeant York* won me an Academy

182

With Noah Beery, Jr., Dickie Moore
and Ward Bond

With Ward Bond

With Alvin C. York

Award, but that's not why it's my favorite. I liked the role because of the background of the picture, and because I was portraying a good, sound American character."

The earlier portions of this film—in the Tennessee Valley—were certainly the most rewarding, although the battle scenes were also excitingly staged. However, the entire film was put in jeopardy when the Hollywood-ized ending was hooked on; it took the air of authenticity right apart. Max Steiner's effective musical score heightened the picture's feeling, but it was Howard Hawks' skillful attention to detail that made his direction so replete with moods, melodrama and meaning.

Cooper won the New York Film Critics award as Best Actor of the Year for his portrayal of York and the Academy Award Oscar. William Holmes also won an Oscar for his superb editing. In addition to the two winners, there were 9 other nominations: Best Picture, Best Supporting Actor (Brennan), Best Supporting Actress (Wycherly), Best Director (Hawks), Best Score (Steiner), Best Sound, Best Photography, (Polito), Best Scenario (the four writers), and Best Art and Set Decoration. *Sergeant York* was 1941's top-grossing film, and Cooper, because of his appearances in this film, *Meet John Doe* and *The Westerner,* was the leading money-making star of the year.

Evaluating Cooper's performance, Howard Barnes in the *New York Herald Tribune* said, "Suffice it to say that it is one of extraordinary versatility and conviction. Whether he is being the gangling hell-raiser of the opening sequences, the hard-working fanatic of the middle portion or the shrewd fighter of the Argonne section, he is always utterly right in the part." Bosley Crowther, in *The New York Times,* noted that the film ". . . has all the flavor of true Americana, the blunt and homely humor of backwoodsmen and the raw integrity peculiar to simple folk," but found that the unnecessary glamorous ending "jars sharply with the naturalness which has gone before. However, the performance of Gary Cooper in the title role holds the picture together magnificently."

Said *Newsweek:* "Cooper's Alvin York is a completely persuasive characterization." Archer Winston in the *New York Post* remarked, "Gary Cooper gives one of his best performances as York, which is saying that it couldn't be done better." Henry T. Murdock in the *Philadelphia Evening Public Ledger* thought "Cooper dominates the scene with his quiet sincerity, which is enhanced by his moments of blazing action."

With Joan Leslie

With Margaret Wycherly

With Barbara Stanwyck

BALL OF FIRE

A Samuel Goldwyn Production
Released by RKO-Radio Pictures, Inc.   1941

CAST:

GARY COOPER (*Prof. Bertram Potts*); BARBARA STAN-WYCK (*Sugarpuss O'Shea*); OSCAR HOMOLKA (*Prof. Gurkakoff*); HENRY TRAVERS (*Prof. Jerome*); S. Z. SAKALL (*Prof. Magenbruch*); TULLY MARSHALL (*Prof. Robinson*); LEONID KINSKEY (*Prof. Quintana*); RICH-ARD HAYDN (*Prof. Oddly*); AUBREY MATHER (*Prof. Peagram*); ALLEN JENKINS (*Garbage Man*); DANA ANDREWS (*Joe Lilac*); DAN DURYEA (*Duke Pastrami*); RALPH PETERS (*Asthma Anderson*); KATHLEEN HOW-ARD (*Miss Bragg*); MARY FIELD (*Miss Totten*); CHARLES LANE (*Larson*); CHARLES ARNT (*McNeary*); ELISHA COOK, JR. (*Cook*); ALAN RHEIN ("*Horseface*"); EDDIE FOSTER (*Pinstripe*); ALDRICH BOWKER (*Justice of the Peace*); ADDISON RICHARDS (*District Attorney*); PAT WEST (*Bum*); KENNETH HOWELL (*College Boy*); TOMMY RYAN (*Newsboy*); TIM RYAN (*Motor Cop*); WILL LEE ("*Benny, the Creep*"); GENE KRUPA AND HIS ORCHES-TRA; OTTO HOFFMANN (*Stage Door Man*); ED MUNDY (*Spieler*); GERALDINE FISSETTE (*Hula Dancer*); JUNE HORNE, ETHELREDA LEOPOLD (*Nursemaids in Park*); WALTER SHUMWAY, GEORGE BARTON (*Garbagemen*); MERRILEE LANNON, DORIA CARON (*Girls in Subway*); HELEN SEAMON, CATHERINE HENDERSON (*College Girls*); JACK PERRY (*Fighting Bum*); LORRAINE MIL-LER (*Girl in Café*); MILDRED MORRIS (*Chorus Girl*); FRANCIS SAYLES (*Taxi Driver*); GERALD PIERCE (*De-livery Boy*); CHET DE VITO (*Toll Keeper*); PAT FLAHERTY, GEORGE SHERWOOD (*Deputies*); DEL LAWRENCE (*Irish Gardener*); EDDY CHANDLER, LEE PHELPS, KEN CHRISTY, DICK RUSH, OSCAR CHALKEE WILLIAMS (*Cops*); JOHNNIE MORRIS (*Justice of Peace Clerk*); EDWARD CLARK (*Proprietor of Motor Court*).

CREDITS:

HOWARD HAWKS (*Director*); SAMUEL GOLDWYN (*Pro-ducer*); CHARLES BRACKETT, BILLY WILDER (*Scenar-*

ists); GREGG TOLAND (*Photographer*); DANIEL MAN-
DELL (*Editor*); ALFRED NEWMAN (*Musical Score*);
PERRY FERGUSON (*Art Director*); THOMAS T. MOULTON
(*Sound Recorder*); JULIA HERON (*Set Decorator*).
SONG: "*Drum Boogie*" *by* GENE KRUPA *and* ROY
ELDRIDGE. *Based on "From A to Z," an original
story, by* THOMAS MONROE *and* BILLY WILDER.

SYNOPSIS:

Professor Bertram Potts, writing a treatise on
slang for an encyclopedia, elicits, for research purposes only, the aid of a burlesque stripper, Sugarpuss O'Shea. Miss O'Shea is hep to the last syllable
of current slang and moves in with the professor
and his seven scholarly associates—when the law
starts moving in on her.

Her presence upsets the stodgy lives of the rather
stuffy gentlemen and their housekeeper, and the
regulated existence to which they are accustomed.
However, they all soon take Sugarpuss to their
hearts and her dialogue down on paper. When
it eventually comes time for her to leave her hideaway and marry her gangster boyfriend, Joe Lilac,
Sugarpuss balks because, by this time, she has fallen
for the good professor.

NOTES:

Ball of Fire, called *The Professor and the Burlesque
Queen* during production, offered a marvelous
change of pace for Cooper, and he responded by
giving one of his most deft characterizations. Barbara Stanwyck, who had been so fine with Cooper
in *Meet John Doe*, was sterling as the sassy Sugarpuss, a performance that won her a second Academy
Award nomination. The supporting cast, including
Richard Haydn in his film debut, was utilized to its
fullest. Besides Miss Stanwyck's nomination, Alfred
Newman's musical score was nominated, as were
Thomas Monroe and Billy Wilder's original story
and the sound recording.

Samuel Goldwyn and director Howard Hawks
remade this delicious comedy, in 1948, as a vehicle
tailored for the unusual talents of comedian Danny
Kaye, then calling it *A Song is Born*. Funny it
wasn't.

Howard Barnes, in his review in the *New
York Herald Tribune*, remarked, "Crowned with
laurels already for his performances in *Meet John
Doe* and *Sergeant York* last year, Gary Cooper
deserves a new wreath, or at least a lei, for his
current make-believe in *Ball of Fire*. . . . It is a

With Richard Haydn, Aubrey Mather,
Leonid Kinskey, S. Z. Sakall,
Kathleen Howard and Tully Marshall

With Barbara Stanwyck

strange role for Cooper, but he handles it with great skill and comic emphasis. His natural diffidence serves him in greater stead than his physique in this comic melodrama about professors and gangsters, but it is sufficient to make his characterization utterly delightful.

". . . While he may not be completely plausible in the preposterous doings of *Ball of Fire* he contributes the sort of amusing and even hilarious performance which one would scarcely have expected from him. Before you know it he'll be a rounded actor as well as a great one. While Cooper is the wheel horse of this Samuel Goldwyn production, Barbara Stanwyck helps out no little as the heroine of the proceedings. . . . when she is playing a night-club stray, with a heart of gold, she is better than any of her sisters in screen make-believe. In any case, *Ball of Fire* is a rattling good comedy."

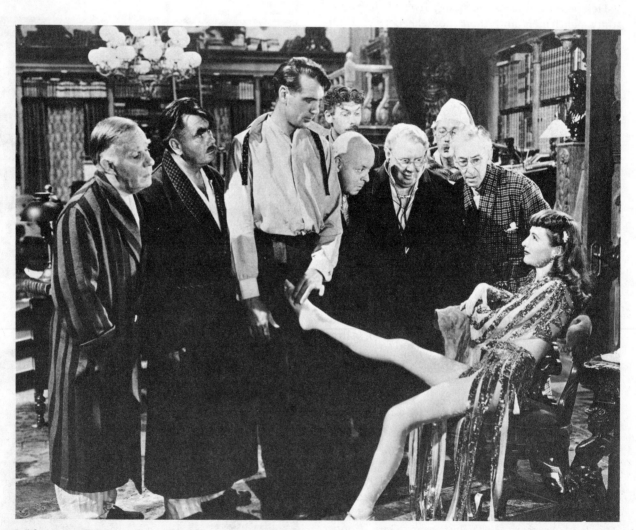

With Henry Travers, Oscar Homolka, Aubrey Mather, Leonid Kinskey, S. Z. Sakall, Richard Haydn, Tully Marshall and Barbara Stanwyck

186

THE PRIDE OF THE YANKEES

A Samuel Goldwyn Production
Released by RKO-Radio Pictures, Inc.   *1942*

CAST:

GARY COOPER (*Lou Gehrig*); TERESA WRIGHT (*Eleanor Gehrig*); WALTER BRENNAN (*Sam Blake*); DAN DURYEA (*Hank Hanneman*); BABE RUTH (*Himself*); ELSA JANSSEN (*Mom Gehrig*); LUDWIG STOSSEL (*Pop Gehrig*); VIRGINIA GILMORE (*Myra*); BILL DICKEY (*Himself*); ERNIE ADAMS (*Miller Huggins*); PIERRE WATKIN (*Mr. Twitchell*); HARRY HARVEY (*Joe McCarthy*); ROBERT W. MEUSEL, MARK KOENIG, BILL STERN (*Themselves*); ADDISON RICHARDS (*Coach*); HARDIE ALBRIGHT (*Van Tuyl*); EDWARD FIELDING (*Clinic Doctor*); GEORGE LESSEY (*Mayor of New Rochelle*); VAUGHAN GLASER (*Doctor in Gehrig Home*); DOUGLAS CROFT (*Lou Gehrig as a boy*); VELOZ & YOLANDA; RAY NOBLE & HIS ORCHESTRA; FRANK FAYLEN (*3rd Base Coach*); LANE CHANDLER (*Player in Locker Room*); EDGAR BARRIER (*Hospital Doctor*); GENE COLLINS (*Billy, age 8*); DAVID HOLT (*Billy, age 17*); GEORGE OFFERMAN, JR. (*Freshman*);

DAVID MANLEY (*Major La Guardia*); ANITA BOLSTER (*Sasha's Mother*); JIMMY VALENTINE (*Sasha*); SPENCER CHARTERS (*Mr. Larsen*); SARAH PADDEN (*Mrs. Roberts*); BERNARD ZANVILLE [*later* DANE CLARK], TOM NEAL (*Fraternity Boys*); LORNA DUNN (*Nurse in Clinic*); EMORY PARNELL (*Cop*); DOROTHY VAUGHAN (*Landlady*); PATSY O'BYRNE (*Scrub Woman*); MATT MC HUGH (*Strength Machine Operator*); WILLIAM CHANEY (*Newsboy*); PAT FLAHERTY (*Baseball Player*); MARY GORDON (*Maid*); FRANCIS SAYLES (*Cab Driver*).

CREDITS:

SAM WOOD (*Director*); SAMUEL GOLDWYN (*Producer*); JO SWERLING, HERMAN J. MANKIEWICZ (*Scenarists*); RUDOLPH MATE (*Photographer*); WILLIAM CAMERON MENZIES (*Producer Designer*); LEIGH HARLINE (*Musi-*

With Teresa Wright

With Elsa Janssen

cal Score); PERRY FERGUSON *(Art Director);* MC CLURE CAPPS *(Associate Art Director);* HOWARD BRISTOL *(Set Director);* RENE HUBERT *(Costumer);* DANIEL MANDELL *(Editor);* JOHN SHERWOOD *(Assistant Director);* FRANK MAKER *(Sound Recorder);* JACK COSGROVE *(Special Photographic Effects);* RAY BINGER *(Special Sound Effects),* SONG: *"Always" by* IRVING BERLIN. *Produced with the assistance of* MRS. LOU GEHRIG, *by arrangement with* CHRISTY WALSH. *From an original story by* PAUL GALLICO.

SYNOPSIS:

As a boy in New York, Lou Gehrig dreams of becoming a big league baseball player, although his parents want him to become an engineer. "Mom" Gehrig, a cook at a Columbia University frat house, sees Lou through school and into Columbia, where he works his way as a waiter at the frat

house. The members, admiring his prowess in sports, pledge Lou to membership, but he clashes with a few snobbish fellows.

Soon after, sports writer Sam Blake recommends him to the New York Yankees and, when he learns his mother requires a costly operation, Gehrig signs with the Yankees to obtain necessary funds. "Mom" believes her son to be at Harvard when Lou is farmed out for experience to the minors. Later, she discovers he's a baseball player.

As first baseman with the team, he becomes an associate of such greats as Babe Ruth, Bill Dickey, Mark Koenig and Bob Meusel. Romance claims him in Chicago when an attractive spectator, Eleanor Twitchell, teases him for awkwardly tripping over a pile of bats. He meets her after the game and their courtship begins. After the Yankees win the World Series, Lou proposes to Eleanor and is accepted. Lou, meanwhile, rises steadily to become the baseball hero of America, and, when he plays his 2000th consecutive game, the whole world honors him. Not long afterwards, however, he goes into a mysterious slump, the victim of amytropic lateral sclerosis, a neurological disease similar to multiple sclerosis. He reluctantly quits the game on July 4, 1939, at Yankee Stadium, before 62,000 saddened fans.

NOTES:

If Cooper had left any doubts before this film that he was an actor as well as a screen personality, he eliminated them completely with his splendid, sensitive and many-faceted performance as Lou Gehrig.

Gehrig, born Henry Louis Gehrig in New York on June 19, 1903, joined the New York Yankees in 1923. After two seasons at Hartford, he went to the Yankees officially on June 2, 1925, and, from then on, he never missed a game. He played in 2,130 consecutive games and participated in seven World Series before he fell victim of the rare paralysis. He died on June 2, 1941, at 37 years old.

Cooper had to be taught how to throw and bunt left-handed, and Lefty O'Doul worked with him for many weeks. His farewell speech in Yankee stadium to his teammates—and thousands of fans—left few dry eyes, and was later a special favorite with GI's during Cooper's South Pacific tours.

The *New York Daily News* critic noted, "Cooper's performance as Gehrig is second only to his characterization of Sergeant York." Archer Winsten in the *New York Post* commented, "The performances are uncommonly fine. Gary Cooper, though entirely lacking the physical equipment of a Gehrig, manages the technical aspects of baseball in a manner which should not be too distracting except to a critical expert. And, on the other hand, his projection of the mental and spiritual side of the man is brilliant." The *New York World-Telegram* added, "Mr. Cooper has seldom been better than he is as Gehrig. His performance grows, as the character grows, from shy gawky undergraduate to modest, unassuming hero of millions."

The Pride of the Yankees received eight Academy Award nominations. Cooper was again nominated —his third time at bat. The picture was nominated, as well as Paul Gallico's original story, Rudolph Mate's photography, Leigh Harline's musical score, the art direction of Perry Ferguson and McClure Capps and the set decoration of Howard Bristol. The eighth nomination was the film's special effects.

With Babe Ruth

With Teresa Wright

On the set with director Sam Wood
and visitor Pola Negri

FOR WHOM
THE BELL TOLLS

A Paramount Picture in Technicolor   1943

CAST:

GARY COOPER *(Robert Jordan);* INGRID BERGMAN *(Maria);* AKIM TAMIROFF *(Pablo);* ARTURO DE CORDOVA *(Agustin);* VLADIMIR SOKOLOFF *(Anselmo);* MIKHAIL RASUMNY *(Rafael);* FORTUNIO BONANOVA *(Fernando);* ERIC FELDARY *(Andres);* VICTOR VARCONI *(Primitivo);* KATINA PAXINOU *(Pilar);* JOSEPH CALLEIA *(El Sordo);* LILO YARSON *(Joaquin);* ALEXANDER GRANACH *(Paco);* ADIA KUZNETZOFF *(Gustavo);* LEONID SNEGOFF *(Ignacio);* LEO BULGAKOV *(Gen. Golz);* DUNCAN RENALDO *(Lt. Berrendo);* GEORGE COULOURIS *(Andre Massart);* FRANK PUGLIA *(Capt. Gomez);* PEDRO DE CORDOBA *(Col. Miranda);* MICHAEL VISAROFF *(Staff Officer);* KONSTANTIN SHAYNE *(Karkov);* MARTIN GARRALAGA *(Capt. Mora);* JEAN DEL VAL *(Sniper);* FEODOR CHALIAPIN *(Kashkin);* PEDRO DE CORDOBA *(Frederico Gonzales);* MAYO NEWHALL *(Ricardo);* MICHAEL DALMATOFF *(Benito Garcia, Mayor);* ANTONIO VIDAL *(Guillermo);* ROBERT TAFUR Faustino Rivero);* ARMAND ROLAND *(Julian);* TRINI VARELA *(Spanish Singer);* DICK BOTILLER *(Sgt. Elias Man);* FRANCO CORSARO, FRANK LACKTEEN *(Elias Men);* GEORGE SOREL *(Bored Sentry);* JOHN BLEIFER *(Peasant-Flails Gonzalez);* HARRY CORDING *(Man-Flails the Mayor);* WILLIAM EDMUNDS, ALBERT MORIN, PEDRO REGAS *(Soldiers);* SOLEDAD JIMINEZ *(Guillermo's Wife);* LUIS ROJAS *(Drunkard);* MANUEL PARIS *(Officer of Civil Guards);* JOSE TORTOSA, ERNESTO MORELLI, MANUEL LOPEZ *(Civil Guards);* YAKIMA CANUTT *(Young Cavalry Man);* TITO RENALDO *(1st Sentry);* MAXINE ARDELL, MARJORIE DEANNE, YVONNE DE CARLO, ALICE KIRBY, MARCELLA PHILLIPS, LYNDA GREY, CHRISTOPHER KING, LOUISE LA PLANCHE *(Girls in Café).*

190

SAM WOOD (*Director and Producer*); DUDLEY NICHOLS (*Scenarist*); BUDDY DE SYLVA (*Executive Producer*); RAY RENNAHAN (*Photographer*); VICTOR YOUNG (*Musical Score*); HANS DREIER, HALDANE DOUGLAS (*Art Directors*); SHERMAN TODD, JOHN LINK (*Editors*); BERT GRANGER (*Set Decorator*); HAROLD C. LEWIS, DON JOHNSON (*Sound Recorders*); WILLIAM CAMERON MENZIES (*Production Designer*); GORDON JENNINGS (*Special Photographic Effects*); FARCIOT EDOUART (*Process Photography*); WALLY WESTMORE (*Makeup Artist*); NATALIE KALMUS, MORGAN PADELFORD (*Technicolor Color Directors*); JAN DOMELA, IRMIN ROBERTS (*Musical Associates*); LEO SHUKEN, GEORGE PARRISH (*Orchestrators*); LONNIE D'ARSA, JOE YOUNGERMAN (*Assistant Directors*); SONGS: "*A Love Like This*" by VICTOR YOUNG *and* NED WASHINGTON; "*For Whom the Bell Tolls*" by MILTON DRAKE *and* WALTER KENT. *From the novel by* ERNEST HEMINGWAY.

With Vladimir Sokoloff

With Ingrid Bergman

191

With Ingrid Bergman

Wood began filming in the beauteous Sierra Nevadas in late 1942. This was the second time Hemingway had been filmed—and the second time with Cooper.

The political significance, *i.e.* the realities of the Spanish Civil War, was reduced to background for the passion-filled romance between Jordan and Maria, and Dudley Nichols' scenario stuck pretty close to Hemingway's original except on these points. However, Fascists became Nationalists and Loyalists became Republicans, causing *The Nation's* critic to comment, "You may easily get the impression that Gary Cooper is simply fighting for the Republican Party in a place where the New Deal has got particularly out of hand."

With Ingrid Bergman

SYNOPSIS:

Robert Jordan, an adventurous American, joins a group of guerrilla fighters during the Spanish Civil War. He is assigned the task of blowing up a strategic bridge in a heavily guarded mountain pass, to stop the enemy's advance. He tries in vain to get assistance from Pablo, the drunken leader, who has become weak. Pablo resents Robert's interest in the lovely Maria, for he himself has become fond of her since she came to live with him and his woman Pilar. Nevertheless, Robert and Maria enjoy a passionate romance in the three days he is with the group.

Pilar, a strong-willed woman, assumes the guerrilla leadership and, along with an old guide, Anselmo, aids Robert in the plan. She arranges for guerrilla fighter El Sordo to supply horses for the group's departure after the bridge has been blown up. However, the enemy gets to El Sordo and he and his band are blown to bits while the others watch helplessly. Robert must still blow up the bridge at a precise moment and, despite everything, accomplishes the feat, dying to do so.

NOTES:

Ernest Hemingway's 1940 novel was purchased by Paramount for a record (at that time) figure of $150,000 and was originally scheduled as an item on Cecil B. DeMille's agenda. What ever happened to those plans is unknown, and director Sam

192

The production was exquisitely mounted by William Cameron Menzies, the genius who made *Gone With the Wind* and *King's Row* (for director Wood) such beautiful productions. The photography and musical score were above reproach, but, regardless of these assets, Wood's film was overlong and dwelled too much on exceedingly long and drawn-out close-ups. (The original running time was 168 minutes). Many a critic commented about the color photography, postulating that black-and-white would have better served the mood. For the record, Hemingway insisted that they use Coop.

The film was re-issued in the mid-1950's in an abridged form, which completely eliminated the roles played by Konstantin Shayne and George Coulouris. This is the version presently available to TV audiences. The story was unofficially reworked as an Allied Artists "B" film, in 1953, called *Fighter Attack*, with Sterling Hayden, Joy Page and Kenneth Tobey.

Bosley Crowther in *The New York Times* wrote, "Gary Cooper as Robert Jordan and Ingrid Bergman as Maria are fine, though limited in their opportunities." Howard Barnes in the *New York Herald Tribune* disagreed, saying, "Gary Cooper and Ingrid Bergman play starring roles with the true stature and authority of stars, while the supporting cast is never far behind them and sometimes a step ahead." *Variety* heralded: *"For Whom the Bell Tolls* is one of the important pictures of all time."

For his vigorous portrayal of Robert Jordan, Cooper received his fourth Academy Award nomination. Bergman was nominated for Best Actress; the film itself for Best Picture; Akim Tamiroff for Supporting Actor; Katina Paxinou for Supporting Actress; Best Art Direction and Set Decoration; Best Editing; Best Photography; and Best Musical Score. Katina Paxinou alone won an Oscar.

Few people remember that Vera Zorina was Paramount's original choice for the role of Maria and had not only been signed but had cut her hair and went on location with Cooper for nearly three weeks. Paramount, upon seeing the rushes, decided to replace her with Bergman. Zorina threatened suit and Paramount paid off.

With Yvonne De Carlo (as an extra) extreme right

THE STORY OF DR. WASSELL

A Paramount Picture in Technicolor   1944

CAST:

GARY COOPER *(Dr. Corydon M. Wassell)*; LARAINE DAY *(Madeleine Day)*; SIGNE HASSO *(Bettina)*; CAROL THURSTON *(Tremartini)*; DENNIS O'KEEFE *(Benjamin "Hoppy" Hopkins)*; CARL ESMOND *(Lt. Dirk Van Daal)*; STANLEY RIDGES *(Cdr. William B. Goggins)*; RENNY MC EVOY *(Joe Leinwerber)*; ELLIOTT REID *(William Anderson)*; MELVIN FRANCIS *(Himself)*; JOEL ALLEN *(Robert Kraus)*; PAUL KELLY *(Murdock)*; OLIVER THORNDIKE *(Alabam)*; JAMES MILLICAN *(Robert Elroy Whaley)*; MIKE KILIAN *(Thomas Borghetti)*; PHILIP AHN *(Ping)*; DOODLES WEAVER *(Harold Hunter)*; BARBARA BRITTON *(Ruth)*; RICHARD LOO *(Dr. Wei)*; DAVIDSON CLARK *(Dr. Holmes)*; SI JENKS *(The Arkansas Mailman)*; MORTON LOWRY *(Lt. Bainbridge)*; RICHARD NUGENT *(Capt. Carruthers)*; LESTER MATTHEWS *(Dr. Wayne)*; VICTOR VARCONI *(Capt. Ryk)*; GEORGE MACREADY *(A Dutch Officer)*; LUDWIG DONATH *(Dr. Vranken)*; FRANK PUGLIA *(Java Temple Guide)*; IRVING BACON *(Missionary)*; OTTOLA NES-MITH *(His Wife)*; JODY GILBERT *(Head Nurse)*; ANTHONY CARUSO *(Male Nurse)*; LOUIS JEAN HEYDT *(Ensign)*; MINOR WATSON *(Rear Admiral)*; ANN DORAN *(Praying Woman)*; JULIA FAYE *(Anne, a nurse)*; RON RANDELL, SARAH EDWARDS, JACK NORTON *(Passengers)*; CARLYLE BLACKWELL *(An American Marine)*; *and* DOUGLAS FOWLEY, MILES MANDER, EDITH BARRETT, WILLIAM HALL, CATHERINE CRAIG, SYBIL MERRITT, MARIE LOREDO, LORETTA LUIZ, LUKE CHAN, ISABEL COOPER, OLGA MARIE THUNIS, SAM FLINT, JACK LUDEN, HUGH BEAUMONT, CHARLES TROWBRIDGE, EDWARD EARLE, CHUCK HAMILTON, SVEN HUGO BORG, BRUCE WARREN, FRANK LACKTEEN, DORIS LILLY, HARVEY STEPHENS, FRED KOHLER, JR., IVAN TRIESAULT, PHILIP VAN ZANDT, GRETL DUPONT, GRIFF BARNETT, MAXINE FIFE, LANE CHANDLER, MILDRED HARRIS, JUNE KILGOUR, YVONNE DE CARLO, JAMES CORNELL, GLORIA DEA, BETH HARTMAN, ISABEL LAMAL.

CREDITS:

CECIL B. DE MILLE *(Director and Producer);* ALAN
LE MAY, CHARLES BENNETT *(Scenarists);* VICTOR MIL-
NER *(Photographer);* ANNE BAUCHENS *(Editor);* HUGO
GRENZBACH *(Sound Recorder);* GORDON JENNINGS,
FARCIOT EDOUART, W. WALLACE KELLEY *(Special
Photographic Effects);* GEORGE DUTTON *(Special
Sound Effects);* HANS DREIER, ROLAND ANDERSON *(Art
Directors);* GEORGE SAWLEY *(Set Decorator);* SIDNEY
BIDDELL *(Associate Producer);* ARTHUR ROSSON *(Sec-
ond Unit Director);* NATALIE KALMUS, WILLIAM
SNYDER *(Technicolor Consultants);* NATALIE VISART
(Costumer); VICTOR YOUNG *(Musical Score);* EDDIE
SALVEN, OSCAR RUDOLPH *(Assistant Directors);* COM-
MANDER CORYDON M. WASSELL *(Technical Consul-
tant);* LT. CDR. H. D. SMITH, U.S.N. (RET.), CAPT. FRED
F. ELLIS, B.M.M. (RET.) *(Technical Supervisors).*
Based on the story by COMMANDER CORYDON M.
WASSELL *and the original story by* JAMES HILTON.

SYNOPSIS:

Dr. Corydon M. Wassell, an obscure country doctor
from Arkansas, becomes a medical missionary in
China. He eventually meets a young nurse, Madeleine Day, with whom he falls in love, but, with
the ever-changing scene in China, they lose touch
with each other. When war is declared between
the United States and Japan, Wassell joins the
Navy and is sent to Java, where he is put in
charge of evacuating marines wounded in the
battle of Macassar.

The Japanese bomb Java and Wassell sees to it
that all of the wounded are evacuated. He stays
behind with ten grievously wounded men, whom
he takes through the jungle with the help of the
Dutch and British soldiers who are still on the
island, and gets them through to Australia, where
he is proclaimed a hero.

NOTES:

In his third film for Cecil B. DeMille, Cooper
played a doctor who was one of the heroes of the
war in the Pacific. The story was woven together
from interviews with Dr. Corydon M. Wassell and
re-worked by novelist James Hilton, at the request
of DeMille. The famed producer-director had
heard President Roosevelt speak of Dr. Wassell
on the radio in April of 1942, and the idea for a
filmed biography of his exploits came to him at

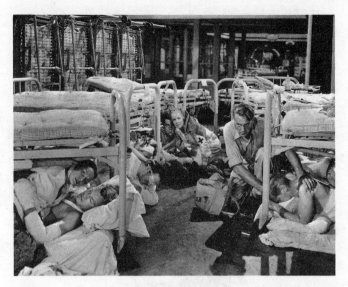

With Carol Thurston, Dennis O'Keefe,
Elliott Reid, Signe Hasso and Paul Kelly

With Elliott Reid and Signe Hasso

With Minor Watson

195

With Laraine Day

that time. After meeting Dr. Wassell himself, DeMille put the production wheels in motion.

Besides the facts surrounding the doctor's exploits on the island of Java, DeMille injected just about every cliché in the book, which the patriotic public didn't seem to mind. Said Bosley Crowther in his *New York Times* review: "Mr Cooper's performance as the good doctor is familiarly shy. Except for an occasional 'Good gravy!' and a startled look, you'd hardly know he was pressed."

Cooper was almost too much of a hero in this picture, but that was his major screen image— the strong, silent man of integrity, sincerity and good deeds. The best performance, however, was turned in by Dennis O'Keefe, as one of the wounded men. O'Keefe, who had appeared in some 200 movies in the 1930's as an extra under his real name, Bud Flannigan (including Cooper's *Mr. Deeds Goes to Town* and *The Plainsman*), came into his own with this film and went on to a lucrative career.

The splendid photographic effects of Gordon Jennings and Farciot Edouart and the sound effects handled by George Dutton were nominated for Academy Awards in their respective categories.

196

With Teresa Wright

CASANOVA BROWN

*A Christie Productions Picture
An International Pictures, Inc. Production
Released by RKO-Radio Pictures, Inc.   1944*

CAST:

GARY COOPER (*Casanova Brown*); TERESA WRIGHT (*Isabel Drury*); FRANK MORGAN (*Mr. Ferris*); ANITA LOUISE (*Madge Ferris*); PATRICIA COLLINGE (*Mrs. Drury*); EDMOND BREON (*Mr. Drury*); JILL ESMOND (*Dr. Zernerke*); EMORY PARNELL (*Frank*); ISABEL ELSOM (*Mrs. Ferris*); MARY TREEN (*Monica*); HALLIWELL HOBBES (*Butler*); LARRY JOE OLSEN (*Junior*); BYRON FOULGER (*Fletcher*); SARAH PADDEN (*Landlady*); ELOISE HARDT (*Doris Ferris*); GRADY SUTTON (*Tod*); FREDERICK BURTON (*Rev. Dean*); ROBERT DUDLEY (*Marriage Clerk*); ISABEL LA MAL (*Clerk's Wife*); FLORENCE LAKE (*Nurse Phillips*); ANN EVERS (*Nurse Petherbridge*); FRANCES MORRIS (*Nurse Gillespie*); NELL CRAIG (*4th Nurse*); LANE CHANDLER (*Orderly*); KAY DESLYS (*Fat Woman Patient*); OTTOLA NESMITH (*Patient's Nurse*); LORNA DUNN, KELLY FLINT, JULIA FAYE (*X-Ray Nurses*); DOROTHY TREE (*Nurse Clark*); ISABEL WITHERS (*Nurse, helps Casanova*); IRVING BACON (*Hotel Manager*); JAMES BURKE (*O'Leary*); FRANCIS SAYLES (*Elevator Operator*); PHIL TEAD (*License Clerk*); SNUB POLLARD (*Father at Baby Window*); GRACE CUNARD, VERNA KORNMAN, ANNA LUTHER, MARIAN GRAY, SADA SIMMONS (*Women at Baby Window*); LELAH TYLER (*Switchboard Operator*); CECIL STEWART (*Organist*); HELEN ST. RAYNER (*Soloist*); STEWART GARNER (*Usher*); MARY YOUNG (*Mrs. Dean*); JOHN BROWN (*Fire Chief*); and JACK GARGAN (*Interne*).

CREDITS:

SAM WOOD (*Director*); NUNNALLY JOHNSON (*Producer and Scenarist*); JOHN SEITZ (*Photographer*); THOMAS NEFF (*Editor*); ARTHUR LANGE (*Musical Score*); PERRY FERGUSON (*Art Director*); JULIA HERON (*Set Decorator*); MURIEL KING (*Costumer*);

BENJAMIN WINKLER (*Sound Recorder*); JOHN SHERWOOD (*Assistant Director*); CHARLES MAXWELL, CLIFFORD VAUGHAN, HOWARD JACKSON (*Musical Associates*). Based on the play *"The Little Accident"* by FLOYD DELL *and* THOMAS MITCHELL.

SYNOPSIS:

During the rehearsal for his wedding to Madge Ferris, timid English teacher Casanova Q. Brown learns that he is about to become a father, the unexpected result of a brief, whirlwind marriage, now annulled, to Isabel Drury. At the maternity hospital, Isabel tells Casanova that she is going to put the baby up for adoption, but after seeing his baby girl, Casanova revolts and kidnaps the child.

In his struggles to be mother as well as father, and to keep the whole thing a secret, the hotel chambermaid, Monica, and a page, Frank, help Casanova to such an extent that he determines to marry Monica to provide his daughter with a lawful mother. Finally, both his ex-bride and bride-to-be descend on him with their respective families and, after a gruelling time, Casanova finds that he and Isabel are still in love.

NOTES:

Casanova Brown was the first production of a newly formed independent group, composed of two expatriates of 20th Century-Fox (Nunnally Johnson and William Goetz) and Leo Spitz, a former RKO president. Their plans were to make two films a year under the International Pictures, Inc. banner.

Cooper's name did much to bolster the box-office business of this little comedy. The truth of the matter is, however, that the film was an engaging story—both ably played and directed (by Sam Wood)—by itself. And it won three Academy Award nominations in the bargain: Perry Ferguson for his art direction and Julia Heron for her set decorations; Arthur Lange for his musical score; and Thomas T. Moulton representing the Goldwyn Sound Department.

While some critics found *Casanova Brown* "trifling," "old fashioned" and an "unimportant bit of fluff," the *New York Morning Telegraph* thought, "The charm and distinctive personality of both Mr. Cooper and Miss Wright do more than a little to help." The *New York Daily News* felt the film was "delightful nonsense."

Alton Cook in the *New York World-Telegram* wrote, "The role is a boon to Gary Cooper, rescuing him from his recent strong dynamic characters in which he is so ineffectual. The very lack of these qualities is the foundation of his great talent. His work in this picture belongs with his best, right up with Mr. Deeds." Bosley Crowther, on the other hand, in *The New York Times* remarked, ". . . Mr. Cooper's somewhat obvious and ridiculous clowning over the babe takes on a silly complexion" and concluded with "All in all, there is so much endeavor with so little subject in this film that one is exposed to the impression that anything went for a laugh."

With Frank Morgan

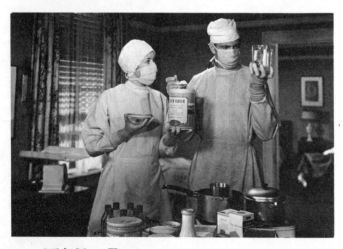

With Mary Treen

With Patricia Collinge, Edmond Breon and Teresa Wright

ALONG CAME JONES

A Cinema Artists Corp. Picture
An International Pictures, Inc. Production
Released by RKO-Radio Pictures, Inc.   1945

CAST:

GARY COOPER (*Melody Jones*); LORETTA YOUNG (*Cherry de Longpre*); WILLIAM DEMAREST (*George Fury*); DAN DURYEA (*Monte Jarrad*); FRANK SULLY (*Cherry's Brother*); RUSSELL SIMPSON (*Pop de Longpre*); ARTHUR LOFT (*Sheriff*); WILLARD ROBERTSON (*Luke Packard*); DON COSTELLO (*Gledhill*); RAY TEAL (*Kriendler*); WALTER SANDE (*Ira Waggoner*); LANE CHANDLER (*Boone*); FRANK CORDELL (*Guard on Coach*); LOU DAVIS, ED RANDOLPH, TOMMY COATES (*Passengers on Coach*); TONY ROUX (*Old Mexican*); ERVILLE ALDERSON (*Bartender*); PAUL SUTTON (*Man at Bar*); HERBERT HEYWOOD, FRANK HAGNEY, RALPH LITTLEFIELD, ERNIE ADAMS (*Townsmen*); LANE WATSON (*Town Character*); PAUL E. BURNS (*Small Man*); CHRIS PIN MARTIN (*Store Proprietor*); JACK BAXLEY (*Rancher on Street*); DOUG MORROW (*Rifleman*); RALPH DUNN (*Cotton*); GEOFFREY INGHAM, JOHN MERTON, TOM HERBERT (*Card Players*); CHARLES MORTON (*Fat Card Player*); LEE PHELPS (*Deputy*); BILLY ENGLE (*Wagon Driver*); BOB KORTMAN, FRANK MC CARROLL, HANK BELL, CHALKY WILLIAMS (*Posse*).

CREDITS:

STUART HEISLER (*Director*); GARY COOPER (*Producer*); NUNNALLY JOHNSON (*Scenarist*); MILTON KRASNER (*Photographer*); ARTHUR LANGE, HUGO FRIEDHOFER, CHARLES MAXWELL (*Musical Score*); THOMAS NEFF (*Editor*); PAUL WEATHERWAX (*Editorial Supervision*) WIARD B. IHNEN (*Production Designer*); JULIA HERON (*Set Decorator*); FRED LAU, ARTHUR JOHNS (*Sound Recorders*); WALTER PLUNKETT (*Costumer*); GUSTAV NORIN (*Makeup Artist*); ART BLACK (*Assistant Director*). *From an original story by* ALAN LE MAY.

SYNOPSIS:

Melody Jones, a mild-mannered cowpoke, drifts into a small town with his sidekick George Fury, innocently precipitating a situation in which he's at once mistaken for notorious road agent Monte Jarrad. Because of a similarity in physique and circumstantial evidence, Jones, who can't even handle a gun, eventually finds himself the unwitting and indirect cause of the slaying of the hold-up man.

As an inevitable result, he gets the latter's girl, Cherry, who, as things turn out, is forced to make a quick decision and drills the gunman right between the eyes just as Jones is about to be killed by the outlaw.

NOTES:

Cooper's association with director Stuart Heisler began back in 1934, when Heisler was editor on King Vidor's *The Wedding Night* with Cooper and Anna Sten. Now, 11 years later, Heisler was directing Cooper in the second film enterprise of International Pictures, Inc. (The firm was soon merged with Universal Pictures, to make Universal-International Pictures, Inc.).

With Loretta Young

Along Came Jones was Cooper's first hand at producing and was, when all the chips were down, a fun-western. It was almost as though Cooper was poking fun at all the beloved saddle tramps, including himself, who ever rode the silver screen. Loretta Young was his lovely co-star; William Demarest was around for laughs; and Dan Duryea added just the right touch of menace to the Old West.

Said *Variety*'s critic: "Cooper plays his usually languid self impressively, while Miss Young is decorative and photographed well. Demarest is in for some comedy relief, of which there is too little, while Dan Duryea is properly menacing as the killer." The *New York Daily News* said, in its 4-star review, "Not since his beloved 'Mr. Deeds' has he [Cooper] been able to expand on all the charm, befuddled naivete and droll humor at his command. That his current Melody Jones has all this, and then some, is perhaps largely due to the astuteness and skill of Nunnally Johnson, who knew not only what to capitalize on in his screenplay for Cooper, but precisely how. Stuart Heisler's direction is commendable."

With Loretta Young and William Demarest

With Dan Duryea

With Loretta Young

With Ingrid Bergman

SARATOGA TRUNK

A Warner Bros. Picture   1945

CAST:

GARY COOPER *(Col. Clint Maroon)*; INGRID BERGMAN *(Clio Dulaine)*; FLORA ROBSON *(Angelique Buiton)*; JERRY AUSTIN *(Cupidon)*; JOHN WARBURTON *(Bartholomew Van Steed)*; FLORENCE BATES *(Mrs. Coventry Bellop)*; CURT BOIS *(Augustin Haussy)*; JOHN ABBOTT *(Roscoe Bean)*; ETHEL GRIFFIES *(Mme. Clarissa Van Steed)*; MARLA SHELTON *(Mrs. Porcelain)*; HELEN FREEMAN *(Mrs. Nicholas Dulaine)*; SOPHIE HUXLEY *(Charlotte Dulaine)*; FRED ESSLER *(Monsieur Begue)*; LOUIS PAYNE *(Raymond Soule)*; SARAH EDWARDS *(Miss Diggs)*; ADRIENNE D'AMBRICOURT *(Grandmother Dulaine)*; JACQUELINE DE WIT *(Guilia Forosini)*; MINOR WATSON *(J. P. Reynolds)*; J. LEWIS JOHNSON, LIBBY TAYLOR, LILLIAN YARBO *(Servants)*; GENEVA WILLIAMS *(Blackberry Woman)*; RUBY DANDRIDGE *(Turbaned Vendor)*; PAUL BRYANT, SHELBY BACON *(Urchins)*; PETER CUSANELLI *(Coffee Proprietor)*; GEORGE HUMBERT *(Jambalaya Proprietor)*; BERTHA WOOLFORD *(Flower Woman)*; GEORGE REED *(Carriage Driver)*; AMELIA LIGGETT *(Mme. Begue)*; GEORGE BERANGER *(Leon, the Headwaiter)*; JOHN SYLVESTER *(Young Man Escort)*; EDMUND BREON *(McIntyre)*; WILLIAM B. DAVIDSON *(Mr. Stone)*; EDWARD FIELDING *(Mr. Bowers)*; THURSTON HALL *(Mr. Pound)*; ALICE FLEMING *(Woman on Piazza)*; RALPH DUNN *(Engineer)*; LANE CHANDLER *(Al)*; GLENN STRANGE *(Cowboy)*; CHESTER CLUTE *(Hotel Clerk)*; THEODORE VON ELTZ *(Hotel Manager)*; MONTE BLUE *(Fireman on Train)*; FRANKLYN FARNUM *(Gambler)*; BOB REEVES *(Soule Bodyguard)*; AL FERGUSON, HANK BELL *(Cowhands)*; DICK ELLIOTT *(Politician)*.

CREDITS:

SAM WOOD *(Director)*; HAL B. WALLIS *(Producer)*; CASEY ROBINSON *(Scenarist)*; ERNEST HALLER *(Photographer)*; MAX STEINER *(Musical Score)*; RALPH DAWSON *(Editor)*; CARL JULES WEYL *(Art Director)*;

With Jerry Austin and Ingrid Bergman

With Flora Robson

With John Warburton,
Jerry Austin
and Ingrid Bergman

FRED MAC LEAN (Set Decorator); JOSEPH ST. AMAND
(Production Designer); PERC WESTMORE (Makeup
Artist); LEAH RHODES (Costumer); LEO F. FORBSTEIN
(Musical Director); ROBERT B. LEE (Sound
Recorder); DALTON S. REYMOND (Technical Adviser);
LAWRENCE BUTLER (Special Effects); PHIL QUINN (Assistant Director). SONGS: "As Long as I Live" and
"Goin' Home" by CHARLES TOBIAS and MAX STEINER
and "Ah Suzette Chére" (sung by Miss Bergman).
From the novel by EDNA FERBER.

202

SYNOPSIS:

Beautiful fortune-hunter Clio Dulaine arrives
back in her native New Orleans, after a long
absence, with her bizarre body servant, the mulatto Angelique, and the dwarf Cupidon. In the
French market, Clio meets Clint Maroon, a cowboy
from Texas, and an immediate and intense mutual
love is ignited, despite Angelique's protests. All of
New Orleans buzzes over this romance, which reminds them all of the old Dulaine family scandal
involving Clio's dead parents.

Clint soon leaves New Orleans for Saratoga
Springs on business and, shortly, informs Clio that
the town is loaded with millionaires. After her
arrival, Clio sets out to ensnare wealthy Bartholomew Van Steed into marriage. Meanwhile,
Clint makes an agreement with Van Steed and
other financiers to clear the Saratoga Trunk Line
of a rival financial combine. In the face of great
opposition, the Texan and his gang save the
Trunk Line through spectacular fighting, although
Cupidon is badly injured.

Back in Saratoga Springs, Van Steed and Clio
are about to announce their engagement at a
fashionable costume ball when Clint staggers in,
carrying the unconscious Cupidon. Clio hurls herself at him with ecstatic relief, loudly proclaiming
her love for him, completely forgetting Van Steed

and hundreds of onlookers. She now knows she will marry Clint Maroon.

NOTES:

Warner Bros. filmed Edna Ferber's *Saratoga Trunk* with Cooper and Ingrid Bergman directly after the stars completed *For Whom the Bell Tolls* at Paramount. In fact, Sam Wood began filming on February 22, 1943, and finishing shooting on May 26, 1943. The film was probably ready for distribution by the end of that year, but, for some unknown reason, the release was held up until November of 1945. Prior to that time, the only audience to see it were the men and women of the Armed Forces, at service theatres.

Bergman was delicious in the wickedly comic part, which she played with great style. Cooper also seemed to be enjoying his role but unfortunately Casey Robinson's script was dull and bored audiences to death. For her marvelous portrayal of the mulatto servant Angelique, Flora Robson was nominated for an Academy Award as Best Supporting Actress of 1945.

Howard Barnes, in his *New York Herald Tribune* review, said "Cooper is perfect as the backwoodsman who tries unsuccessfully not to become entangled with the scheming spitfire. . . . It is a prodigal show, distinguished by several superior performances." Bosley Crowther, in *The New York Times* thought, ". . . it lacks a logical pattern of drama and character that the competent playing of Ingrid Bergman and Gary Cooper cannot supply. Mr. Cooper, while pleasantly roguish, has an air of substantial piety. *Saratoga Trunk*, however, is a piece of baggage labelled solely for its two stars."

With Ingrid Bergman

With Lilli Palmer

CLOAK AND DAGGER

*A United States Pictures Production
Released by Warner Bros.   1946*

CAST:

GARY COOPER *(Prof. Alvah Jesper)*; LILLI PALMER *(Gina)*; ROBERT ALDA *(Pinkie)*; VLADIMIR SOKOLOFF *(Polda)*; J. EDWARD BROMBERG *(Trenk)*; MARJORIE HOSHELLE *(Ann Dawson)*; LUDWIG STOSSEL *(The German)*; HELENE THIMIG *(Katerin Lodor)*; DAN SEYMOUR *(Marsoli)*; MARC LAWRENCE *(Luigi)*; JAMES FLAVIN *(Col. Walsh)*; PAT O'MOORE *(The Englishman)*; CHARLES MARSH *(Erich)*; DON TURNER *(Lingg)*; CLIFTON YOUNG *(American Commander)*; ROSS FORD *(Paratrooper)*; ROBERT COOTE *(Cronin)*; HANS SCHUMM, PETER MICHAEL *(German Agents)*; YOLA D'AVRIL, CLAIRE DU BREY, LOTTIE STEIN *(Nurses)*; LYNNE LYONS *(Woman in Bank, Double)*; RORY MALLINSON *(Paul)*; ED PARKER, GIL PERKINS *(Gestapo)*; BRUCE LESTER *(British Officer)*; LEON LENOIR *(Italian Soldier)*; OTTO REICHOW, ARNO FREY *(German Soldiers)*; MARIA MONTEIL, LILLIAN NICHOLSON *(Nuns)*; BOBBY SANTON *(Italian Boy)*; ELVIRA CURCI *(Woman in Street)*; HELLA CROSSLEY *(Rachele)*; DOUGLAS WALTON *(British Pilot)*; VERNON DOWNING *(British Sergeant)*; HOLMES HERBERT *(British Officer)*; FRANK WILCOX *(American Officer)*; MICHAEL BURKE *(OSS Agent)*.

CREDITS:

FRITZ LANG *(Director)*; MILTON SPERLING *(Producer)*; ALBERT MALTZ, RING LARDNER, JR. *(Scenarists)*; SOL POLITO *(Photographer)*; MAX STEINER *(Musical Score)*; HUGO FRIEDHOFER *(Orchestrator)* CHRISTIAN NYBY *(Editor)*; MAX PARKER *(Art Director)*; FRANCIS J. SCHEID *(Sound Recorder)*; WALTER TILFORD *(Set Decorator)*; LEAH RHODES *(Costumer)*; HARRY BARNDOLLAR, EDWIN B. DU PAR *(Special Effects)*; PERC WESTMORE *(Makeup Artist)*; LEO F. FORBSTEIN *(Musical Director)*; RUSSELL SAUNDERS *(Assistant Director)*; MICHAEL BURKE *(Technical Adviser)*. *From an Original Story by* BORIS INGSTER *and* JOHN LARKIN.

Suggested by the book by COREY FORD *and* ALASTAIR MAC BAIN.

SYNOPSIS:

Mild-mannered Alvah Jesper, a professor of physics at a leading university, is drafted by the OSS to enter first Switzerland, then Italy, just prior to the end of World War II. His mission is to locate Dr. Polda, an atomic scientist being held captive by the Nazis. While in Switzerland, he contacts Austrian scientist Katerin Lodor to get information on Polda's whereabouts, but is spotted and followed by Ann Dawson, a Nazi spy. Shortly thereafter, Katerin Lodor is brutally murdered.

Quickly moving on to Italy, Jesper has a romance with an Italian partisan named Gina, who —along with Pinkie—has been assigned to aid him in locating Dr. Polda. In disguise, Jesper visits the scientist who, like Katerin Lodor, fears for his life. Jesper is determined to remove Polda to the safety of the United States and, through a carefully worked out plan, the group smuggles Polda to a deserted farmhouse near a landing strip where a plane is to pick them up. Although their escape is nearly averted by the enemy, Jesper and Polda board the plane, but not before Jesper promises Gina that he will return to her after the war.

NOTES:

As a change of pace, Cooper played a man drafted into service for the OSS (Office of Strategic Services) during the latter years of World War II. He wasn't bad in the role, but his total American demeanor was a bit hard to accept when one knew he wasn't supposed to be detected.

Cloak and Dagger's ad campaign stressed: "The Moment He Fell in Love Was His Moment of Greatest Danger!" The woman he fell in love with was Lilli Palmer, making her American film debut, due largely to her superb portrayal in *The Rake's Progress* (*Notorious Gentleman*) with Rex Harrison.

Variety noted "Cooper fits requirements of his role, turning in his usual topnotch job." Howard Barnes was more explicit in his *New York Herald Tribune* review, saying, "The presence of Gary Cooper in the starring role is more important to the entertainment than his simulated activities. Cooper is not altogether at ease as a counter-intelligence agent. . . . He has a tendency to back away from test-tubes and he han-

dles the subdued romance gingerly. It is only when he is involved in the considerable violence of the production that he lends it unerring authority."

The New York Times' Bosley Crowther said, "As the hero, Gary Cooper—an old hand at partisan war—gives a good Gary Cooper performance, which is what was expected of him. Mr. Lang, being wise and experienced, has not pretended to show any more than a romantic thriller, which is what his writers prepared."

With Marjorie Hoshelle

With Robert Alda, Vladimir Sokoloff and Lilli Palmer

On the set with Lilli Palmer and director Fritz Lang

With Katherine De Mille

UNCONQUERED

A Paramount Picture in Technicolor 1947

CAST:

GARY COOPER (*Capt. Christopher Holden*); PAULETTE GODDARD (*Abigail Martha Hale*); HOWARD DA SILVA (*Martin Garth*); BORIS KARLOFF (*Guyasuta, Chief of the Senecas*); CECIL KELLAWAY (*Jeremy Love*); WARD BOND (*John Fraser*); KATHERINE DE MILLE (*Hannah*); HENRY WILCOXON (*Capt. Steele*); SIR C. AUBREY SMITH (*Lord Chief Justice*); VICTOR VARCONI (*Capt. Simeon Ecuyer*); VIRGINIA GREY (*Diana*); PORTER HALL (*Leach*); MIKE MAZURKI (*Dave Bone*); ROBERT WARWICK (*Pontiac, Chief of the Ottawas*); RICHARD GAINES (*Col. George Washington*); VIRGINIA CAMPBELL (*Mrs. Fraser*); GAVIN MUIR (*Lt. Fergus McKenzie*); ALAN NAPIER (*Sir William Johnson*); NAN SUTHERLAND (*Mrs. Pruitt*); MARC LAWRENCE (*Sioto*); JANE NIGH (*Evelyn*); GRIFF BARNETT (*Brother Andrews*); JOHN MYLONG (*Col. Henry Bouquet*); LLOYD BRIDGES (*Lt. Hutchins*); OLIVER THORNDIKE (*Lt. Baillie*); JACK PENNICK (*Jim Lovat*); PAUL E. BURNS (*Dan McCoy*); DAVIDSON CLARK (*Mr.* *Carroll*); DOROTHY ADAMS (*Mrs. Bront*); CLARENCE MUSE (*Jason*); RAYMOND HATTON (*Venango Scout*); JULIA FAYE (*The Widow Swivens*); CHIEF THUNDERCLOUD (*Chief Killbuck*); CHARLES B. MIDDLETON (*Mulligan*); TINY JONES (*Bondswoman*); FRED KOHLER, JR. (*Sergeant*); *and* IRON EYES CODY, OLAF HYTTEN, ERIC ALDEN, FRANK HAGNEY, RAY TEAL, EDGAR DEARING, NOBLE JOHNSON, SALLY RAWLINSON, CHUCK HAMILTON, BYRON FOULGER, ETHEL WALES, BOB KORTMAN, FRANCIS MC DONALD, JUNE HARRIS, WILLIAM HAADE, JEFF COREY, ERVILLE ALDERSON, LEX BARKER, MIKE KILIAN, LANE CHANDLER, ANNA LEHR, JAY SILVERHEELS, ISABEL CHABING COOPER, CHARMIENNE HARKER, BELLE MITCHELL, FERNANDA ELISCU, CLAIRE DU BREY, MIMI AGUGLIA, INEZ PALANGE, ROSE HIGGINS, CONSTANCE PURDY, AL FERGUSON, OTTOLA NESMITH, GRETA GRANSTEDT, GERTRUDE VALERIE, CHRISTOPHER CLARK, FRANK WILCOX, BILL MURPHY.

With Paulette Goddard

With Paulette Goddard

With Henry Wilcoxon,
Howard Da Silva, Victor Varconi
and Paulette Goddard

With Boris Karloff
and Marc Lawrence

With Virginia Grey

CREDITS:

CECIL B. DE MILLE *(Director and Producer)*; CHARLES BENNETT, FREDERIC M. FRANK, JESSE LASKY, JR. *(Scenarists)*; RAY RENNAHAN *(Photographer)*; ANNE BAUCHENS *(Editor)*; HANS DREIER, WALTER TYLER *(Art Directors)*; ARTHUR ROSSON *(Second Unit Director)*; VICTOR YOUNG *(Musical Score)*; SAM COMER, STANLEY JAY SAWLEY *(Set Decorators)*; GORDON JENNINGS, FARCIOT EDOUART, W. WALLACE KELLEY, PAUL LERPAE, DEVEREUX JENNINGS *(Special Photographic Effects)*; GEORGE DUTTON *(Special Sound Effects)*; EDWARD SALVEN *(Assistant Director)*; GWEN WAKELING, MME. BARBARA KARINSKA *(Costumers)*; WALLY WESTMORE *(Makeup Artist)*; HUGO GRENZBACH, JOHN COPE *(Sound Recorders)*; JACK CROSBY *(Choreographer)*; SONG: *"Whippoorwills-a-Singing"* by RAY EVANS, JAY LIVINGSTON; CAPT. FRED F. ELLIS, B.M.M. (RET.), IRON EYES CODY *(Technical Supervisors)*; NATALIE KALMUS, ROBERT BROWER *(Technicolor Consultants)*. *Based on a novel by* NEIL H. SWANSON.

SYNOPSIS:

Abigail Martha Hale, a young English girl accused unjustly of a crime, is sentenced to fourteen years' slavery in North America in the early 1760's. At the auction block, the highest bid comes from Captain Christopher Holden, a Virginia militiaman whom she had met aboard the ship. Holden, a true patriot, is aware of Martin Garth's trading with the restless Indians, because of his marriage to Hannah, a Chief's daughter.

Garth plays an important role in the historic "Pontiac Conspiracy" in which eighteen Indian nations pledge their allegiance to the great chief of the Ottawas, thus joining him in his plan to drive the colonists out of their land.

Adventures and misadventures result in Holden being court-martialed for desertion and sentenced to death. Since he had already saved her from the Indians, Abigail helps him escape to a military fort, where he gets men enough to put down the rebellion.

NOTES:

Americana was again invaded by Cecil B. DeMille, Cooper and Paulette Goddard—joined this trip by Boris Karloff, as a campy Indian chief and DeMille's adopted daughter Katherine, as his spitfire daughter. Despite its flaws, which critics insisted were many, *Unconquered* is a most enjoyable piece of semi-history, even after repeated viewings. There's something about DeMille's treatment of historical subjects and/or events that is always satisfying.

Time magazine called it "Cecil Blount De Mille's florid, $5,000,000, Technicolored celebration of Gary Cooper's virility, Paulette Goddard's femininity, and the American Frontier Spirit." The critic for the *Baltimore Sun* noted that "In some ways *Unconquered* is better than anything Mr. DeMille has done. Although some scenes are improbable to the point of absurdity, the picture, in the main, sticks closer to the main current of history than has been the case with most of his productions. Mr. Cooper has a field day with this role, he looks and acts the part. . . ." *The New Yorker* just thought it a "flaccid epic."

Bosley Crowther in *The New York Times*, while describing *Unconquered*'s virtues, remarked, ". . . isn't the chance of watching Gary Cooper, in a colonial costume and tri-corner hat, acting the gallant frontiersman sufficient for anyone? If it isn't, there's Paulette Goddard as the red-headed, flashing-eyed slave, exhibited in numerous situations, from a bathtub to an Indian torture stake."

One of the spectacular sequences had Cooper and Goddard go over the rapids in a canoe, a feat that helped earn an Academy Award nomination for the Special Effects crew.

208

1. WILLIAM BENDIX	9. GEORGE REEVES	17. DOROTHY BARRETT	25. VIRGINIA FIELD	33. GARY COOPER	41. LUCILLE BARKLEY
2. HOWARD DA SILVA	10. WILLIAM DEMAREST	18. JUNE HARRIS	26. BURT LANCASTER	34. DOROTHY LAMOUR	42. NANETTE PARKS
3. MACDONALD CAREY	11. RICHARD WEBB	19. PATRIC KNOWLES	27. LIZABETH SCOTT	35. JOAN CAULFIELD	43. WANDA HENDRIX
4. BARRY FITZGERALD	12. JOHNNY COY	20. MAVIS MURRAY	28. BOB HOPE	36. WILLIAM HOLDEN	44. MONA FREEMAN
5. CECIL KELLAWAY	13. RAE PATTERSON	21. JOHN LUND	29. OLGA SAN JUAN	37. SONNY TUFTS	45. STANLEY CLEMENTS
6. MARILYN GRAY	14. ROGER DANN	22. MIKHAIL RASUMNY	30. MARY HATCHER	38. SALLY RAWLINSON	46. ANDRA VERNE
7. STERLING HAYDEN	15. BILLY DeWOLFE	23. FRANK FAYLEN	31. BING CROSBY	39. ALAN LADD	47. GAIL RUSSELL
8. CATHERINE CRAIG	16. RENEE RANDALL	24. ARLEEN WHELAN	32. JANET THOMAS	40. VERONICA LAKE	48. PAT WHITE

With some of the stars and starlets

VARIETY GIRL

A Paramount Picture   1947

CAST:

MARY HATCHER (*Catherine Brown*); OLGA SAN JUAN (*Amber La Vonne*); DE FOREST KELLEY (*Bob Kirby*); WILLIAM DEMAREST (*Barker*); FRANK FAYLEN (*Stage Manager*); FRANK FERGUSON (*J. R. O'Connell*); GLENN TRYON (*Bill Farris*); NELLA WALKER (*Mrs. Webster*); TORBEN MEYER (*Headwaiter, Brown Derby*); JACK NORTON (*Busboy*); ELAINE RILEY (*Cashier*); CHARLES VICTOR (*O'Connell's Assistant*); GUS TAUTE (*Assistant's Assistant*); HARRY HAYDEN (*Stage Manager, Grauman's Chinese*); JANET THOMAS, ROBERTA JONAY (*Girls*); WALLACE EARL (*Girl with Sheep Dog*); DICK KEENE (*Dog Trainer*); ANN DORAN (*Hairdresser*); JERRY JAMES (*Assistant Director*); ERIC ALDEN (*Makeup Man*); FRANK MAYO (*Director*); RUSSELL HICKS, CHARLES COLEMAN, EDDIE FETHERSTON (*Men in Steam Bath*); FRANK HAGNEY (*Attendant*).

GUEST STARS (AS THEMSELVES):

BING CROSBY, BOB HOPE, GARY COOPER, RAY MILLAND, ALAN LADD, BARBARA STANWYCK, PAULETTE GODDARD, DOROTHY LAMOUR, SONNY TUFTS, JOAN CAULFIELD, WILLIAM HOLDEN, LIZABETH SCOTT, BURT LANCASTER, GAIL RUSSELL, DIANA LYNN, STERLING HAYDEN, ROBERT PRESTON, VERONICA LAKE, JOHN LUND, WILLIAM BENDIX, BARRY FITZGERALD, CASS DALEY, HOWARD DA SILVA, MACDONALD CAREY, *and* BILLY DE WOLFE, PATRIC KNOWLES, MONA FREEMAN, CECIL KELLAWAY, VIRGINIA FIELD, RICHARD WEBB, ARLEEN WHELAN, JOHNNY COY, STANLEY CLEMENTS, WANDA HENDRIX, MIKAIL RASUMNY, GEORGE REEVES, CECIL B. DE MILLE, MITCHELL LEISEN, FRANK BUTLER, GEORGE MARSHALL, PEARL BAILEY, SPIKE JONES & HIS CITY SLICKERS, ROGER DANN, JIM & MILDRED MULCAY *and* BARNEY DEAN.

CREDITS:

GEORGE MARSHALL (*Director*); DANIEL DARE (*Producer*); EDMUND HARTMANN, FRANK TASHLIN, ROBERT WELCH, MONTE BRICE (*Scenarists*); LIONEL LINDON, STUART THOMPSON (*Photographers*); HANS DREIER, ROBERT CLATWORTHY (*Art Directors*); SAM COMER, ROSS DOWD (*Set Decorators*); JOSEPH J. LILLEY (*Musical Score*); EDITH HEAD (*Star's Costumer*); DOROTHY O'HARA (*Production Costumer*); WALDO ANGELO (*Chorus Costumer*); TROY SANDERS (*Musical Associate*); LE ROY STONE (*Editor*); THORNTON HEE, WILLIAM COTTRELL (*Special Puppetoon Sequence*); VAN CLEAVE (*Special Orchestral Arrangements*); WALLY WESTMORE (*Makeup Artist*); GEORGE TEMPLETON (*Assistant Director*); GORDON JENNINGS (*Special Photographic Effects*); FARCIOT EDOUART (*Process Photography*); EUGENE MERRITT, JOHN COPE (*Sound Recorders*); SONGS: "*Tallahassee*," "*He Can Waltz*," "*Your Heart Calling Mine*," "*I Must Have Been Madly in Love*," "*Impossible Things*," "*The French*," and "*I Want My Money Back*" by FRANK LOESSER; "*Harmony*" by JOHNNY BURKE and JAMES VAN HEUSEN; "*Tired*" by ALLAN ROBERTS and DORIS FISHER; "*Romeow and Julicat*" by EDWARD PLUMB; "*Mildred's Boogie*" by MILDRED and JIM MULCAY; "*Tiger Rag*" by the ORIGINAL DIXIELAND JAZZ BAND. BILLY DANIELS, BERNARD PEARCE (*Choreographers*).

SYNOPSIS:

Catherine Brown and Amber La Vonne are in Hollywood seeking screen careers. They visit Grauman's Chinese Theatre, the Brown Derby and other Hollywood landmarks before crashing the gate at Paramount Studios, where they become involved in numerous comic situations with various actors and technicians on the lot. At the climactic Variety Club show, both girls are vindicated—for it is learned that Catherine is really the original Variety Girl.

NOTES:

This musical extravaganza, based on the founding of the Variety Clubs of America, dates back to 1928 when a group of theatre men in Pittsburgh adopted a foundling and formed the first Variety Club for the aid of underprivileged children. Just about every Paramount star and featured player, plus scores of young tyros—together with some Technicolor cartoon sequences—were used to help fill out the flimsy storyline. Cooper, as one of the many guest stars, appeared in several scenes on and about the Paramount lot.

Otis L. Guernsey, in the *New York Herald Tribune*, noted "Many guest appearances are more or less on a level with a scene showing Gary Cooper unhappily astride a merry-go-round horse. The foundation of the humor here is a Hollywood attempt to kid itself, but the film's incidents rarely rise above a half-hearted slapstick." On the other hand, the *New York Times* critic thought "*Variety Girl* is hodge-podge, to be sure. But let's not quibble about its lack of form, because it is a hearty slam-bang entertainment wherein the good very definitely outweighs the poor."

With Ann Sheridan

GOOD SAM

*A Rainbow Productions, Inc. Picture
Released by RKO-Radio Pictures, Inc.*   *1948*

CAST:

GARY COOPER (*Sam Clayton*); ANN SHERIDAN (*Lu Clayton*); RAY COLLINS (*Reverend Daniels*); EDMUND LOWE (*H. C. Borden*); JOAN LORRING (*Shirley Mae*); CLINTON SUNDBERG (*Nelson*); MINERVA URECAL (*Mrs. Nelson*); LOUISE BEAVERS (*Chloe*); DICK ROSS (*Claude*); LORA LEE MICHEL (*Lulu*); BOBBY DOLAN, JR. (*Butch*); MATT MOORE (*Mr. Butler*); NETTA PACKER (*Mrs. Butler*); RUTH ROMAN (*Ruthie*); CAROL STEVENS (*Mrs. Adams*); TODD KARNS (*Joe Adams*); IRVING BACON (*Tramp*); WILLIAM FRAWLEY (*Tom*); HARRY HAYDEN (*Banker*); IRMGARD DAWSON, JANE ALLAN (*Girls*); TOM DUGAN (*Santa Claus*); SARAH EDWARDS (*Mrs. Gilmore*); RUTH SANDERSON (*Sam's Secretary*); MARTA MITROVICH (*Mysterious Woman*); MIMI DOYLE (*Red Cross Nurse*); FRANKLIN PARKER (*Photographer*); IDA MOORE (*Old Lady*); FLORENCE AUER (*Woman on Bus*); DICK WESSELL (*Bus Driver*); SEDAL BENNETT (*Woman Chasing Bus*); JACK GARGAN, BESS FLOWERS (*Parents*); ALMIRA SESSIONS (*Landlady*); GARRY OWENS (*Taxi Driver*); STANLEY MC KAY (*Young Minister*); BERT ROACH (*Whispering Usher*); BOB TIDWELL (*Telegraph Boy*); ANN LAWRENCE (*Salvation Army Girl*); JOE HINDS, FRANCIS STEVENS (*Salvation Army Workers*); JOSEPH CREHAN (*Casey*); WILLIAM HAADE (*Taxi Driver*).

CREDITS:

LEO MC CAREY (*Director and Producer*); KEN ENGLUND (*Scenarist*); GEORGE BARNES (*Photographer*); JAMES MC KAY (*Editor*); ROBERT EMMETT DOLAN (*Musical Score*); JOHN B. GOODMAN (*Art Director*); RUSSELL A. CULLY (*Special Effects*); JESSE HIBBS (*Assistant Director*); JOHN L. CASS, CLEM PORTMAN (*Sound Recorders*). *Based on a story by* LEO MC CAREY *and* JOHN KLORER.

With Joan Lorring

SYNOPSIS:

Everyone but his wife, Lu, thinks Sam Clayton is a good Samaritan; she calls him a soft touch. Sam loans a neighbor his car and ends up paying the garage bill and asking the repairman to dinner. He lends money that he and Lu were saving for a new home to a young couple, to enable them to buy a business and have a baby. Sam even takes on Lu's brother Claude, a no-good sponger who won't work once Sam gets him a job. Sam even prevents Shirley Mae, a sassy salesgirl working in the store in which Sam is General Manager, from committing suicide.

Yet, when Sam needs money badly, no one comes forth to offer aid. Disgusted, he goes on a binge and ends up in a rescue mission. However, his friends belatedly rally around him and he is made vice president of the store and returns home.

NOTES:

This engaging little comedy had some very funny moments in it, but director Leo McCarey got

trapped by his own ideas. Cooper was more or less a straight man to a line-up of supporting and/or character actors who seemed to get the best business, best lines and the best of everything. One can look befuddled for only so long and then, where does one go?

Said *The New Yorker:* "The picture, strung together like a vaudeville show, gives all hands a chance to do a turn with Mr. Cooper. Toward the end of the piece, he looked pretty tired to me, and I can't say that I blamed him." *Cue* magazine reported "It may be unkind to quote vital statistics to make the point, but Mr. Cooper is by now a grown man, and his boyish bashfulness, sheepish grins, trembling lip and fluttering eyelids are actor's tricks he can surely do without." *Time* thought, "Gary Cooper is probably better qualified than most Hollywood leading men, to suggest a nice guy who cannot say no. Until it comes to share, with the picture as a whole, its air of haggard and ill-concealed desperation, he does a beautiful job."

With Almira Sessions

With Ann Sheridan

With Edmund Lowe and Sarah Edwards

On the set with director Leo McCarey

On the set with director King Vidor
and author Ayn Rand

THE FOUNTAINHEAD

A Warner Bros. Picture   1948

CAST:

GARY COOPER *(Howard Roark);* PATRICIA NEAL *(Dominique);* RAYMOND MASSEY *(Gail Wynand);* KENT SMITH *(Peter Keating);* ROBERT DOUGLAS *(Ellsworth Toohey);* HENRY HULL *(Henry Cameron);* RAY COLLINS *(Enright);* MORONI OLSEN *(Chairman);* JEROME COWAN *(Alvah Scarret);* PAUL HARVEY *(A Business Man);* HARRY WOODS *(The Superintendent);* PAUL STANTON *(The Dean);* BOB ALDEN *(Newsboy);* TRISTRAM COFFIN *(Secretary);* ROY GORDON *(Vice-President);* ISABEL WITHERS *(Secretary);* ALMIRA SESSIONS *(Housekeeper);* TITO VUOLO, WILLIAM HAADE *(Workers);* GAIL BONNEY *(Woman);* THURSTON HALL *(Businessman);* DOROTHY CHRISTY *(Society Woman);* HARLAN WARDE *(Young Man);* JONATHAN HALE *(Guy Franchon);* FRANK WILCOX *(Gordon Prescott);* DOUGLAS KENNEDY *(Reporter);* PIERRE WATKIN, SELMER JACKSON *(Officials);* JOHN DOUCETTE *(Gus Webb);* JOHN ALVIN *(Young Intellectual);* GERALDINE WALL *(Woman);* FRED KELSEY *(Old Watchman);* PAUL NEWLAND GEORGE SHERWOOD *(Policemen);* LOIS AUSTIN *(Woman Guest);* JOSEPHINE WHITTELL *(Hostess);* LESTER DORR *(Man);* BILL DAGWELL *(Shipping Clerk);* CHARLES TROWBRIDGE, RUSSELL HICKS, RAYMOND LARGAY, CHARLES EVANS *(Directors);* MORRIS ANKRUM *(Prosecutor);* GRIFF BARNETT *(Judge);* G. PAT COLLINS *(Foreman);* ANN DORAN, RUTHELMA STEVENS *(Secretaries);* CREIGHTON HALE *(Clerk);* PHILO MC CULLOUGH *(Bailiff).*

CREDITS:

KING VIDOR *(Director);* HENRY BLANKE *(Producer);* AYN RAND *(Scenarist);* ROBERT BURKS *(Photographer);* DAVID WEISBART *(Editor);* EDWARD CARRERE *(Art Director);* MAX STEINER *(Musical Score);* OLIVER S. GARRETSON *(Sound Recorder);* WILLIAM KUEHL *(Set Dec-

214

With Henry Hull

With Kent Smith

orator); JACK DANIELS (Dialogue Director); MURRAY CUTTER (Orchestrator); WILLIAM MCGANN, EDWIN DU PAR, H. F. KOENEKAMP, JOHN HOLDEN (Special Effects); MILO ANDERSON (Costumer); PERC WESTMORE, JOHN WALLACE (Makeup Artists); DICK MAYBERRY (Assistant Director); ERIC STACEY (Production Manager); GERTRUDE WHEELER (Hair Stylist); HAROLD NOYSE (Grip); EARL ELLWOOD (Gaffer); JACK WOODS (Still Man); JAMES BELL (Operating Cameraman); and RITA MICHAELS (Script Supervisor). From the novel "The Fountainhead" by AYN RAND.

SYNOPSIS:

Howard Roark, an idealistic and highly unorthodox architect with financial difficulties, takes a job in a stone quarry where he meets Dominique, a beautiful heiress. Mutual attraction soon becomes love, but Roark ends the affair abruptly and returns to New York when he is offered an architectural commission. Dominique, meanwhile, weds newspaper tycoon Gail Wynand, whose paper, "The Banner," wages a violent campaign against Roark's ideas.

Soon, Peter Keating, a society architect, enlists Roark's aid in the design of a proposed public-housing project. Roark agrees, although he insists that, once his designs are accepted, nothing can be changed. Much later, after returning from a trip with Wynand, now his ally, Roark discovers innumerable changes in his original conception and, in a rage, destroys the unfinished structure with dynamite.

At his trial, Roark wins an acquittal by a brilliant self-defense. Wynand, frantic because he was unable to help his friend, kills himself, but commissions Roark to build the world's highest building as his memorial. Roark—with Dominique, now his wife, beside him—begins working on this assignment.

NOTES:

The film version of Ayn Rand's 1943 novel, *The Fountainhead*, was almost nothing like the original book. Miss Rand's philosophy, Objectivism, was only hinted at in this initial effort, although it was later fully documented in three non-fiction works. With Ayn Rand herself writing the screenplay, one could easily have expected a little more of her original concepts.

Cooper was the wrong choice, of course, and

216

he didn't seem to understand, or care, about the deeper philosophical meanings and drives which motivated architectural-genius Howard Roark from one plane to another. Director King Vidor later said, in *Sight and Sound,* "I didn't think that Cooper was well cast, but he was cast before I was. I thought it should have been someone like Bogart, a more arrogant type of man. But after I forgot all that and saw it several years later I accepted Cooper doing it. Pat Neal I thought marvellous, splendid. I liked her tremendously."

Screenland magazine quipped, "If you like deep thinking, hidden meanings, plus pure modern architecture, this is something for which you have been waiting a long time." Another critic felt, "Cooper has an uneasy time in the miscasting as the plot's hero. Given lengthy sides to read, Cooper fails to sustain the mood demanded and the faltering delivery emphasizes his bent for the monosyllabic."

With Patricia Neal and Ray Collins

217

With Dennis Morgan

IT'S A GREAT FEELING

A Warner Bros. Picture in Technicolor   1949

CAST:

DENNIS MORGAN *(Himself);* DORIS DAY *(Judy Adams);*
JACK CARSON *(Himself);* BILL GOODWIN *(Arthur
Trent);* IRVING BACON *(Information Clerk);* CLAIRE
CARLETON *(Grace);* HARLAN WARDE *(Publicity Man);*
JACQUELINE DE WIT *(Trent's Secretary);* THE
MAZZONE-ABBOTT DANCERS; WILFRED LUCAS *(Mr.
Adams);* PAT FLAHERTY *(Gate Guard);* WENDY LEE
(Manicurist); NITA TALBOT, EVE WHITNEY, CAROL
BREWSTER, SUE CASEY, JOAN VOHS *(Models);* LOIS
AUSTIN *(Saleslady);* TOM DUGAN *(Wrestling Fan in
Bar);* JAMES HOLDEN *(Soda Jerk);* JEAN ANDREN
(Headwaitress); DUDLEY DICKERSON *(Porter);* SANDRA
GOULD *(Train Passenger, upper berth);* SHIRLEY BAL-
LARD *(Beautiful Girl on Bike);* and ERROL FLYNN
(The Groom, Jeffrey Bushfinkle).

GUEST STARS (AS THEMSELVES):

GARY COOPER, JOAN CRAWFORD, SYDNEY GREENSTREET,

DANNY KAYE, PATRICIA NEAL, ELEANOR PARKER, RON-
ALD REAGAN, EDWARD G. ROBINSON, JANE WYMAN, *and
directors* DAVID BUTLER, MICHAEL CURTIZ, KING VIDOR
and RAOUL WALSH.

CREDITS:

DAVID BUTLER *(Director);* ALEX GOTTLIEB *(Producer);*
JACK ROSE, MEL SHAVELSON *(Scenarists);* WILFRID M.
CLINE *(Photographer);* STANLEY FLEISCHER *(Art Di-
rector);* IRENE MOORE *(Editor);* DOLPH THOMAS, DAVID
FORREST *(Sound Recorders);* WILLIAM MC GANN, H. F.
KOENEKAMP *(Special Effects);* HERSCHEL DAUGHERTY
(Dialogue Director); LYLE B. HEIFSNIDER *(Set Deco-
rator);* RAY HEINDORF *(Musical Director);* SIDNEY
CUTNER, LEO SHUKEN *(Orchestrators);* LE ROY PRINZ
(Choreographer); MILO ANDERSON *(Costumer);* PERC
WESTMORE *(Makeup Artist);* NATALIE KALMUS,
MITCHELL KOVALESKI *(Technicolor Consultants);*

218

PHIL QUINN (*Assistant Director*); FRANK MATTISON (*Unit Manager*). SONGS: *"It's a Great Feeling," "Give Me a Song with a Beautiful Melody," "Fiddle Dee Dee," "At the Café Rendezvous," "That Was a Big Fat Lie," "There's Nothing Rougher than Love" and "Blame My Absent-Minded Heart" by* JULE STYNE *and* SAMMY CAHN. *From a story by* I. A. L. DIAMOND.

SYNOPSIS:

Jack Carson promises waitress Judy Adams a film career if she'll pose as his pregnant wife to win the sympathy of actor Dennis Morgan, who Carson wants to star in a picture which he is to direct. Taking pity on Carson, Morgan signs. However, they soon find out that no female star will work under Carson's direction. Morgan then suggests Judy, who no longer wants the bright lights of Hollywood and wants to return to Wisconsin and marry her childhood sweetheart, Jeffrey Bushfinkle.

Together, Carson and Morgan push Judy at producer Arthur Trent, thus alienating him completely—until he hears Judy sing. He sends the boys after her, but they're too late, for Judy is on her way home. They follow her and arrive just as she's being married to Jeffrey Bushfinkle.

NOTES:

Since Cooper was now a star on the Warner roster, he again was asked to do "box office duty." He appeared on the Warner lot, had a soda with Dennis Morgan, and, for authenticity, a scene from the then-filming *The Fountainhead* with Patricia Neal, being directed by King Vidor, was used. The *New York Times* critic said, "The feeling it leaves may not be great precisely, but it is pleasant."

On the set with Dennis Morgan
and director David Butler

With Jane Wyatt

TASK FORCE

A Warner Bros. Picture   1949

CAST:

GARY COOPER *(Jonathan L. Scott);* JANE WYATT *(Mary Morgan);* WAYNE MORRIS *(McKinney);* WALTER BRENNAN *(Pete Richard);* JULIE LONDON *(Barbara McKinney);* BRUCE BENNETT *(McCluskey);* JACK HOLT *(Reeves);* STANLEY RIDGES *(Bentley);* JOHN RIDGELY *(Dixie Rankin);* RICHARD ROBER *(Jack Southern);* ART BAKER *(Senator Vincent);* MORONI OLSEN *(Ames);* RAY MONTGOMERY *(Pilot);* HARLAN WARDE *(Timmy);* JAMES HOLDEN *(Tom Cooper);* RORY MALLINSON *(Jerry Morgan);* JOHN GALLAUDET *(Jennings);* WARREN DOUGLAS *(Winston);* CHARLES WALDRON, JR. *(Aide);* ROBERT ROCKWELL *(Lt. Kelley);* WILLIAM GOULD *(Mr. Secretary);* SALLY CORNER *(Mrs. Secretary);* KENNETH TOBEY *(Capt. Williamson);* TETSU KOMAI *(Japanese Representative);* BEAL WONG *(Japanese Naval Attaché);* LAURA TREADWELL *(Mrs. Ames);* ROSCOE J. BEHAN *(Ames' Attaché);* BASIL RUYSDAEL *(Admiral);* REED HOWES *(Officer);* EDWIN FOWLER *(Commander Price);* WILLIAM HUDSON *(Lt. Leenhouts);* MARY LAWRENCE *(Ruth Rankin);* JOHN MC GUIRE *(Supply Officer);* CHARLES SHERLOCK *(Capt. Wren);* CHARLES WILLIAMS *(Luggage Clerk);* BRAD EVANS, GERARD WALLER *(Midshipmen);* RICHARD A. PAXTON *(Pilot);* TOMMY WALKER *(Lieutenant).*

CREDITS:

DELMER DAVES *(Director and Scenarist);* JERRY WALD *(Producer);* ROBERT BURKS, WILFRID M. CLINE *(Photographers);* ALAN CROSLAND, JR. *(Editor);* FRANZ WAXMAN *(Musical Score);* LEONID RAAB *(Orchestrator);* LEAH RHODES *(Costumer);* LEO K. KUTER *(Art Director);* GEORGE JAMES HOPKINS *(Set Decorator);* CHARLES LANG *(Sound Recorder);* ROY DAVIDSON, EDWIN DU PAR *(Special Effects);* NATALIE KALMUS, WILLIAM FRITZSCHE *(Technicolor Consultants);* PERC WESTMORE *(Makeup Artist);* CAPT. S. G. MITCHELL,

With Jane Wyatt and Julie London

U.S.N., CAPT. JAMES DYER, U.S.N. (RET.) *(Technical Advisers);* BILL KISSELL *(Assistant Director);* ERIC STACEY *(Production Manager).*

SYNOPSIS:

Admiral Jonathan L. Scott, about to retire from the Navy, recalls the struggle he and a group of Navy men had in 1921, when they were striving to prove the importance of carrier-launched aircraft. At that time, Scott and his friend Pete Richard, were among the few eager young officers who could land on the short deck of the carrier Langley.

When he is in Washington to gain friends for naval aviation, Scott is re-united with Mary Morgan, the widow of a flying buddy, at a party. Later, that evening, an argument develops over the value of carriers and Scott insults a Japanese diplomat. He is promptly assigned a desk job in Panama.

The following year, he reports for duty aboard a new carrier, the U.S.S. *Saratoga.* During a Naval exercise, he is wounded and, once released from the hospital, he and Mary wed. He is at sea when the Japanese bomb Pearl Harbor and, soon, he is commanding his own carrier. At the climactic Okinawa battle, Scott's ship is seriously damaged by *kamikaze* planes, but, instead of abandoning ship, he guides her back to the U.S., where the crew is received with cheers as a symbol of America's determination and spirit.

NOTES:

Task Force was a grand Navy actioner which utilized some splendid Technicolor newsreel footage of World War II to highlight the production. Cooper gave a fine performance as a seasoned Naval officer and the supporting cast was excellent.

221

This was one of his most popular films of the late 1940's, with critics and public alike.

Said Bosley Crowther in *The New York Times:* "Gary Cooper, after mushing the romantic scenes, does a pretty tight job of imitating an air officer and then a captain in the midst of war. His scenes as the operating officer in the Yorktown at the Battle of Midway are some of the best in the picture, so far as personal drama is concerned." Howard Barnes, in the *New York Herald Tribune,*

commented, "Cooper and the documentary shots are the chief mainstays of the production. The star plays a stubborn advocate of air power on the high seas with commanding persuasion. His characterization . . . is rigidly correct, but extremely sympathetic." *Photoplay* felt, "Gary Cooper effectively portrays a Navy man who winds up a rear Admiral. . . . A classic of its kind, *Task Force* ranks among the most authentic war pictures ever made. A magnificant movie."

With Jane Wyatt and Kenneth Tobey

With John Ridgely and Bruce Bennett

With Walter Brennan

222

With Lauren Bacall

BRIGHT LEAF

A Warner Bros. Picture   1950

CAST:

GARY COOPER (*Brant Royle*); LAUREN BACALL (*Sonia Kovac*); PATRICIA NEAL (*Margaret Jane*); JACK CARSON (*Chris Malley*); DONALD CRISP (*Major Singleton*); GLADYS GEORGE (*Rose*); ELIZABETH PATTERSON (*Tabitha Jackson*); JEFF COREY (*John Barton*); TAYLOR HOLMES (*Lawyer Calhoun*); THURSTON HALL (*Phillips*); JAMES GRIFFITH (*Ellery*); MARIETTA CANTY (*Queenie*); WILLIAM WALKER (*Simon*); CHARLES MEREDITH (*Pendleton*); LESLIE KIMMEL (*Hokins*); JOHN PICKARD (*Devers*); ELZIE EMANUEL (*Negro Boy*); JAMES ADAMSON, IRA BUCK WOODS (*Negro Peddlers*); PAUL NEWLAND (*Blacksmith*); J. LEWIS JOHNSON (*Negro Grandpa*); JESSIE LEE HUNT (*Boy*); LYLE LATELL (*Clay*); EDDIE PARKES (*Hotel Clerk*); CELIA LOVSKY (*Dressmaker*); SELBY BACON (*Fauntleroy*); PAT FLAHERTY (*Farmer*); PETER KELLETT, HUBERT KERNS (*Farmer's sons*); RENE DE VOUX (*Cousin Emily*); EILEEN COUGHLAN (*Cousin Pearl*); CLEO MOORE (*Cousin Louise*); NITA TALBOT (*Cousin Theodora*); PAT GOLDIN (*Cousin Arthur*); CHALKY WILLIAMS (*Sheriff*); CHICK CHANDLER (*Tobacco Auctioneer*); MARSHALL BRADFORD (*Farmer*); JOHN ALVIN, JOHN MORGAN, BENNY LONG (*Poker Players*); ED PEIL, SR. (*Conductor*); CHARLES CONRAD (*Edwards*); SAM FLINT (*Johnson*); BOYD DAVIS (*Official*); KERMIT WHITFIELD (*Detective Curson*).

CREDITS:

MICHAEL CURTIZ (*Director*); HENRY BLANKE (*Producer*); RANALD MAC DOUGALL (*Scenarist*); KARL FREUND (*Photographer*); OWEN MARKS (*Editor*); STANLEY FLEISHER (*Art Director*); BEN BONE (*Set Decorator*); VICTOR YOUNG (*Musical Score*); SIDNEY CUTNER, LEO SHUKEN (*Orchestrators*); NORMAN STUART (*Dialogue Director*); STANLEY JONES (*Sound Recorder*); LEAH RHODES, MARJORIE BEST (*Costumers*);

With Patricia Neal

With Jack Carson and Patricia Neal

DAVID GARDNER (Second Unit and Montage Director); PERC WESTMORE, RAY ROMERO, JOHN WALLACE (Makeup Artists); SHERRY SHOURDS (Assistant Director); MYRL STOLTZ (Hair Stylist); WARREN YAPLE (Grip); PAUL BUTNER (Gaffer); JACK WOODS (Still Man). From the novel by FOSTER FITZ-SIMONS.

SYNOPSIS:

Although driven out of his home town years before by tobacco tycoon Major James Singleton for paying too much attention to the magnate's daughter, tenant-farmer Brant Royle returns. He meets John Barton, inventor of a cigarette-making machine, and Chris Malley, a medicine show man. Impressed with the invention, Brant asks an old flame, Sonia Kovac, for funds enough to produce

it. A partnership is formed and, soon, this revolutionary discovery wipes out all their competitors, including the Major.

Brant still loves Margaret Singleton, to the dismay of Sonia, and Margaret, in order to save her father's fortune, offers to marry Brant. Mortified, Major Singleton commits suicide. After a few loveless months of marriage, Brant learns that his vindictive wife has almost ruined him and that government officials are now after him with a monopoly suit. Brant throws Margaret out of his mansion, which accidently burns to the ground. He then bids Sonia farewell and rides away, knowing that someday he'll return to her.

NOTES:

Bright Leaf is the sort of routine romantic drama that is fun to sit through if you're the kind of person who likes to know what's coming next. Forget any extra special thrills or surprises, because there weren't any. The production itself, however, was well mounted, directed in proper style by Michael Curtiz and had the distinction of being photographed by Karl Freund and scored by Victor Young.

Cooper was really quite good as Brant Royle, especially so, considering that Patricia Neal was allowed to overact with too much flair, Lauren Bacall's role of the madame was played down and the audience was treated to too much Donald Crisp and not enough Gladys George. Cooper did get fine support from Jack Carson, a truly good performer, who was always underrated because of his slapstick beginnings.

Howard Barnes in the *New York Herald Tribune* said, "Cooper does an extraordinary job. Miss Neal is a bit on the vague side. *Bright Leaf* is grim, but it is a dramatic account of the changing of the South at the turn of the century." *The New York Times*' Bosley Crowther observed that "Although Mr. Cooper does a commendably strong and vivid job as a man wracked by agitating passions which propel him to his doom, Patricia Neal plays his female tormentor as though she were some sort of vagrant lunatic. Her eyes pop and gleam in crazy fashion, her face wreathes in idiotic grins and she drawls with a Southern accent that sounds like a dim-wit travesty. It is hard to perceive how this lady could fascinate anyone. Lauren Bacall is torpid and dull—not much more of a charmer, indeed, than the aberrant Miss Neal."

DALLAS

A Warner Bros. Picture in Technicolor   1950

CAST:

GARY COOPER (*Blayde [Reb] Hollister*); RUTH ROMAN (*Tonia Robles*); STEVE COCHRAN (*Brant Marlow*); RAYMOND MASSEY (*Will Marlow*); BARBARA PAYTON (*Flo*); LEIF ERICKSON (*Martin Weatherby*); ANTONIO MORENO (*Felipe*); JEROME COWAN (*Matt Coulter*); REED HADLEY (*Wild Bill Hickok*); GIL DONALDSON (*Luis*); ZON MURRAY (*Cullen Marlow*); WILL WRIGHT (*Judge Harper*); MONTE BLUE (*The Sheriff*); BYRON KEITH (*Jason Trask*); STEVE DUNHILL (*Dink*); CHARLES WATTS (*Bill Walters*); JOSE DOMINGUEZ (*Carlos*); GENE EVANS (*Drunk*); JAY "SLIM" TALBOT (*Stage Driver*); BILLIE BIRD (*School Teacher*); FRANK KREIG (*Politician*); TOM FADDEN (*Mountaineer*); HAL K. DAWSON (*Drummer*); BUDDY ROOSEVELT (*Northerner*); ALEX MONTOYA (*Vaquero*); DOLORES CORVALL (*Mexican Servant*); FRED GRAHAM (*Lou*); CHARLES HORVATH, WINN WRIGHT, CARL ANDRE (*Cowpunchers*); ANN LAWRENCE (*Mrs. Walters*); O. Z. WHITEHEAD (*Settler*); MIKE DONOVAN (*Citizen*); GLENN THOMPSON (*Guard*); FRANK MC CARROLL, LARRY MC GRATH, AL FERGUSON (*Citizens*); DEWEY ROBINSON, ROY BUCKO, BUDDY SHAW, DAVE DUNBAR, OSCAR WILLIAMS (*Prisoners*); FRED KELSEY (*Carter*); BENNY CORBETT (*Bystander*).

CREDITS:

STUART HEISLER (*Director*); ANTHONY VEILLER (*Producer*); JOHN TWIST (*Scenarist*); ERNEST HALLER (*Photographer*); DOUGLAS BACON (*Art Director*); MAX STEINER (*Musical Score*); CLARENCE KOLSTER (*Editor*); OLIVER S. GARETSON (*Sound Recorder*); MARJORIE BEST (*Costumer*); MURRAY CUTTER (*Orchestrator*); GEORGE JAMES HOPKINS (*Set Decorator*); B. REEVES EASON (*Second Unit Director*); CHUCK HANSEN (*Assistant Director*); MITCHELL KOVALESKI (*Technicolor Color Consultant*).

With Ruth Roman
and Leif Erickson

With Steve Cochran, Benny Corbett
and Raymond Massey

226

Blayde Hollister, an ex-Confederate officer, comes to Dallas seeking revenge on the three brothers who plundered his land and murdered his family. In order to trap the killers, he enlists the aid of Martin Weatherby, the newly-appointed U.S. Marshal and the two switch identities. However, at the hacienda of a wealthy Spanish rancher, Weatherby explains Hollister's plan to Tonia, the man's daughter, whom he is courting.

Hollister rides to town and kills the first brother in a gun duel. Wounded in the fight, he recovers at the hacienda. Soon, he and Tonia are in love. Well again, he goes after the second brother and, eventually, kills him too. Will, the oldest and wisest of the Marlow clan, leads a band of renegades to the hacienda and holds the family hostage. However, Hollister returns and, in a fierce struggle, slays the third brother.

NOTES:

Despite its swift pace and shoot-'em-up action, its Technicolor photography (by expert Ernest Haller), its sweeping and melodic musical score (by Max Steiner) and a competent supporting cast, *Dallas* was, and still is, an undistinguished western melodrama.

Howard Barnes in the *New York Herald Tribune* felt, "[*Dallas*] gains special flavor and melodramatic impact from the star's coiled-spring performance. Ruth Roman is quietly ornamental." Bosley Crowther in *The New York Times*, noted that "There is something about the sadness that appears in Mr. Cooper's eyes, something about the slowness and the weariness of his walk, something about his manner that is not necessarily in the script which reminds the middle-aged observer that Mr. Cooper has been at it a long time."

With Ruth Roman
and Leif Erickson

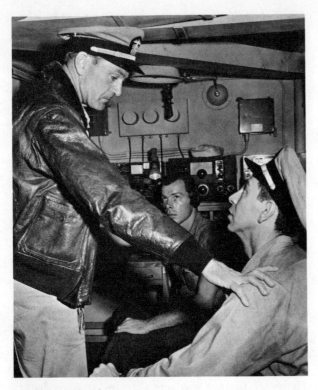

With Lee Marvin
and Jack Webb

YOU'RE IN THE NAVY NOW

A 20th Century-Fox Picture   1951
First released under the title: U.S.S. Teakettle

CAST:

GARY COOPER *(Lt. John Harkness);* JANE GREER *(Ellie);* MILLARD MITCHELL *(Larrabee);* EDDIE ALBERT *(Lt. Bill Barron);* JOHN MC INTYRE *(Commander Reynolds);* RAY COLLINS *(Admiral Tennant);* HARRY VON ZELL *(Capt. Eliot);* JACK WEBB *(Ensign Anthony Barbo);* RICHARD ERDMAN *(Ensign Chuck Dorrance);* HARVEY LEMBECK *(Norelli);* HENRY SLATE *(Ryan-Chief Engineer);* ED BEGLEY *(Commander);* FAY ROOPE *(Battleship Admiral);* CHARLES TANNEN *(Houlihan);* CHARLES BUCHINSKI *[later* BRONSON*] (Wascylewski);* JACK WARDEN *(Morse);* KEN HARVEY, LEE MARVIN, JERRY HAUSNER, CHARLES SMITH *(Crew Members);* JAMES CORNELL *(New Boy-Sailor);* GLEN GORDON, LAURENCE HUGO *(Shore Patrolmen);* DAMIAN O'FLYNN *(Doctor);* BIFF MC GUIRE *(Sailor Messenger);* NORMAN MC KAY *(Admiral's Aide);* JOHN MC GUIRE *(Naval Commander);* ELSA PETERSON *(Admiral's Wife);* JOEL FLUELLEN *(Mess Boy);* HERMAN CANTON *(Naval Captain);* RORY MALLINSON *(Lieutenant Commander);* WILLIAM LEICESTER *(C.P.O.);* TED STANHOPE *(Naval Officer).*

CREDITS:

HENRY HATHAWAY *(Director);* FRED KOHLMAR *(Producer);* RICHARD MURPHY *(Scenarist);* JOE MAC DONALD *(Photographer);* CYRIL MOCKRIDGE *(Musical Score);* LYLE WHEELER, J. RUSSELL SPENCER *(Art Directors);* THOMAS LITTLE, FRED J. RODE *(Set Decorators);* JAMES B. CLARK *(Editor);* CHARLES LE MAIRE *(Costumer);* LIONEL NEWMAN *(Musical Director);* EDWARD POWELL *(Orchestrator);* BEN NYE *(Makeup Artist);* FRED SERSEN, RAY KELLOGG *(Special Photographic Effects);* W. D. FLICK, ROGER HEMAN *(Sound Recorders);* JOSEPH WARREN LOMAX, U.S.N. *(Technical Adviser). From an article in "The New Yorker" by* JOHN W. HAZARD.

SYNOPSIS:

During World War II, the Navy puts a steam turbine, instead of a diesel engine, in a patrol craft (PC1168) for experimental purposes. Lt. John Harkness, a Reserve officer with little naval experience, is assigned as her skipper. He quickly learns that his entire crew are "90-day wonders," like himself, except for the Chief Boatswain's Mate, Larrabee.

Trouble plagues the craft from the start and, after numerous mishaps, new boilers are finally installed. Harkness is then notified that the PC1168 will participate in an official test conducted by the Admiral's Board, slated to be held in two days. During this rigorous test, the engine's valves get stuck and the U.S.S. *Teakettle,* as she has been dubbed by her crew, races ahead, madly out of control.

Back at the base, waiting for the Board's report, Harkness goes to Captain Eliot's office (his wife Ellie is the base commander's secretary) prepared to speak his mind, but is surprised when the Captain gives him, and his crew, a commendation for gallant efforts. Later, aboard ship, as he reads the commendation to his men, a diesel is being lowered into the engine room.

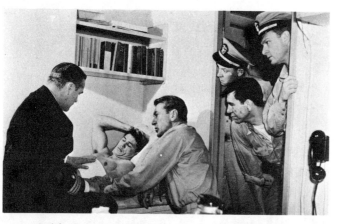

With Damian O'Flynn, Charles Buchinski (Bronson), Richard Erdman, Jack Webb and Eddie Albert

With Jane Greer

NOTES:

Henry Hathaway was one director who could get just about any kind of performance out of Cooper. In this film, he got a rich assortment of comic mannerisms which jelled beautifully with the contrivances of the script—Never was Cooper more delightful or winning. The most was made of the supporting men, but Jane Greer was wasted in a minute role as Cooper's wife ashore.

Originally filmed as *U.S.S. Teakettle,* 20th Century-Fox actually released the film with this title in February of 1951. Despite glowing reviews, the audience response was nil and a change of title was thought necessary. Immediately thereafter, it came out as *You're in the Navy Now.*

The part was Cooper's first starring role at 20th Century-Fox and marked his first visit to that great studio since the early days of his career (1925), when he rode as an extra in Tom Mix's film, *The Lucky Horseshoe.*

Said The *New York Times* (Bosley Crowther): "To dish it out, Mr. Hathaway has a wonderfully able cast, headed up by Gary Cooper as the skipper of the Teakettle tub. Through 20th Century-Fox, which make this sparkler, they are contributing the best comedy of the year." "Gary Cooper is ideally cast," said Otis L. Guernsey, Jr. in the *New York Herald Tribune.* "His acting is of the economical and yet clear and versatile type that would make any audience identify itself with his frustration."

With Eddie Albert
and Millard Mitchell

With Phil Harris,
Virginia Gibson and Frank Lovejoy

STARLIFT

A Warner Bros. Picture   1951

CAST:

DORIS DAY, GORDON MAC RAE, VIRGINIA MAYO, GENE NELSON, RUTH ROMAN (*Themselves*); JANICE RULE (*Nell Wayne*); DICK WESSON (*Sgt. Mike Nolan*); RON HAGERTHY (*Cpl. Rick Williams*); RICHARD WEBB (*Col. Callan*); HAYDEN RORKE (*Chaplain*); HOWARD ST. JOHN (*Steve Rogers*); ANN DORAN (*Mrs. Callan*); TOMMY FARRELL (*Turner*); JOHN MAXWELL (*George Norris*); DON BEDDOE (*Bob Wayne*); MARY ADAMS (*Sue Wayne*); BIGELOWE SAYRE (*Dr. Williams*); ELEANOR AUDLEY (*Mrs. Williams*); PAT HENRY (*Theatre Manager*); GORDON POLK (*Chief Usher*); ROBERT HAMMACK (*Piano Player*); RAY MONTGOMERY (*Capt. Nelson*); BILL NEFF (*Co-Pilot*); STAN HOLBROOK (*Ground Officer*); JILL RICHARDS (*Flight Nurse*); JOE TURKEL (*Litter Case*); RUSH WILLIAMS (*Virginia Boy*); BRIAN MC KAY (*Pete*); JACK LARSON (*Will*); LYLE CLARK (*Nebraska Boy*); DOROTHY KENNEDY, JEAN DEAN, DOLORES CASTLE (*Nurses*); WILLIAM HUNT (*Boy with Cane*); ELIZABETH FLOURNOY (*Army Nurse*); WALTER BRENNAN, JR. (*Driver*); ROBERT KARNS, JOHN HEDLOE (*Lieutenants*); STEVE GREGORY (*Boy with Camera*); RICHARD MONOHAN (*Morgan*); JOE RECHT, HERB LATIMER (*Soldiers in Bed*); DICK RYAN (*Doctor*); BILL HUDSON (*Crew Chief*); SARAH SPENCER (*Miss Parson's Asst.*); JAMES BROWN (*Non-Com*); EZELLE POULE (*Waitress*).

GUEST STARS: JAMES CAGNEY, GARY COOPER, VIRGINIA GIBSON, PHIL HARRIS, FRANK LOVEJOY, LUCILLE NORMAN, LOUELLA PARSONS, RANDOLPH SCOTT, JANE WYMAN *and* PATRICE WYMORE.

CREDITS:

ROY DEL RUTH (*Director*); ROBERT ARTHUR (*Producer*);

229

JOHN KLORER, KARL KAMB *(Scenarists);* TED MC CORD *(Photographer);* CHARLES H. CLARKE *(Art Director);* WILLIAM ZIEGLER *(Editor);* G. W. BERNTSEN *(Set Decorator);* RAY HEINDORF *(Musical Director);* FRANCIS J. SCHEID, DAVID FORREST *(Sound Recorders);* LEAH RHODES *(Costumer);* LE ROY PRINZ *(Choreographer);* GORDON BAU *(Makeup Artist);* MEL DELLAR *(Assistant Director);* MAJOR JAMES G. SMITH, USAF, M.A.T.S., MAJOR GEORGE E. ANDREWS, USAF, S.A.C. *(Technical Advisers).* SONGS: *" 'Swonderful"* and *"Liza"* by IRA *and* GEORGE GERSHWIN; *"You Do Something to Me"* and *"What Is This Thing Called Love?"* by COLE PORTER; *"You're Gonna Lose Your Gal"* by JOE YOUNG *and* JIMMY MONACO; *"You Ought to Be in Pictures"* by EDWARD HEYMAN *and* DANA SUESSE; *"It's Magic"* by SAMMY CAHN *and* JULE STYNE; *"Good Green Acres of Home"* by IRVING KAHAL *and* SAMMY FAIN; *"I May Be Wrong, but I Think You're Wonderful"* by HARRY RUSKIN *and* HENRY SULLIVAN; *"Look Out, Stranger, I'm a Texas Ranger"* by RUBY RALESIN *and* PHIL HARRIS; *"Noche Carib"* by PERCY FAITH. *From a story by* JOHN KLORER.

SYNOPSIS:

Movie stars Ruth Roman, Doris Day, and Nell Wayne are making personal appearances in San Francisco when they meet G.I.s Mike Nolan and Rick Williams. Since his buddy has a crush on Nell, Mike tells the girls that they will soon be leaving for Korea (not explaining that they are actually crew members on a regular transport run). The girls agree to accompany them to Travis Air Force Base, where Nell kisses Rick goodbye before he and Mike take off. Their appearance causes a sensation and, moved by the reception, Ruth and Doris plan to return.

Meanwhile, Nell's love affair with the young airman is publicized in Louella Parsons' column and soon, such stars as Gary Cooper, Jane Wyman, James Cagney, Randolph Scott, Gordon MacRae and others, visit the base and present a show of songs and comic sketches for the servicemen.

NOTES:

Cooper again was called upon to lend his name to a downright second-rate musical-comedy—the kind of film that is more often bad than good, as a general rule. In the sketch done for the servicemen—in the film's story—Cooper, Frank Lovejoy, Phil Harris and Virginia Gibson team up in a burlesque of a bar-room shooting. The song "Look Out, Stranger, I'm a Texas Ranger" was sung by the foursome. James Barstow, Jr. in the *New York Herald Tribune* observed that "Gary Cooper looks patiently uneasy in a travesty of the iron-jawed marshal of the standard western."

Bosley Crowther in *The New York Times* said, "Let's be brief about it: the performances given by Miss Rule and Ron Hagerthy as the flier are as sappy as they could possibly be, and Dick Wesson as a pushy pal of the flier is downright insufferable."

IT'S A BIG COUNTRY

A Metro-Goldwyn-Mayer Picture   1951

CAST:

ETHEL BARRYMORE *(Mrs. Brian Patrick Riordan);* KEEFE BRASSELLE *(Sgt. Maxie Klein);* GARY COOPER *(Texas);* NANCY DAVIS *(Miss Coleman);* VAN JOHNSON *(Adam Burch);* GENE KELLY *(Icarus Xenophon);* JANET LEIGH *(Rosa Szabo);* MARJORIE MAIN *(Mrs. Wrenley);* FREDRIC MARCH *(Papa Esposito);* GEORGE MURPHY *(Mr. Callaghan);* WILLIAM POWELL *(Professor);* S. Z. SAKALL *(Stefan Szabo);* LEWIS STONE *(Sexton);* JAMES WHITMORE *(Mr. Stacey);* KEENAN WYNN *(Michael Fisher);* LEON AMES *(Secret Service Man);* ANGELA CLARKE *(Mama Esposito);* BOBBY HYATT *(Joseph Esposito);* SHARON MC MANUS *(Sam Szabo);* ELISABETH RISDON *(Woman);* BILL BALDWIN *(Austin);* MICKEY MARTIN *(Copy Boy);* WILLIAM H. WELSH *(Official);* NED GLASS *(Receptionist);* SHERRY HALL, FRED SANTLEY, HENRY SYLVESTER, ROGER MOORE, ROGER COLE, HARRY STANTON *(Officials);* JUNE HEDIN *(Kati);* LUANA MEHLBERG *(Lenka);* JERALYN ALTON *(Yolande);* JACQUELINE KENLEY *(Margit);* TONY TAYLOR *(Baby Sitter);* BENNY BURT *(Soda Jerk);* GEORGE ECONOMIDES *(Theodore);* HAL HATFIELD, GEORGE CONRAD, RICHARD GRINDLE, ANTHONY LAPPAS, TOM NICKOLS, COSTAS MORFIS *(Greek Athletes);* A. CAMERON GRANT *(Proprietor of Inn);* DAVID ALPERT *(Greek Athlete);* DON FIELDS *(George);* JERRY HUNTER *(Frank Grillo);* DONALD GORDON *(Mervin);* LUCILE CURTIS *(Miss Bloomburg);* DOLLY ARRIAGE *(Concetta Esposito);* ELENA SAVANAROLA *(Amelia Esposito);* CAROL NUGENT *(Girl);* GEORGE MC DONALD, CHARLES MYERS, DAVID WYATT, MICKEY LITTLE *(Boys);* TINY FRANCONE *(Girl in Classroom);* RHEA MITCHELL *(School Teacher).*

CREDITS:

RICHARD THORPE, JOHN STURGES, CHARLES VIDOR, DON WEIS, CLARENCE BROWN, WILLIAM A. WELLMAN, DON

HARTMAN (*Directors*); ROBERT SISK (*Producer*); WILLIAM LUDWIG, HELEN DEUTSCH, GEORGE WELLS, ALLEN RIVKIN, DOROTHY KINGSLEY, DORE SCHARY, ISOBEL LENNART (*Scenarists*); JOHN ALTON, RAY JUNE, WILLIAM MELLOR, JOSEPH RUTTENBERG (*Photographers*); BEN LEWIS, FREDERICK Y. SMITH (*Editors*); DOUGLAS SHEARER (*Sound Recorder*); JOHNNY GREEN (*Musical Supervisor*); ALBERTO COLOMBO, ADOLPH DEUTSCH, LENNIE HAYTON, BRONISLAU KAPER, RUDOLPH G. KOPP, DAVID RAKSIN, DAVID ROSE, CHARLES WOLCOTT (*Musical Arrangers*); CEDERIC GIBBONS, MALCOLM BROWN, WILLIAM FERRARI, EDDIE IMAZU, ARTHUR LONERGAN, GABRIEL SCOGNAMILLO (*Art Directors*). *Some segments based on stories by* EDGAR BROOKE, RAY CHORDES, JOSEPH PETRACCA, LUCILLE SCHLOSSBERG, CLAUDIA CRANSTON, *and* JOHN MC NULTY.

NOTES:

It's A Big Country was an eight-episode look at America and, like all composite-films, some episodes were better than others. Cooper appeared in Episode 6, called "Texas," which was directed by Clarence Brown and written especially for the film by scenarist Dorothy Kingsley. As a Texan named Texas, Cooper's delightful monologue has him boasting about the state of Texas by pretending not to. He explains at length that Texas isn't all that big and newsreel shots are interpolated, showing that the opposite is true.

Said Bosley Crowther in *The New York Times*: "Gary Cooper delivers an amusingly sly speech on the modesty of Texas and that rounds out the show." Otis L. Guernsey, Jr., in the *New York Herald Tribune* noted ". . . a comedy monologue belittling Texas, and spoken by Gary Cooper, with inserts of Texas grandeur giving his words the little white lie . . ." John Beaufort in the *Christian Science Monitor* said, "Gary Cooper spikes a number of false rumors which have been allowed to grow up about the sovereign state of Texas."

232

With Richard Webb

DISTANT DRUMS

*A United States Pictures Production
Released by Warner Bros. Pictures, Inc.
in Technicolor   1951*

CAST:

GARY COOPER *(Capt. Quincy Wyatt)*; MARI ALDON *(Judy Beckett)*; RICHARD WEBB *(Lt. Richard Tufts)*; RAY TEAL *(Private Mohair)*; ARTHUR HUNNICUTT *(Monk)*; ROBERT BARRAT *(General Zachary Taylor)*; CLANCY COOPER *(Sgt. Shane)*; LARRY CARPER *(Chief Ocala)*; DAN WHITE *(Cpl. Peachtree)*; MEL ARCHER *(Pvt. Jeremiah Hiff)*; ANGELITA MC CALL *(Amelia)*; LEE ROBERTS *(Pvt. Tibbett)*; GREGG BARTON *(Pvt. James Tasher)*; SHEB WOOLEY *(Pvt. Jessup)*; WARREN MAC GREGOR *(Pvt. Sullivan)*; GEORGE SCANLAN *(Bosun)*; CARL HARBAUGH *(M. Duprez)*; BEVERLY BRANDON *(Mme. Duprez)*; SIDNEY CAPO *(Indian Boy)*.

CREDITS:

RAOUL WALSH *(Director)*; MILTON SPERLING *(Producer)*; NIVEN BUSCH, MARTIN RACKIN *(Scenarists)*; SID HICKOX *(Photographer)*; DOUGLAS BACON *(Art Director)*; FOLMER BLANGSTED *(Editor)*; MAX STEINER *(Musical Score)*; WILLIAM WALLACE *(Set Decorator)*; MARJORIE BEST *(Costumer)*; GORDON BAU *(Makeup Artist)*; OLIVER S. GARETSON *(Sound Recorder)*; RUSS SAUNDERS *(Assistant Director)*. *From a story by* NIVEN BUSCH.

SYNOPSIS:

In this exciting story of the swamp fighters who turned the tide of the savage Seminole Indian War, Captain Quincy Wyatt, an experienced Indian fighter, leads a small force deep into the Florida Everglades to put down a Seminole uprising. During the arduous journey, the men come upon a beautiful captive girl, who, with her servant, joins the men on their mission.

NOTES:

This "exciting" Technicolored adventure was filmed on location in the Florida Everglades. Besides its

With Richard Webb, Mari Aldon
and Angelita McCall

appeal for the action-lovers, it boasted fine photography by Sid Hickox and vigorous direction by Raoul Walsh. Cooper gave one of his standard interpretations in a role which offered him little challenge.

Cooper was given a second-string supporting cast and, while they performed satisfactorily, there were few memorable moments. Max Steiner again provided one of his seemingly endless line of lush musical scores, which—if you were lucky—would sweep you along with the action, helping you forget the inept storyline.

Bosley Crowther in *The New York Times* could only say, "Don't look for surprises . . . Raoul Walsh, who directed, did so in precisely the same way that he has been directing such pictures for a matter of some twenty-five years. That is to say, Mr. Cooper is kept steady and laconic throughout, the action is serio-comic, and the pace is conventionally maintained."

With Clancy Cooper
and Arthur Hunnicutt

With Mari Aldon

234

With Grace Kelly

HIGH NOON

A Stanley Kramer Production
Released Thru United Artists   1952

CAST:

GARY COOPER *(Will Kane)*; THOMAS MITCHELL *(Jonas Henderson)*; LLOYD BRIDGES *(Harvey Pell)*; KATY JURADO *(Helen Ramirez)*; GRACE KELLY *(Amy Kane)*; OTTO KRUGER *(Percy Mettrick)*; LON CHANEY *(Martin Howe)*; HENRY MORGAN *(William Fuller)*; IAN MAC-DONALD *(Frank Miller)*; EVE MC VEAGH *(Mildred Fuller)*; HARRY SHANNON *(Cooper)*; LEE VAN CLEEF *(Jack Colby)*; BOB WILKE *(James Pierce)*; SHEB WOOL-LEY *(Ben Miller)*; TOM LONDON *(Sam)*; TED STANHOPE *(Station Master)*; LARRY BLAKE *(Gillis)*; WILLIAM PHILLIPS *(Barber)*; JEANNE BLACKFORD *(Mrs. Henderson)*; JAMES MILLICAN *(Baker)*; CLIFF CLARK *(Weaver)*; RALPH REED *(Johnny)*; WILLIAM NEWELL *(Drunk)*; LUCIEN PRIVAL *(Bartender)*; GUY BEACH *(Fred)*; HOWLAND CHAMBERLIN *(Hotel Clerk)*; MOR-GAN FARLEY *(Minister)*; VIRGINIA CHRISTINE *(Mrs. Simpson)*; VIRGINIA FARMER *(Mrs. Fletcher)*; JACK ELAM *(Charlie)*; PAUL DUBOV *(Scott)*; HARRY HARVEY *(Coy)*; TIM GRAHAM *(Sawyer)*; NOLAN LEARY *(Lewis)*; TOM GREENWAY *(Ezra)*; DICK ELLIOTT *(Kibbee)*; JOHN DOUCETTE *(Trumbull)*.

CREDITS:

FRED ZINNEMANN *(Director)*; STANLEY KRAMER *(Producer)*; CARL FOREMAN *(Scenarist)*; FLOYD CROSBY *(Photography)*; RUDOLPH STERNAD *(Art Director)*; DIMITRI TIOMKIN *(Musical Score)*; ELMO WILLIAMS *(Editor)*; HARRY GERSTAD *(Associate Editor)*; JEAN SPEAK *(Sound Recorder)*; EMMETT EMERSON *(Set Decorator)*. SONG: *"Do Not Forsake Me Oh My Darlin'"* by DIMITRI TIOMKIN *and* NED WASHINGTON; *Sung by* TEX RITTER. *Based on the story "The Tin Star"* by JOHN W. CUNNINGHAM.

235

SYNOPSIS:

At 10:30 a.m. on an otherwise quiet morning in the peaceful prairie town of Hadleyville, ex-Marshal Will Kane marries Amy, a pretty young Quaker girl. They are about to leave town when news comes that Frank Miller, whom Kane helped send to prison five years earlier, has just been pardoned and is headed for Hadleyville to settle the score with Kane. Will and his bride leave town with happy thoughts of the general store they will open in a nearby community, but Kane's strong sense of duty compels him to turn back and face Miller, despite Amy's pleas of non-violence.

Miller is slated to arrive on the train due at high noon, and three members of his old gang are already awaiting his arrival at the depot, so the middle-aged Kane sets out to get support from the townspeople, but, one by one, they turn their backs on him, each with a different excuse. Left alone, Kane faces the four men when the train arrives and the deserted streets soon become a battlefield. Once the last shot has been fired and calm replaces tension in the air, the pious citizens rush to congratulate their victorious ex-Marshal. Without looking back, however, Will and Amy Kane leave Hadleyville.

With Grace Kelly and Howland Chamberlin

With Lloyd Bridges

With Katy Jurado

With Lon Chaney, Jr., Thomas Mitchell,
Henry (Harry) Morgan,
Eve McVeagh, Otto Kruger
and Grace Kelly

With Grace Kelly

NOTES:

This drama of moral courage ushered in a new brand of "adult" western. It wasn't the first, of course, but it did give impetus to the trend. No longer was the cowboy-hero of stereotype dimensions; he became the aging lawman fighting for principles against all odds. *High Noon's* storyline was basically simple, but artful direction, astute editing and a haunting minstrel-like tune raised it from the commonplace.

Cooper's magnificently understated performance of Will Kane was universally acclaimed. He won his second Academy Award, gaining another foothold in his lengthy career. Dimitri Tiomkin won two Oscars (for both his song and musical score), and Elmo Williams and Harry Gerstad won for their superb editing.

Life thought that "although *High Noon* has some defects, few recent Westerns have gotten so much tension and excitement into the classic struggle between good and evil." *Films in Review* said, "It is astonishing how much of the simple Western story is told visually by means of rapid cross-cutting. Fred Zinnemann, who directed, and Elmo Williams, who edited, cannot be praised too highly for sheer virtuosity."

John McCarten, in *The New Yorker*, commented, "Gary Cooper, who has stalked desperadoes down many a deserted cowtown street, never took a more effective stroll than he does in *High Noon*. [It] isn't quite on a par with *Stagecoach*, that excellent variation on the theme of de Maupassant's "Boule de Suif," but, even so, all those who had a hand in it should get our warmest thanks."

SPRINGFIELD RIFLE

A Warner Bros. Picture in WarnerColor 1952

CAST:

GARY COOPER *(Major Alex Kearney)*; PHYLLIS THAX-TER *(Erin Kearney)*; DAVID BRIAN *(Austin McCool)*; PAUL KELLY *(Lt. Col. Hudson)*; PHILIP CAREY *(Capt. Tennick)*; LON CHANEY *(Elm)*; JAMES MILLICAN *(Matthew Quint)*; MARTIN MILNER *(Olie Larsen)*; GUINN "BIG BOY" WILLIAMS *(Sgt. Snow)*; JERRY O'SUL-LIVAN *(Lt. Evans)*; JAMES BROWN *(Pvt. Ferguson)*; JACK WOODY *(Sims)*; ALAN HALE, JR. *(Mizzell)*; VINCE BARNETT *(Cook)*; FESS PARKER *(Jim Randolph)*; RICHARD BENJAMIN *[later* LIGHTNER*] (Lt. Johnson)*; EWING MITCHELL *(Spencer)*; POODLES HANNEFORD *(Cpl. Hamel)*; GEORGE ROSS *(Riley)*; ERIC HOEG *(South-erner)*; WILTON GRAFF *(Col. Sharpe)*; NED YOUNG *(Sgt. Poole)*; WILLIAM FAWCETT *(Cpl. Ramsey)*; RICHARD HALE *(General Halleck)*; BEN CORBETT *(Sgt. Major)*; GUY E. HEARNE *(Calhoun)*; GEORGE ELDREDGE *(Judge Advocate)*; RORY MALLINSON *(Barfly)*; PAULA SOWL *(Bit Woman)*; RIC ROMAN, JACK MOWER *(Guards)*; MICHAEL RAGAN *[later* HOLLY BANE*] (Red)*; RAY BEN-NETT *(Commissioner)*; MICHAEL CHAPIN *(Jamie)*; RALPH SANFORD *(Barfly)*.

CREDITS:

ANDRE DE TOTH *(Director)*; LOUIS F. EDELMAN *(Pro-ducer)*; CHARLES MARQUIS WARREN, FRANK DAVIS *(Scenarists)*; EDWIN DU PAR *(Photographer)*; ROBERT L. SWANSON *(Editor)*; MAX STEINER *(Musical Score)*; JOHN BECKMAN *(Art Director)*; CHARLES LANG *(Sound Recorder)*; G. W. BERNTSEN *(Set Decorator)*; MURRAY CUTTER *(Orchestrator)*; GORDON BAU *(Makeup Artist)*; FRANK MALLISON *(Assistant Director)*; BEN CORBETT *(Technical Adviser)*. *From a story by* SLOAN NIBLEY.

SYNOPSIS:

Major "Lex" Kearney, a foresighted Union Officer, masterminds a counter-espionage scheme to un-

238

cover the reasons why a Northern cavalry post is unable to supply the mounts needed to keep the government's army on the move in the Southern states.

Every time the cavalry outpost tries to move a string of horses, renegades, tipped to the plan, ambush the soldiers and sell the horses to the Confederacy. Personal difficulties arise with the Major's wife and son, who are unaware of the undercover part he is playing.

NOTES:

Normally, this actioner would have been well received by the press and the public alike, but it followed *High Noon* in release and didn't fare too well. The story was above the average of action films being offered to Cooper at that time and Warner Bros. gave the production a good mounting and topped it off with a vivid musical score by Max Steiner, whose scoring usually makes ordinary pictures seem better than they are and great films even greater.

The supporting cast was more than adequate. Phyllis Thaxter, who performed in the small part of the wife, was most effective in her scenes with Cooper. The men of the cast—headed by David Brian, Paul Kelly and Philip Carey—were all excellent, contributing greatly to the rough-'n'-ready atmosphere. *Variety* lauded, "Cooper handles himself easily in the top role." *Film Daily* remarked, "This is a well-told tale that was concocted by Sloan Nibley and it received able direction from the hand of Andre de Toth. The narrative is projected with imagination and suspense. Gary Cooper in the saddle, and a good cast of worthies to back him up, gives *Springfield Rifle* solid entertainment substance to render satisfaction."

With Guinn "Big Boy" Williams
and Martin Milner

With Phyllis Thaxter
and Michael Chapin

RETURN TO PARADISE

*An Aspen Productions Picture
Released Through United Artists
in Technicolor   1953*

CAST:

GARY COOPER *(Mr. Morgan);* ROBERTA HAYNES *(Maeva);* BARRY JONES *(Pastor Corbett);* MOIRA MAC-DONALD *(Turia);* JOHN HUDSON *(Harry Faber);* VA'A *(Rori, age 9);* HANS KRUSE *(Rori, age 21);* MAMEA MATAUMUA *(Tonga);* HERBERT AH SUE *(Kura);* HEN-REETTA GODINET *(Povana);* LA'ILI *(Kim Ling);* EZRA WILLIAMS *(Interpreter);* GEORGE MIEDESKE *(Hawkins);* DONALD ASHFORD *(Cutler);* TERRY DUNLEAVY *(Mac);* HOWARD POULSON *(Russ);* MALIA *(Maeva's Aunt);* WEBB OVERLANDER *(Will Talbot);* FRANCES GOW *(Mrs. Talbot);* BRIAN MC EWEN *(Hank Elliott);* KATHLEEN NEWICK *(Mrs. Elliott);* KALAPU *(Tomare).*

CREDITS:

MARK ROBSON *(Director);* THERON WARTH, ROBERT WISE, *and* MARK ROBSON *(Producers);* CHARLES KAUF-MAN *(Scenarist);* WINTON HOCH *(Photographer);* DI-MITRI TIOMKIN *(Musical Score);* DANIEL MANDELL *(Editor);* HARRY SMITH *(Sound Recorder);* HARRY LENART *(Associate Producer). Based on the book by* JAMES A. MICHENER.

SYNOPSIS:

In 1929, Mr. Morgan, an American wanderer, arrives on the Polynesian island of Matareva, which is ruled by Pastor Corbett, a half-crazy puritan and son of a long-dead missionary. Corbett has the entire community under his dictatorship, using wardens who enforce, among other things, close attention while the pastor preaches in church.

The type of man who isn't pushed around, Morgan defies Corbett from the start and even marries Maeva, a Polynesian beauty. Later, he even helps to focus the islanders' latent revolutionary feelings. When he eventually leaves Matareva, the natives are blissfully free and the former dictator has mellowed. Years later, Morgan returns to find a

With Roberta Haynes

daughter, Turia, for whom he is responsible, and saves her from a fate worse than death.

NOTES:

Cooper again gave a performance that fully exceeded the script. All the elements were in James Michener's original short story "Mr. Morgan" (part of his book *Return to Paradise*), but scenarist Charles Kaufman failed to incorporate them in the film version. Instead, we were treated to a vapid South Seas Island tale with little else to offer but gorgeous scenery.

Bosley Crowther in *The New York Times* felt that "While Mr. Cooper is excellent as a bare-footed hedonist, he is obvious and unimpressive as a shod and reponsible man." Otis L. Guernsey, Jr., in the *New York Herald Tribune*, found that "The new film at Loew's State puts Gary Cooper to the embarrassment of a script which fails to develop even the nostalgic romance it had on the printed page."

Family Circle, however, felt differently, informing its readers "For our money, this film is worth three African Queens. Cooper—funny how we always get around to saying it in much the same words—is no great actor, but how good he is, anyway!".

With Barry Jones (center)

242   With Roberta Haynes

BLOWING WILD

A United States Pictures Production
Released by Warner Bros. Pictures, Inc.   *1953*

CAST:

GARY COOPER *(Jeff Dawson)*; BARBARA STANWYCK *(Marina Conway)*; RUTH ROMAN *(Sal)*; ANTHONY QUINN *(Ward "Paco" Conway)*; WARD BOND *(Dutch)*; IAN MAC DONALD *(Jackson)*; RICHARD KARLAN *(Henderson)*; JUAN GARCIA *(El Gavilan)*.

CREDITS:

HUGO FREGONESE *(Director)*; MILTON SPERLING *(Producer)*; PHILIP YORDAN *(Scenarist)*; SID HICKOX *(Photographer)*; AL YBARRA *(Art Director)*; ALAN CROSLAND, JR. *(Editor)*; WILLIAM WALLACE *(Set Decorator)*; DIMITRI TIOMKIN *(Musical Score)*; MANUEL TOPETE BLAKE, MC CLUER MERRICK *(Sound Recorders)*; KAY NELSON, MARJORIE BEST *(Costumers)*; GORDON BAU *(Makeup Artist)*; DON PAGE *(Assistant Director)*. SONG: *"Blowing Wild—The Ballad of Black Gold" by* DIMITRI TIOMKIN *and* PAUL FRANCIS WEBSTER; *Sung by* FRANKIE LAINE.

SYNOPSIS:

Wildcatter Jeff Dawson finds the going rough in Mexico, because of continual bandit raids, and turns to his former boss, Ward Conway, for help. Conway, whose petroleum company has made him a rich man, refuses to re-hire Dawson because of an affair the wildcatter had with his wife, Marina, a tempestuous and unscrupulous woman. Although Dawson now ignores her advances, and has fallen in love with Sal, a stranded American girl, Marina determines to get him for herself.

Soon, El Gavilan, the bandit chief, threatens to blow up Conway's wells unless he is paid $50,000, but Conway, angered by his wife's flirtations, refuses to comply. Later, Marina, watching for her chance, pushes Conway into an oil well, where he is killed by the pump. When Dawson arrives, she boldly admits her deed and begs him to take her away. Horrified, he almost strangles her, but is interrupted by a bandit attack. During the fight, he kills El Gavilan, but not before a dynamite blast

243

blows the Conway well—and the no-good Marina —sky high.

NOTES:

Assembling four stars couldn't—and indeed didn't —help this potboiler. Designed strictly for action fans, the cast fought a losing battle from the beginning. The Mexican scenery was well captured in the Sid Hickox photography; the Alan Crosland, Jr., editing was expert; and the musical score by Dimitri Tiomkin made up for a sagging script. *Blowing Wild* was filmed on location in Mexico, with all interior shots made at the Churubusco Studios in Mexico City.

Said *Family Circle:* "Cooper remains strong fairly silent, the man of action; Quinn is seized as readily as with rage; Miss Stanwyck is more of a nympho, and more obvious about it than ever; and Miss Roman is merely around for the final fade out."

With Barbara Stanwyck and Anthony Quinn

With Barbara Stanwyck

With Ruth Roman

244

With Susan Hayward

GARDEN OF EVIL

*A 20th Century-Fox Picture
in CinemaScope and Technicolor   1954*

CAST:

GARY COOPER *(Hooker);* SUSAN HAYWARD *(Leah Fuller);* RICHARD WIDMARK *(Fiske);* HUGH MARLOWE *(John Fuller);* CAMERON MITCHELL *(Luke Daly);* RITA MORENO *(Singer);* VICTOR MANUEL MENDOZA *(Vicente Madariaga);* FERNANDO WAGNER *(Captain);* ARTURO SOTO BANGEL *(Priest);* MANUEL DONDE *(Waiter);* ANTONIO BRIBIESCA *(Bartender);* SALVADO TERROBA *(Victim).*

CREDITS:

HENRY HATHAWAY *(Director);* CHARLES BRACKETT *(Producer);* FRANK FENTON *(Scenarist);* BERNARD HERRMANN *(Musical Score);* MILTON KRASNER, JORGE STAHL, JR. *(Photographers);* LYLE WHEELER, EDWARD FITZGERALD *(Art Directors);* PABLO GALVAN *(Set Decorator);* RAY KELLOGG *(Special Photographic Effects);* JAMES B. CLARK *(Editor);* CHARLES LE MAIRE *(Wardrobe Director);* TRAVILLA *(Costumer);* BEN NYE *(Makeup Artist);* HELEN TURPIN *(Hair Stylist);* NICOLAS DE LA ROSA, JR., ROGER HEMAN *(Sound Recorders);* SAUL WURTZEL *(Associate Producer);* STANLEY HOUGH *(Assistant Director);* CINEMASCOPE LENSES by BAUSCH & LOMB. SONGS: *"La Negra Noche"* by EMILIO D. URANGA; *"Aqui"* by KEN DARBY *and* LIONEL NEWMAN. *From a story by* FRED FREIBERGER *and* WILLIAM TUNBERG.

SYNOPSIS:

While stranded in a Mexican fishing village, Hooker, Fiske and Daly, soldiers of fortune bound for the California gold mines, are approached by Leah Fuller, an American, who offers to pay them handsomely to escort her through hazardous Indian territory to rescue her husband, who is trapped in a gold mine cave-in. *Gold* being the deciding factor, they agree and, together with a Mexican guide,

245

With Richard Widmark

begin their arduous journey. Emotions become tense when Leah discovers the Mexican marking trails and, later, finds herself fighting off Daly's crude advances.

Soon, the group arrives at what the Indians call "the Garden of Evil"—sacred grounds atop a high mountain—where the mine is located. Finding Fuller, they learn that the angry Indians are everywhere. On the return trip, Fuller is the first killed by the savages, then Daly, then the Mexican. Surrounded, Hooker and Fiske draw cards to see who takes Leah to safety and who stays to cover their escape. Hooker and Leah depart. Once they are a safe distance away, she tells him that Fiske cheated. Hooker returns, but finds Fiske dying in a clearing strewn with the bodies of Indians he had slain.

NOTES:

This was Gary Cooper's 81st film and his first in CinemaScope. It was also a reunion with co-star Susan Hayward, who had only begun her career in films when she appeared in Cooper's *Beau Geste* at Paramount, in 1939. Director Henry Hathaway directed in his best adventure style, which provided action fans with another hit. The critics, however, always more concerned with the script, were unimpressed.

Said *Films in Review:* ". . . The script, by Frank Fenton, is twaddle . . . But there are gropings after deeper motivations than are common in Westerns." Otis L. Guernsey, Jr., in his *New York Herald Tribune* review, commented, "Gary Cooper's hair is gray under his broad-brimmed hat, and he preserves a level, fatherly demeanor through most of the story." *Garden of Evil* did boast some beautiful Technicolor photography, and a rousing musical score to help carry the action along.

With Cameron Mitchell,
Victor Manuel Mendoza,
Richard Widmark
and Susan Hayward

246

With Richard Widmark and Susan Hayward

With Burt Lancaster

VERA CRUZ

*A Hecht-Lancaster Production
Released Through United Artists
in SuperScope and Technicolor   1954*

CAST:

GARY COOPER (*Benjamin Trane*); BURT LANCASTER (*Joe Erin*); DENISE DARCEL (*Countess Marie Duvarre*); CESAR ROMERO (*Marquis de Labordere*); SARITA MONTIEL (*Nina*); GEORGE MACREADY (*Emperor Maximilian*); ERNEST BORGNINE (*Donnegan*); HENRY BRANDON (*Danette*); CHARLES BUCHINSKY [*later* BRONSON] (*Pittsburgh*); MORRIS ANKRUM (*General Aguilar*); JAMES MC CALLION (*Little-Bit*); JACK LAMBERT (*Charlie*); JACK ELAM (*Tex*); JAMES SEAY (*Abilene*); ARCHIE SAVAGE (*Ballard*); CHARLES HORVATH (*Reno*); JUAN GARCIA (*Pedro*).

CREDITS:

ROBERT ALDRICH (*Director*); JAMES HILL (*Producer*); HAROLD HECHT, BURT LANCASTER (*Co-Producers*); ROLAND KIBBEE, JAMES R. WEBB (*Scenarists*); ERNEST LASZLO (*Photographer*); ALAN CROSLAND, JR. (*Editor*); HUGO FRIEDHOFER (*Musical Score*); RAUL LAVISTA (*Orchestrator and Conductor*); MANUEL TOPETE, GALDINO SAMPERIO (*Sound Recorders*); NATE EDWARDS (*Production Manager*); SONG: "*Vera Cruz*" by HUGO FRIEDHOFER *and* SAMMY CAHN. *From a story by* BORDEN CHASE.

SYNOPSIS:

During the Mexican revolution of 1866, Benjamin Trane and Joe Erin, two American adventurers, decide to join forces and fight for whichever side pay them the most. The saucy Nina, who has fallen for Trane, implores them to fight for the rebels, while the Marquis de Labordere, an aide to the Emperor Maximilian, asks them to fight on his side.

At a ball in the sumptuous Chapultepec Palace, the pair meet the beautiful Countess Marie Duvarre, and soon agree to escort her on the hazardous journey to Vera Cruz. Later, she informs

With Denise Darcel

them that she is actually transporting a gold shipment to the Emperor's forces. Shortly after, she offers to steal the gold and split it with the Americans. Overhearing this plan, the Marquis flees with the shipment, but Trane and Erin, with their men, storm the fort and Erin gets the gold.

Nina convinces Trane that the gold rightfully belongs to the people, and, in a final showdown, Trane is forced to kill his friend Erin, who has refused to give it up.

NOTES:

For his third film in two years, Cooper returned to Mexico, this time to film *Vera Cruz* for the independent producing team of Harold Hecht, James Hill and Burt Lancaster. Lancaster gladly took second billing, to get the box-office pull of

Cooper's name, and the advantage of a strong actor to appear opposite him. They proved to be a good combination.

The production values were of a high order. Robert Aldrich directed this adventure yarn with great flourish; Ernest Laszlo uncovered hidden beauty in the many Mexican locales used, especially the glorious Chapultepec Palace of the Emperor Maximilian; Alan Crosland, Jr. edited with a fine hand; and Hugo Friedhofer provided an exciting musical score.

As is typical with this type of action piece, the public loved it while the critics boo-ed. Said *The New York Times:* "Guns are more important in this shambles than Mr. Cooper or Mr. Lancaster. In short, there is nothing to redeem this film—not even the spirit of the season. Some Christmas show, indeed!"

With **Burt Lancaster**

With Henry Brandon
and Burt Lancaster

With Sarita Montiel

With Ralph Bellamy

THE COURT-MARTIAL OF BILLY MITCHELL

A United States Pictures Production
Released by Warner Bros. Pictures, Inc.
in CinemaScope and WarnerColor

CAST:

GARY COOPER *(Billy Mitchell)*; CHARLES BICKFORD *(General Guthrie)*; RALPH BELLAMY *(Congressman Reid)*; ROD STEIGER *(Allan Guillion)*; ELIZABETH MONTGOMERY *(Margaret Lansdowne)*; FRED CLARK *(Colonel Moreland)*; JAMES DALY *(Colonel White)*; JACK LORD *(Zach Lansdowne)*; PETER GRAVES *(Captain Elliott)*; HERBERT HEYES *(General John J. Pershing)*; DARREN MC GAVIN *(Russ Peters)*; ROBERT SIMON *(Admiral Gage)*; CHARLES DINGLE *(Senator Fullerton)*; WILL WRIGHT *(Admiral William S. Sims)*; DAYTON LUMMIS *(General Douglas MacArthur)*; IAN WOLFE *(President Coolidge)*; GRIFF BARNETT *(Civilian Steno)*; EDWARD KEANE, ANTHONY HUGHES, JOHN MAXWELL, EWING MITCHELL *(Court Judges)*; MAX WAGNER *(Sergeant Major)*; ADAM KENNEDY *(Yip Ryan)*; STEVE HOLLAND *(Stu Stewart)*; MANNING ROSS *(Ted Adams)*; JACK PERRIN *(Court Reporter)*; GREGORY WALCOTT *(Reporter Millikan)*; ROBERT WILLIAMS *(Reporter Tuttle)*; EDNA HOLLAND *(Woman Secretary)*; WILLIAM FORREST *(Commandant F.S.H.)*; FRANK WILCOX *(Officer Tom)*; CARLETON YOUNG *(Pershing's Aide)*; TOM MC KEE *(Capt. Eddie Rickenbacker)*; PHIL ARNOLD *(Fiorello LaGuardia)*; ROBERT BRUBAKER *(Major Hap Arnold)*; WILLIAM HENRY, PETER ADAMS *(Officers)*; CHARLES CHAPLIN, JR., JOEL SMITH, AL PAGE, JORDAN SHELLEY, FRED PERCE, WILLIAM FOX, LARS HANSEN, GEORGE MAYON, MICHAEL LALLY, CY MALIS *(Reporters)*.

CREDITS:

OTTO PREMINGER *(Director)*; MILTON SPERLING *(Producer)*; MILTON SPERLING, EMMET LAVERY *(Scenarists)*; SAM LEAVITT *(Photographer)*; MALCOLM BERT *(Art Director)*; FOLMAR BLANGSTED *(Editor)*; STANLEY JONES *(Sound Recorder)*; WILLIAM KUEHL *(Set Decorator)*; HOWARD SHOUP *(Costumer)*; DIMITRI TIOMKIN

(Musical Score); RUSS SAUNDERS *(Second Unit Director);* H. F. KOENEKAMP *(Special Effects);* GORDON BAU *(Makeup Artist);* JACK MC EDWARDS *(Assistant Director);* MAJOR-GENERAL KEENEY, USAF, *Res. (Ret.) (Technical Adviser). From an original story by* MILTON SPERLING *and* EMMET LAVERY.

SYNOPSIS:

After World War I, assistant Chief of the Army Air Service, Brig. Gen. Billy Mitchell, tries to convince disbelieving officials of the Army and Navy of the importance of air power. For his vain attempts, he is relieved of his command, reduced to Colonel and exiled to Texas. Undeterred, Mitchell begins a letter-writing campaign to bring attention to the inadequacy of the U.S. air defenses, but this, too, fails.

After a series of air disasters, one killing a friend, Mitchell publicly charges the War and Navy Departments with "incompetence and criminal negligence." He is arrested and his court-martial is held in a warehouse, in an effort to avoid further attention, but the controversy has already aroused public awareness. Even a Congressman comes to Mitchell's aid, as civilian counsel.

Top brass are called in to bear witness, but the Army's tough prosecutor, Major Guillon, makes a malaria-weakened Mitchell look foolish and appear to be merely a publicity seeker. Mitchell is found guilty and suspended for five years.

NOTES:

What was intended to be a film of the most important episode in the life of General Billy Mitchell, along with the events leading up to it, resulted in a dull, almost boring treatment in what was an otherwise thoroughly exciting life story.

Otto Preminger's direction lacked drive, and the notable cast he had assembled wallowed in an inept script. Cooper, who perhaps wasn't the right choice to play Mitchell, kept his performance on one level throughout. There were fine performances from Charles Bickford, Ralph Bellamy and Rod Steiger, and this was the film debut of Elizabeth Montgomery (Robert's 22-year old daughter), who had made a name for herself on the stage and in various TV dramas.

Said *Films in Review:* "Gary Cooper, who plays Mitchell, was miscast and does not convey the general's zeal and flamboyance. One reason is that the script contains nothing about Mitchell as a man,

With James Daly and Ralph Bellamy

With Elizabeth Montgomery

253

and he is made to appear almost as a toy soldier of small dimension, instead of as a dedicated man sacrificing himself for the defense of his country and his people." William K. Zinsser in the *New York Herald Tribune* noted that "Cooper gives a likable, though somewhat tight-lipped performance, with none of the fanatical flair which the real Mitchell apparently had." However, *The New Yorker*

thought, "As a maverick militarist, Mitchell was a compelling figure, and Gary Cooper, who portrays him here, works up considerable sympathy for his cause."

Despite what critics and/or the public thought of this screen treatment, Milton Sperling and Emmet Lavery's story and screenplay won an Academy Award nomination.

With Rod Steiger, Ralph Bellamy
and Charles Bickford
(extreme right)

With Marjorie Main

FRIENDLY PERSUASION

A William Wyler Production
An Allied Artists Pictures Corp Film
in CinemaScope and Eastmancolor   1956

CAST:

GARY COOPER (*Jess Birdwell*); DOROTHY MC GUIRE (*Eliza Birdwell*); MARJORIE MAIN (*Widow Hudspeth*); ANTHONY PERKINS (*Josh Birdwell*); RICHARD EYER (*Little Jess*); PHYLLIS LOVE (*Mattie Birdwell*); ROBERT MIDDLETON (*Sam Jordan*); MARK RICHMAN (*Gard Jordan*); WALTER CATLETT (*Professor Quigley*); RICHARD HALE (*Elder Purdy*); JOEL FLUELLEN (*Enoch*); THEODORE NEWTON (*Army Major*); JOHN SMITH (*Caleb*); MARY CARR (*Quaker Woman*); EDNA SKINNER, MARJORIE DURANT, FRANCES FARWELL (*Widow Hudspeth's daughters*); SAMANTHA (*The Goose*); RUSSELL SIMPSON, CHARLES HALTON, EVERETT GLASS (*Elders*); RICHARD GARLAND (*Bushwhacker*); JAMES DOBSON (*Rebel Soldier*); JOHN COMPTON (*Rebel Lieutenant*); JAMES SEAY (*Rebel Captain*); DIANE JERGENS (*Young Girl-Elizabeth*); RALPH SANFORD (*Business Man*); JEAN INNESS (*Mrs. Purdy*); NELSON LEIGH (*Minister*); HELEN KLEEB (*Old Lady*); WILLIAM SCHALLERT (*Young Husband*); JOHN CRAVEN (*Leader*); FRANK JENKS (*Shell Game Man*); FRANK HAGNEY (*Lemonade Vendor*); JACK MC CLURE (*Soldier*); CHARLES COURTNEY (*Reb Courier*); TOM IRISH (*Young Rebel*); MARY JACKSON (*Country Woman*).

CREDITS:

WILLIAM WYLER (*Director and Producer*); ROBERT WYLER (*Associate Producer*); ELLSWORTH FREDRICKS (*Photographer*); ROBERT SWINK, EDWARD A. BIERY, ROBERT A. BELCHER (*Editors*); EDWARD S. HAWORTH (*Art Director*); JOE KISH (*Set Decorator*); AUGUST LOHMAN (*Special Effects*); DOROTHY JEAKINS (*Costumer*); EMILE LA VIGNE (*Makeup Artist*); DIMITRI TIOMKIN (*Musical Score*); ALLEN K. WOOD (*Production Manager*); STUART MILLER (*Assistant to Producer*); RICHARD MAYBERY (*Production Assistant*); JESSAMYN WEST (*Technical Adviser*); AGNES FLANIGAN (*Hair Stylist*); AUSTEN JEWELL (*Assistant Director*);

With Dorothy McGuire

RICHARD C. HARRIS *(Music Editor)*; RALPH BUTLER *(Sound Recorder)*; DEL HARRIS *(Sound Editor)*; HARRY HOGAN *(Script Supervisor)*. SONGS: *"Friendly Persuasion (Thee I Love),"* *"Mocking Bird in a Willow Tree,"* *"Coax Me a Little,"* *"Indiana Holiday,"* *"Marry Me, Marry Me"* by DIMITRI TIOMKIN *and* PAUL FRANCIS WEBSTER. *Title Song sung by* PAT BOONE. *From "The Friendly Persuasion" by* JESSAMYN WEST.

SYNOPSIS:

In 1862, the peaceful existence of the Quaker family of Jess Birdwell is threatened by the coming of the Civil War to Southern Indiana. A Union officer appears at a First Day Meeting, begging the young men to join up and take arms against the South. Young Josh Birdwell is troubled by this, for, although he does not believe in fighting, he begins to doubt his own courage.

When word comes that Morgan's raiders are approaching, Josh decides to join the Home Guard, preparing to defend the community at a nearby river. His mother, Eliza, holds that no man should ever harm another, but his father, Jess, realizes that a man must be guided by his own conscience. Later, Josh is wounded and Jess goes out to find him, but first comes upon his friend, Sam Jordan, who is dying. He trails the bushwhacker, but cannot kill him and lets him go. Jess brings his boy home and Josh, convinced he is not a coward, recovers from his wounds.

NOTES:

This portrait of an Indiana Quaker family during the Civil War was Cooper's second-best film of the 1950's and was one of the most celebrated motion pictures made in 1956. It had originally been adapted for the screen by screenwriter Michael Wilson, in 1946, for Liberty Films. The property was then sold to Paramount Pictures, where William Wyler first saw it. He wanted Cooper in the role of Jess Birdwell but, since the star was tied up with commitments for several years, Wyler shelved the project.

Finally, in 1956, Wyler got Cooper and produced the film himself for Allied Artists Picture Corporation. The only writing credit that appears on this film reads *From the Book by Jessamyn West.* Michael Wilson's name was withheld, because Allied Artists chose "the right to deny credit to a writer revealed to be a member of the Communist

With Anthony Perkins,
Phyllis Love, Richard Eyer
and Dorothy McGuire

With Dorothy McGuire

With Mark Richman, Dorothy McGuire and Samantha

party or one who refused to answer charges of Communist affiliations." Wilson invoked the self-incrimination clause of the Fifth Amendment when he was summoned as a witness by the House Committee on Un-American Activities in 1951.

Wilson's script was even nominated for an Academy Award in the "Best Screenplay-adapted" category, but was rendered ineligible for nomination under the Academy by-laws. Other nominations included: Best Picture; Best Supporting Actor (Anthony Perkins); Best Sound Recording; Best Song "Friendly Persuasion (Thee I Love);" and Wyler's contribution, for Best Direction.

Friendly Persuasion made many "Ten Best" lists and "the spare yet appealing integrity projected by Dorothy McGuire as the Quaker wife . . .

was so functional a part of this film, and so pleasing to all kinds of audiences," she was voted the Best Actress of the Year by the National Board of Review.

Films in Review, commented, in part, "*Friendly Persuasion* is one of Wyler's better, not one of his best, films . . . [It] is not meant to be an informed and informing exposition of the practices and satisfactions of the 'friendly persuasion,' i.e. of the Society of Friends. It is intended as nostalgic entertainment for Americans, and, since a disgracefully small number of films now provide this, *Friendly Persuasion* is an exceptional film. Gary Cooper as the loving and loved Quaker husband and father has never more aptly utilized his great American face, nor acted more ably."

With Dorothy McGuire and Anthony Perkins

With Audrey Hepburn

LOVE IN
THE AFTERNOON

A Billy Wilder Production
An Allied Artists Pictures Corp Film   *1957*

CAST:

GARY COOPER *(Frank Flannagan)*; AUDREY HEPBURN *(Ariane Chavasse)*; MAURICE CHEVALIER *(Claude Chavasse)*; JOHN MC GIVER *(Monsieur X)*; LISE BOURDIN *(Madame X)*; BONIFAS *(Commissioner of Police)*; AUDREY WILDER *(Brunette)*; GYULA KOKAS, MICHEL KOKAS, GEORGE COCOS *and* VICTOR GAZZOLI— THE FOUR GYPSIES *(Themselves)*; OLGA VALERY *(Lady Hotel Guest)*; LEILA CROFT, VALERIE CROFT *(Swedish Twins)*; CHARLES BOUILLARD *(Valet at the Ritz)*; MINERVA PIOUS *(Maid at the Ritz)*; FILO *(Flannagan's Chauffeur)*; ANDRE PRIEZ *(First Porter at the Ritz)*; GAIDON *(Second Porter at the Ritz)*; GREGORY GRO- MOFF *(Doorman at the Ritz)*; JANINE DARD, CLAUDE ARIEL *(Existentialists)*; FRANCOIS MOUSTACHE *(Butch- er)*; GLORIA FRANCE *(Client at Butcher's)*; JEAN SYL- VAIN *(Baker)*; ANNIE ROUDIER *(First Client at Baker's)*; JEANNE CHARBLAY *(Second Client at Baker's)*; ODETTE CHARBLAY *(Third Client at Baker's)*; GILBERT CONSTANT, MONIQUE SAINTEY *(Lovers on Left Bank)*; JACQUES PRÉBOIST, ANNE LAURENT *(Lovers near the Seine)*; JACQUES ARY, SIMONE VANLANCKER *(Lovers on Right Bank)*; RICHARD FLAGY *(Husband)*; JEANNE PAPIR *(Wife)*; MARCELLE BROC, MARCELLE PRAINCE *(Rich Women)*; GUY DELORME *(Gigolo)*; OLIVIA CHEVALIER, SOLON SMITH *(Little Children in the Gardens)*; EVE MARLEY, JEAN RIEUBON *(Tande- mists)*; CHRISTIAN LUDE, CHARLES LEMONTIER, EMILE MYLOS *(Generals)*; ALEXANDER TRAUNER *(Ártist)*; BETTY SCHNEIDER, GEORGES PERRAULT, VERA BOCCA- DORO, MARC AURIAN *(Couples under Water Wagon)*; BERNARD MUSSON *(Undertaker)*; MICHÈLE SELIGNAC *(Widow)*.

CREDITS:

BILLY WILDER *(Director and Producer)*; BILLY WILDER, I. A. L. DIAMOND *(Scenarists)*; WILLIAM MELLOR *(Photographer)*; LEONID AZAR *(Editor)*; ALEXANDRE

With Maurice Chevalier

With Audrey Hepburn

With Audrey (Young) Wilder

TRAUNER *(Art Director)*; NOEL HOWARD *(Second Unit Director)*; WILLIAM SCHORR, DOANE HARRISON *(Associate Producers)*; PAUL FEYDER *(Assistant Director)*; JO DE BRETAGNE *(Sound Recorder)*; DEL HARRIS *(Sound Editor)*; FRANZ WAXMAN *(Musical Adaptation)*; ROBERT TRANY *(Music Editor)*. MUSICAL COMPOSITIONS: *"Fascination" by* F. D. MARCHETTI *and* MAURICE DE FERAUDY; *"C'est Si Bon" by* HENRI BETTI *and* ANDRE HORNEZ; *"L'ame Des Poetes" by* CHARLES TRENET; *"Love in the Afternoon," "Ariane," "Hot Paprika" by* MATTY MALNECK. *Based on the novel Ariane by* CLAUDE ANET.

SYNOPSIS:

Ariane Chavasse, daughter of a French detective, loves to read her father's private dossiers. She becomes fascinated with the file concerning American playboy Frank Flannagan and a certain Madame X. She soon learns that Monsieur X has sworn to kill the American, so she goes to his hotel suite to warn him. Flannagan, intrigued by the girl, dates her for the following afternoon. She is captured by his sophistication, and many an afternoon rendezvous follows.

Concealing her identity, she tells him of the many lovers in her past. He now becomes concerned about her. One day, in a steam bath, Flannagan meets Monsieur X, who advises him to consult detective Chavasse. He does, asking the detective to find out about the mysterious girl. Chavasse later reports that the girl is his own, innocent daughter and that he must leave Paris to save her. By this time, however, Flannagan has fallen in love with Ariane, and, at the last minute, takes her with him as the train departs.

NOTES:

Love in the Afternoon had a great many delightful things going for it, but, unhappily, Cooper was not comfortable with his part and looked—most of the time—just plain tired. It wasn't that he was too old to appear opposite Audrey Hepburn (as any young woman, and Miss Hepburn herself, will surely tell you). Rather, it was just that he was again cast in the sort of role in which he could project very little and still be effective, *i.e.,* the mature American roué.

Billy Wilder still injected many wonderfully romantic touches, had a first-rate cameraman

260

(William Mellor) and had gorgeous sets constructed for him (by art director Alexandre Trauner) at the Studios de Boulogne, as well as exteriors shot in and around Paris. Wilder's wife Audrey, the former Audrey Young when at Paramount, played the brief part of Cooper's companion at the opera.

Said William K. Zinsser in the *New York Herald Tribune:* "Cooper, under Audrey Hepburn's influence, swiftly declines from the suave libertine to the perplexed schoolboy, and there is a quiet humor in the quizzical look that crosses his face as he ponders the strange forces that are assailing him. . . . Some people may feel that the picture drags . . . it probably is the kind of movie that you either like or dislike emphatically."

Bosley Crowther in *The New York Times* noted, ". . . What charming performances Audrey Hepburn and Gary Cooper give as the cleverly calculating couple who spar through the amorous afternoons." *Family Circle* observed that "By keeping Gary Cooper mostly in shadow, Wilder nearly makes one forget that Coop may be a little mature for the part of an American playboy who woos and wins Audrey Hepburn, utterly charming as a little Parisian girl, with the aid of soft lights, champagne and a waltz called 'Fascination.'"

On the set with director Billy Wilder,
Audrey Hepburn and Maurice Chevalier

With Suzy Parker

TEN NORTH FREDERICK

*A 20th Century-Fox Picture
in CinemaScope   1958*

CAST:

GARY COOPER *(Joe Chapin)*; DIANE VARSI *(Ann Chapin)*; SUZY PARKER *(Kate Drummond)*; GERALDINE FITZGERALD *(Edith Chapin)*; TOM TULLY *(Slattery)*; RAY STRICKLYN *(Joby)*; PHILIP OBER *(Lloyd Williams)*; JOHN EMERY *(Paul Donaldson)*; STUART WHITMAN *(Charley Bongiorno)*; LINDA WATKINS *(Peg Slattery)*; BARBARA NICHOLS *(Stella)*; JOE MC GUINN *(Dr. English)*; JESS KIRKPATRICK *(Arthur McHenry)*; NOLAN LEARY *(Harry Jackson)*; HELEN WALLACE *(Marian Jackson)*; BEVERLY JO MORROW *(Waitress)*; BUCK CLASS *(Bill)*; RACHEL STEPHENS *(Salesgirl)*; BOB ADLER *(Farmer)*; LINC FOSTER *(Peter)*; JOHN HARDING *(Robert Hooker)*; DUDLEY MANLOVE *(Ted Wallace)*; MACK WILLIAMS *(General Coates)*; VERNON RICH *(Board Chairman)*; MARY CARROLL *(Nurse)*; GEORGE DAVIS *(Waiter)*; JOEY FAYE *(Taxi Driver)*; FRED ESSLER *(Hoffman)*; IRENE SEIDNER *(Wife)*; MELINDA BYRON *(Hope)*; SEAN MEANEY *(Sax Player)*; JOHN INDRISANO, MICHAEL PATAKI, MICHAEL MORELLI *(Men)*.

CREDITS:

PHILIP DUNNE *(Director and Scenarist)*; CHARLES BRACKETT *(Producer)*; JOE MAC DONALD *(Photographer)*; LEIGH HARLINE *(Musical Score)*; LYLE R. WHEELER, ADDISON HEHR *(Art Directors)*; WALTER M. SCOTT, ELI BENNECHE *(Set Decorators)*; LIONEL NEWMAN *(Musical Director)*; DAVID BRETHERTON *(Editor)*; CHARLES LE MAIRE *(Costumer)*; L. B. ABBOTT *(Special Photographic Effects)*; BEN NYE *(Makeup Artist)*; HELEN TURPIN *(Hair Stylist)*; HAL HERMAN *(Assistant Director)*; ALFRED BRUZLIN *(Sound Recorder)*; EDWARD B. POWELL *(Orchestrator)*; CINEMASCOPE LENSES by BAUSCH & LOMB. *From the novel by* JOHN O'HARA.

SYNOPSIS:

Edith Chapin has ambitious plans for her husband Joe, which extend as far as the White House. She goads him into visiting a conniving politician and donates a large sum to the Party, in return for a nomination. Meanwhile, Joe's daughter Ann

With Geraldine Fitzgerald

With Diane Varsi and John Emery

With Buck Class and Suzy Parker

becomes involved with a dance band musician, whom she marries. After a tense scene with her mother, Ann suffers a miscarriage. Dad buys off the young husband and Ann leaves home. The politician double-crosses Joe by making the events public and Joe's wife taunts him with news of her infidelity.

His whole world crumbling around him, Joe takes off for New York to get his daughter back, but falls in love with her beautiful roommate, whom he takes to a cabin in the mountains. The difference in their ages becomes so apparent that Joe eventually relinquishes the only love he has ever known. Joe soon becomes very ill and his son Joby summons Ann home, reconciling father and daughter before he dies.

NOTES:

This film of one of John O'Hara's routine novels hardly met the occasion; it was a one-dimensional character analysis of a man born out of his time. Cooper, playing a most-difficult part, seemed to find the middle ground and stay there for the entire film. His only rich moments were opposite Suzy Parker, who turned in the film's best performance.

Said Paul V. Beckley in the *New York Herald Tribune:* "In spite of my tendency to find Cooper's manner essentially Western, I felt his portrait of an Eastern gentleman quite effective." Henry Hart in *Films in Review* noted "Gary Cooper has the role of Joe Chapin, 'the gentleman who could not take advantage of anyone' and the protagonist of the book O'Hara intended to write. Cooper's portrayal of him is as mixed-up as O'Hara's."

Cooper originally met O'Hara when the novelist was on a visit to his friend Clifford Odets in Hollywood, back in 1936. O'Hara then appeared in Cooper's *The General Died at Dawn* as an extra.

With Barbara Nichols

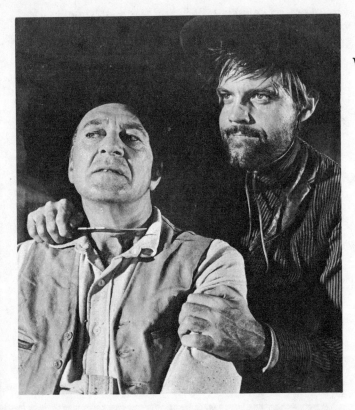

With Jack Lord

MAN OF THE WEST

An Ashton Picture
A Walter M. Mirisch Production
Released Thru United Artists
in CinemaScope and Color by DeLuxe   1958

CAST:

GARY COOPER (*Link Jones*); JULIE LONDON (*Billie Ellis*); LEE J. COBB (*Dock Tobin*); ARTHUR O'CONNELL (*Sam Beasley*); JACK LORD (*Coaley*); JOHN DEHNER (*Claude*); ROYAL DANO (*Trout*); ROBERT WILKE (*Ponch*); JACK WILLIAMS (*Alcutt*); GUY WILKERSON (*Conductor*); CHUCK ROBERSON (*Rifleman*); FRANK FERGUSON (*Marshal*); EMORY PARNELL (*Gribble*); TINA MENARD (*Mexican Woman*); JOE DOMINQUEZ (*Mexican Man*).

CREDITS:

ANTHONY MANN (*Director*); WALTER M. MIRISCH (*Producer*); REGINALD ROSE (*Scenarist*); ERNEST HALLER (*Photographer*); RICHARD HEERMANCE (*Editor*); LEIGH HARLINE (*Musical Score*); ED BOYLE (*Set Decorator*); YVONNE WOOD (*Costumer*); JACK SOLOMON (*Sound Recorder*); HILLYARD BROWN (*Art Director*); ALLEN K. WOOD (*Production Manager*); RICHARD MODER (*Assis-*

tant Director); EMIL LA VIGNE (*Makeup Artist*); SONG: *"Man of the West" by* BOBBY TROUP, *sung by* JULIE LONDON. *Based on a novel by* WILL C. BROWN.

SYNOPSIS:

Link Jones, a reformed prairie bandit and killer, who has since married and gone straight, is on a stagecoach in Eastern Arizona looking to hire a school teacher for his community when the stage is held up. He recognizes the men as his old gang and, to save the other passengers (Billie Ellis, a dance hall singer, and Sam Beasley, a card sharp), Link pretends to rejoin his former cronies, a gang of sadists run by his uncle, Dock Tobin.

Dock orders Link to participate in a bank robbery and sends two of his henchmen with him to case the bank in nearby Lassoo. However, hatred between Link and some of the gang soon leads to bloodshed. Link kills one of the men and, later, in a gun duel, kills his uncle. Billie goes her way, respecting Link; he goes his way in search of a school-teacher.

NOTES:

This violence-ridden western actioner earned the distinction of being the first Cooper feature not to open on Broadway in over three decades. It's biggest business was definitely in the action-and-grind houses and, later, on television screens.

As a film, this Anthony Mann-production has little to offer for comment. What a waste of time for Cooper, to say nothing of a top-notch photographer like Ernest Haller. Howard Thompson in *The New York Times* remarked "Not only does he [Cooper] still ride as if a horse taught him, but he also mops up the prairie in one of the meanest fist-scrounging duels we've seen in years."

Julie London, a fine actress who is usually miscast or wasted, was both in this instance. Her rendition of the title song did give her a free moment away from the script, however, which afforded audiences a brief, but pleasant moment.

With Lee J. Cobb and Julie London

With Julie London

With Maria Schell

THE HANGING TREE

A Baroda Production
A Warner Bros. Picture in Technicolor   1959

CAST:

GARY COOPER *(Doc Joseph Frail);* MARIA SCHELL *(Elizabeth Mahler);* KARL MALDEN *(Frenchy Plante);* BEN PIAZZA *(Rune);* GEORGE C. SCOTT *(Dr. George Grubb);* KARL SWENSON *(Tom Flaunce);* VIRGINIA GREGG *(Edna Flaunce);* JOHN DIERKES *(Society Red);* KING DONOVAN *(Wonder);* SLIM TALBOT *(Stage Driver);* GUY WILKERSON *(Home Owner);* BUD OSBORNE *(Horseman);* ANNETTE CLAUDIER *(Dance Hall Girl);* CLARENCE STRAIGHT *(Dealer).*

CREDITS:

DELMER DAVES *(Director);* MARTIN JUROW, RICHARD SHEPHERD *(Producers);* WENDELL MAYES, HALSTED WELLES *(Scenarists);* TED MC CORD *(Photographer);* DANIEL B. CATHCART *(Art Director);* OWEN MARKS *(Editor);* STANLEY JONES *(Sound Recorder);* MAX STEINER *(Musical Score);* MURRAY CUTTER *(Orchestrator);* RUSSELL LLEWELLYN *(Assistant Director);* ORRY-KELLY *(Miss Schell's Costumes);* MARJORIE BEST *(Costumer);* FRANK MILLER *(Set Decorator);* GORDON BAU *(Makeup Artist);* LEW LEARY *(Unit Production Manager);* SONG: *"The Hanging Tree" by* MACK DAVID *and* JERRY LIVINGSTON, *sung by* MARTY ROBBINS. *From the Novelette "The Hanging Tree" by* DOROTHY M. JOHNSON.

SYNOPSIS:

Doc Joe Frail, a frontier doctor running away from a personal tragedy, now takes his Hippocratic oath with a little gambling and gunfighting in Skull Creek, a wild gold camp in the territory of Montana. He saves an accused thief from a posse and, after healing the lad, they become friends. Next the Doc treats a young Swiss girl, Elizabeth Mahler, for shock and blindness suffered from exposure to the sun after a stage holdup.

Frail aides Elizabeth in a grubstake and, with

267

her partners Frenchy and Rune, she soon strikes it rich. Frenchy tries to force his attentions on Elizabeth, but just then Doc Frail rides up. Frail kills Frenchy and the town takes him to the hanging tree. However, Elizabeth stops them by offering them her rich mine. The townspeople accept and, with the help of Rune, she cuts down Frail.

NOTES:

The screen version of Dorothy M. Johnson's novelette "The Hanging Tree," which won the Western Writers of America's Spur Award, was one of 1959's "sleepers;" no one expected it to be as good or as well played as it was. Warner Bros. gave it a first class production, utilizing talents like photographer Ted McCord, composer Max Steiner and editor Owen Marks. Furthermore, Art Director Daniel B. Cathcart built an entire mining camp in mountains some 40 miles from Yakima, Washington—where all exteriors were filmed.

The acting was quite good all around, and Mack David and Jerry Livingston's title song won an Academy Award nomination. Said *Variety:* "Cooper has one of his best roles. His mystery and tight-lipped refusal to discuss it [his past] perfectly suit his laconic style." The critic for the *London Observer* observed that "As the psychiatric doctor, Mr. Cooper is still one of the most reliable cowboy heroes on the screen. Miss Schell, comporting herself quietly, has an obstinate little something that one must admire. As the youth, Ben Piazza, whom we saw last year in the Canadian film *A Dangerous Age* still strikes me as a promising actor in the James Dean way."

With Maria Schell

With Clarence Straight,
Karl Malden, and Annette Claudier

With Ben Piazza and Karl Malden

ALIAS JESSE JAMES

*A Hope Enterprises, Inc. Production
Released Through United Artists
Color By DeLuxe   1959*

CAST:

BOB HOPE (*Milford Farnsworth*); RHONDA FLEMING (*The Duchess*); WENDELL COREY (*Jesse James*); JIM DAVIS (*Frank James*); GLORIA TALBOTT (*Indian Maiden*); WILL WRIGHT (*Titus Queasley*); MARY YOUNG (*"Ma" James*); SID MELTON (*Fight Fan*); GEORGE E. STONE (*Gibson Girl Fan*); JAMES BURKE (*Charlie, bartender*); JOE VITALE (*Sam Hiawatha*); LYLE LATELL (*Conductor*); HARRY TYLER (*Elmo, station master*); MIKE MAZURKI, MICKEY FINN (*Toughs*); NESTOR PAIVA (*Bixby*); MIKE ROSS (*Killer*); EMORY PARNELL (*Sheriff*); STAN JOLLEY (*Conductor*); DICK ALEXANDER (*Jeremiah Cole*); OLIVER BLAKE (*Undertaker*); JACK LAMBERT (*Snake Brice*); ETHAN LAIDLAW, GLENN STRANGE (*Henchmen*); J. ANTHONY HUGHES (*Dirty Dog Saloonkeeper*); *and* BOB GUNDERSON, FRED KOHLER, JR., IRON EYES CODY.

GUEST STARS (UNBILLED):

HUGH O'BRIAN (*Wyatt Earp*); WARD BOND (*Major Seth Adams*); JAMES ARNESS (*Matt Dillon*); ROY ROGERS (*himself*); FESS PARKER (*Davy Crockett*); GAIL DAVIS (*Annie Oakley*); JAMES GARNER (*Bret Maverick*); GENE AUTREY (*himself*); JAY SILVERHEELS (*Tonto*); BING CROSBY (*himself*); GARY COOPER (*himself*).

CREDITS:

NORMAN MC LEOD (*Director*); JACK HOPE (*Producer*); BOB HOPE (*Executive Producer*); WILLIAM BOWERS, DANIEL D. BEAUCHAMP (*Scenarists*); LIONEL LINDON (*Photographer*); HAL PEREIRA, ROLAND ANDERSON (*Art Directors*); JOHN P. FULTON (*Special Photographic Effects*); FARCIOT EDOUART (*Process Photography*); SAM COMER, BERTRAM GRANGER (*Set Decorators*);

EDITH HEAD (Costumer); MARVIN COIL and JACK BACHOM (Editors); LYLE FIGLAND and CHARLES GRENZBACH (Sound Recorders); JOSEPH J. LILLEY (Music Arranger/Conductor). SONGS: "Ain't-A-Hankerin'" and "Protection" by ARTHUR ALTMAN (Music) and BUD BURTSON (Lyrics), sung by Bob and Rhonda; "Alias Jesse James Theme" by MARILYN and JOE HOOVEN (Music) and DUNHAM (Lyrics), sung by GUY MITCHELL over title credits. DANIEL MCCAULEY (Assistant Director). Based on a story by ROBERT ST. AUBREY and BERT LAWRENCE.

SYNOPSIS:

A greenhorn insurance salesman, Milford Farnsworth, sells a paid-up policy to a T. J. James, who he soon discovers is actually Jesse James. The beneficiary is Jesse's girl, Cora Lee Collins, a dance hall queen better known as "The Duchess."

Milford is sent West to retrieve the policy and get his company off the hook and he joins the James gang, to protect Jesse. Milford then begins to emulate the notorious outlaw, which gives Jesse the idea that he can substitute Milford for himself and thus collect the $100,000 insurance and flee to California with the Duchess.

Jesse's plans are carried out and Milford is left in a ditch for dead. However, his bullet-proof vest saves the day. He and the Duchess, who by this time loves him, hold off the James gang until reinforcements arrive.

NOTES:

This extremely mild Bob Hope comedy contained a surprise gag ending with the aforementioned Guest Stars making brief appearances. Cooper, doing a favor for his longtime friend Hope, was one of them.

On the set with director
Norman McLeod (smoking)

THEY CAME TO CORDURA

A Goetz-Baroda Production
A Columbia Picture
in CinemaScope and Eastman Color
by Pathé   1959

CAST:

GARY COOPER (*Major Thomas Thorn*); RITA HAYWORTH (*Adelaide Geary*); VAN HEFLIN (*Sgt. John Chawk*); TAB HUNTER (*Lt. William Fowler*); RICHARD CONTE (*Cpl. Milo Trubee*); MICHAEL CALLAN (*Pvt. Aubrey Hetherington*); DICK YORK (*Pvt. Renziehausen*); ROBERT KEITH (*Colonel Rogers*); CARLOS ROMERO (*Arrsaga*); JAMES BANNON (*Capt. Raltz*); EDWARD PLATT (*Colonel DeRose*); MAURICE JARA (*Mexican Federale*); SAM BUFFINGTON (*1st Correspondent*); ARTHUR HANSON (*2nd Correspondent*).

CREDITS:

ROBERT ROSSEN (*Director*); WILLIAM GOETZ (*Producer*); IVAN MOFFAT, ROBERT ROSSEN (*Scenarists*); BURNETT GUFFEY (*Photographer*); WILLIAM A. LYON (*Editor*); ELIE SIEGMEISTER (*Musical Score*); CARY ODELL (*Art Director*); FRANK A. TUTTLE (*Set Decorator*); MILTON FELDMAN (*Assistant Director*); CLAY CAMPBELL (*Makeup Artist*); HELEN HUNT (*Hair Stylist*); JOHN LIVADARY (*Sound Recorder*); JAMES HAVENS (*Second Unit Director*); FRANK G. CARSON (*Second Unit Photographer*); CARTER DE HAVEN, JR. (*Assistant Director*); HENRI JAFFA (*Color Consultant*); MORRIS STOLOFF (*Musical Director*); ARTHUR MORTON (*Orchestrator*); COL. PAUL DAVISON, U.S.A. (RET.) (*Technical Adviser*). PHOTOGRAPHIC LENSES by PANAVISION. *From the novel by* GLENDON SWARTHOUT.

SYNOPSIS:

Due to showing cowardice in battle, Major Thomas Thorn has been assigned the degrading task of "Awards Officer" to the Mexican expedition of 1916 against Pancho Villa. Thorn witnesses an attack on a ranch house which results in an American victory, and selects five men as candidates for the Congressional Medal of Honor. Since Washington wants

With Rita Hayworth

With Van Heflin, Tab Hunter,
Dick York, Michael Callan,
Richard Conte and Rita Hayworth

heroes in a hurry, for a World War I recruiting campaign, Thorn has to guide these men through the perilous border country to the safety of a rear base at Cordura.

Since Villa's men were given haven in the ranch house of the beautiful Adelaide Geary, she is accused of treason and is forced to accompany the men on their difficult journey. Before the seven get to the Texas border town, the five heroes are given ample time to show their true characters, as does the Major.

NOTES:

They Came to Cordura was a box-office disaster despite the presence of the big-name cast. The chief fault lay in the script, with plodding direction running a close second. The actors seemed bored and listless throughout and displayed little interest in their respective assignments. It was downright embarrassing to watch them wallow through such ludicrous situations, speaking inane dialogue to one another. Cooper didn't look well and his mind seemed miles away from his work. The only one to come out of this hodge-podge with dignity was Rita Hayworth.

The color photography of Burnett Guffey—and the second unit work of Frank G. Carson and James Havens—in and around St. George, Utah, were wasted on this film. After its initial release, Robert Rossen gained rights to the film with hopes of re-editing it according to his original plan. However, Rossen is now dead and it hasn't been seen commercially for years. Let's hope it never is.

Variety noted that "Gary Cooper is very good as the central figure, although he is somewhat too old for the role. It is a little hard to believe that a man of his maturity would only then be finding out the things about himself which Cooper explores as part of his character. Miss Hayworth, looking haggard, drawn and defeated, gives the best performance of her career. If she shows only half the beauty she usually does, she displays twice the acting." *Cue* magazine concurred, saying "The picture is long, draggy, generally tiresome and monotonous—although well enough acted by a first-rate cast."

Films in Review declared: "Gary Cooper is much too old for the part of the cowardly officer assigned to make heroes out of riff-raff—Van Heflin, Richard Conte, Michael Callan and Dick York—with only one performance at all credible [Heflin's]. Rita

272

Hayworth *did* endeavor to substitute acting for sex and glamour, but her part was too inadequately written. And Robert Rossen's direction was downright incompetent . . ." *The New Yorker* opined, *"They Came to Cordura* . . . is not even mildly diverting. Mr. Cooper gets to reflecting on courage, and as the action proceeds, he discovers that his clutch of heroes aren't all they're cracked up to be. He is rather a slow study, as I think you'll be inclined to agree after accompanying him and his companions over a bleak landscape for a couple of hours. As played by Rita Hayworth, the lady on the team is much less complex. She just wants to keep the boys from getting any ideas."

With Rita Hayworth and Richard Conte

273

THE WRECK
OF THE MARY DEARE

A Blaustein-Baroda Production
A Metro-Goldwyn-Mayer Picture
in CinemaScope and Metrocolor   1959

CAST:

GARY COOPER *(Gideon Patch);* CHARLTON HESTON *(John Sands);* MICHAEL REDGRAVE *(Mr. Hyland);* EMLYN WILLIAMS *(Sir Wildred Falcett);* CECIL PARKER *(The Chairman);* ALEXANDER KNOX *(Petrie);* VIRGINIA MC KENNA *(Janet Taggart);* RICHARD HARRIS *(Higgins);* BEN WRIGHT *(Mike Duncan);* PETER ILLING *(Gunderson);* TERENCE DE MARNEY *(Frank);* ASHLEY COWAN *(Burrows);* CHARLES DAVIS *(Yules);* ALEXANDER ARCHDALE *(Lloyd's Counsel);* JOHN LE MESURIER *(M.O.A. Lawyer);* LOUIS MERCIER *(Com. de Police);* ALBERT CARRIER *(Ambulance Attendant);* LILYAN CHAUVIN *(Nun);* PAUL BRYAR *(Port Official);* LOMAX STUDY *(Photographer);* JEAN DEL VAL *(Javot);* KALU K. SONKUR *(Lascar);* NOEL DRAYTON *(Bell);* CHARLES LAMB *(Count Clerk);* JOHN DEARTH *(Reporter);* GEORGE DEE *(French Captain).*

CREDITS:

MICHAEL ANDERSON *(Director);* JULIAN BLAUSTEIN *(Producer);* ERIC AMBLER *(Scenarist);* JOSEPH RUTTENBERG *(Photographer);* GEORGE DUNING *(Musical Score);* HANS PETERS, PAUL GROESSE *(Art Directors);* HENRY GRACE, HUGH HUNT *(Set Decorators);* FREDERICK A. YOUNG, HAROLD E. WELLMAN *(Associate Photographers);* EDA WARREN *(Editor);* ROBERT SAUNDERS *(Assistant Director);* FRANKLIN MILTON *(Sound Recorder);* A. ARNOLD GILLESPIE, LEE LE BLANC *(Special Effects);* WILLIAM TUTTLE *(Makeup Artist);* CHARLES K. HAGEDON *(Color Consultant).* PHOTOGRAPHIC LENSES *by* PANAVISION. *Based on the novel by* HAMMOND INNES.

SYNOPSIS:

The freighter Mary Deare is set afire and abandoned

by its crew during a storm on the English Channel. Gideon Patch is the only man aboard, until he is joined by John Sands, whose salvage boat has been rammed by the freighter. Sands believes Patch is deliberately trying to wreck the Mary Deare.

At a London Court of Inquiry, Patch is faced by many accusers and the mystery of the Mary Deare becomes a major news item. At first, Patch does little to aid himself, giving only evasive testimony. Finally, he and Sands swim beneath the wreckage on the reefs in search of evidence. The riddle of how the Captain died, what caused the crew to mutiny, and the contents of the vital cargo the Mary Deare carried are eventually revealed.

NOTES:

The Wreck of the Mary Deare was an above-average sea saga with fine suspense values, good color photography and an able cast. One might say it was *The Court-Martial of Billy Mitchell* gone to sea. The scripts and characterizations involving Cooper were almost identical. Charlton Heston was a marvelous counterpart and the two played well together. It was a popular film, since sea sagas were becoming rarer in those days, as today.

Said Howard Thompson in *The New York Times:* "As the dour, hard-headed, aging Captain, Mr. Cooper looks emotionally exhausted, and rightly so, if a bit mature for underwater combat." Paul V. Beckley in the *New York Herald Tribune* felt, "It is, in other words, just what it pretends to be, no more but no less, and anyone looking for a muscular and uncomplicated seagoing adventure movie should find this exciting."

Hazel Flynn, in the *Beverly Hills Citizen,* commented, "Unfortunately the action calls on Gary to save the obviously younger and stronger Heston's life . . . to engage in a fist fight with him (Gary has already been injured) and to worst him in a somewhat preposterous manner. Thus those in charge of *Mary Deare* have made the same mistake as a number of other filmmakers recently where Cooper is concerned. They insist on presenting him as oh so noble . . . oh so virile . . . oh so pathetic and misunderstood because of his reticence . . . giving him things to do which would be more credible if handled by (alas) his younger companion and (at first) adversary."

On the other hand, John L. Scott in the *Los Angeles Times* thought, "Cooper emerges with the stronger role, but both he and Heston have been well chosen for their robust characterizations."

With Virginia McKenna

With Charlton Heston

With Alexander Knox and Charlton Heston

With Deborah Kerr

THE NAKED EDGE

A Pennebaker-Baroda Production
Released Through United Artists   1961

CAST:

GARY COOPER *(George Radcliffe)*; DEBORAH KERR *(Martha Radcliffe)*; ERIC PORTMAN *(Jeremy Clay)*; DIANE CILENTO *(Mrs. Heath)*; HERMIONE GINGOLD *(Lilly Harris)*; PETER CUSHING *(Mr. Wrack)*; MICHAEL WILDING *(Morris Brooke)*; RONALD HOWARD *(Mr. Claridge)*; RAY MC ANALLY *(Donald Heath)*; SANDOR ELES *(Manfridi)*; WILFRID LAWSON *(Mr. Pom)*; HELEN CHERRY *(Miss Osborne)*; JOYCE CAREY *(Victoria Hicks)*; DIANE CLARE *(Betty)*; FREDERICK LEISTER *(Judge)*; MARTIN BODDEY *(Jason Roote)*; PETER WAYN *(Chauffeur)*.

CREDITS:

MICHAEL ANDERSON *(Director)*; WALTER SELTZER, GEORGE GLASS *(Producers)*; MARLON BRANDO, SR. *(Executive Producer)*; JOSEPH STEFANO *(Scenarist)*; EDWIN HILLIER *(Photographer)*; GORDON PILKINGTON *(Editor)*; WILLIAM ALWYN *(Musical Score)*; CARMEN DILLON *(Art Director)*; NORMAN COGGS *(Sound Recorder)*; PETER BOLTON *(Assistant Director)*; JOCK MC GREGOR *(Assistant Producer)*; BILLY KIRBY *(Production Supervisor)*; MUIR MATHIESON *(Conductor, Sinfonia of London)*. *Based on the novel "First Train to Babylon" by* MAX EHRLICH.

SYNOPSIS:

American business executive George Radcliffe becomes a witness against Donald Heath, a man accused of murder and robbery. Heath is convicted and sentenced to life imprisonment. Suddenly, however, George and a partner amass a large sum of money and start a new business. Six years later, his wife Martha shows him a letter that has been in a missing mailbag for 5 years. In the letter, a lawyer accuses George of the murder.

Martha wants to believe her husband but, the strong evidence causes her to distrust him, and

276

With Deborah Kerr and Eric Portman

the situation leads to mounting tension between them. Playing detective, Martha discovers that George stressed "an accomplice," in his testimony against Heath, although one was never found. At home, Martha tells George she can't help but believe the accusations against him, so he leaves. Meanwhile, a man sneaks up the stairs into the bathroom and picks up George's razor. Martha calls and George answers, but they do not continue speaking. Then, Martha goes to take her bath. . . . and. . . .

NOTES:

The Naked Edge, drawn from Max Ehrlich's highly suspenseful novel *First Train to Babylon,* was the 92nd—and final—film in Cooper's lengthy career. It was neither the best nor the worst of his films but, as a suspenser, it could really have used the nimble touch of Alfred Hitchcock. Director Michael Anderson, who was better at directing such things as *Around the World in 80 Days,* seemed to employ every trick of suspense he could come up with. The

With Deborah Kerr

results were good, but not extraordinary. Filming was done entirely in England at the Elstree Studios and the finished film wasn't released until after Cooper's death.

Brendan Gill, in *The New Yorker* declaimed, "A thriller in which, for a wonder, Cooper himself is suspected of having committed a dastardly murder, it consists of a wholly synthetic piling up of the palest pink herrings. The qualities that made Cooper a great star had little to do with acting, and since he must have been very uncomfortable in this absurd and unpleasant role, he leaves the make-believe largely to Deborah Kerr, as his distracted wife, and Eric Portman, as a loony ex-barrister."

Variety thought: "The picture that winds up Gary Cooper's long list of credits is neatly constructed, thoroughly professional little suspense meller that may seem anti-climactic only because it climaxes a great career." *Time* complained, "*Naked Edge,* the whodunit that is the late Gary Cooper's last picture, is a waste of a good man."

TWO TRIBUTES

"He was a poet of the real. He knew all about cows, bulls, cars and ocean tides. He had the enthusiasm of a boy. He could always tell you his first vivid impression of a thing. He had an old-fashioned politeness, but he said nothing casually."

—CLIFFORD ODETS

"He is one of the most beloved illiterates
this country has ever known."

—CARL SANDBURG